TIME TO LISTEN

TIME TO LISTEN

Confronting Child Sexual Abuse by Catholic Clergy in Ireland

Helen Goode, Hannah McGee and Ciarán O'Boyle
Royal College of Surgeons in Ireland

The Liffey Press

Published by
The Liffey Press
Ashbrook House, 10 Main Street
Raheny, Dublin 5, Ireland
www.theliffeypress.com

© 2003 Helen Goode, Hannah McGee and Ciarán O'Boyle

A catalogue record of this book is
available from the British Library.

ISBN 1-904148-38-7

Printed in the Republic of Ireland by ColourBooks Ltd.

CONTENTS

Health Services Research Centre, Department of Psychology, Royal College of Surgeons in Ireland

The Health Services Research Centre (HSRC) was established in 1997 at the Department of Psychology, Royal College of Surgeons in Ireland. Its aim is to promote quality in Irish healthcare through research. Its work facilitates co-operation among researchers, health professionals, policy makers and health service users. Recently completed projects include assessments of the health status and healthcare access of homeless men and women; of those infected by hepatitis C through State-provided blood products; of Travellers; of cardiac patients; and of older people in Ireland. The HSRC produced the first national study on the lifetime prevalence of sexual abuse and violence in Ireland (SAVI) in 2002 and recently completed an evaluation of client experiences of the National Counselling Service (a service established by the government for those abused in institutional care in Ireland). Ongoing work includes evaluation of barriers to organ donation; public attitudes to, and experiences of, crisis pregnancy; and public views on the use of human organs and tissue in research. Its work is funded by Government agencies and voluntary bodies. [www.rcsi.ie]

Helen Goode MSc is Research Co-ordinator for the clerical sexual abuse study. Hannah McGee PhD is Professor of Psychology and Director of the Health Services Research Centre. Ciarán O'Boyle PhD is Professor of Psychology and Chairman of the Department of Psychology, Royal College of Surgeons in Ireland.

FOREWORD

The clerical sexual abuse problem in the Roman Catholic Church has dominated media attention during recent years in Ireland, the United Kingdom, Australia, the United States, and elsewhere. Few stories have received the kind of laser beam focus for so long as this story has. In fact, the Catholic sexual abuse scandal was front-page news in the *New York Times* 41 days in a row during the first half of 2002.

The story of Catholic priests sexually abusing children is a remarkable story for several important reasons. First, it appears to be the height of hypocrisy and contradiction to learn that Catholic priests, who are important moral, ethical, and religious leaders and who take a vow of celibacy, would sexually engage themselves with children. Second, it is shocking to learn that religious superiors (such as local bishops) knew of this abhorrent behaviour among priests under their supervision and did nothing (or very little) to stop it from continuing. Finally, it is amazing that many Church leaders did not follow the wisdom and instruction of the Gospel message of Jesus by not treating the victims of clergy abuse (and their families) with compassion, love, justice and understanding.

While we hear so much about the problem of sex offending Catholic clergy, we actually know very little about it.[1] Why might this be the case? First, very few Church officials have been willing to open their records to researchers. Second, there are very few researchers who have had both the skill and interest in this area. It is surprising that the number of professional researchers and clinicians who have any expertise in the area of Catholic clerical sexual abuse is incredibly small, numbering just a few dozen in the world.[2] Third, professional organisations as well as professional journals and scholarly book publishers have been generally uninterested in this topic. Finally, few clerical sexual abuse perpetrators and victims have been willing to participate in research, preferring to keep their stories and experiences private affairs.

What is clearly needed is comprehensive research that maintains the co-operation and collaboration of the Catholic Church, the academic community who have the skill and independence to conduct the research, and appropriate government agencies (e.g. law enforcement, child protection services). The study reported and discussed in this book is the first groundbreaking, comprehensive, country-wide, and collaborative empirical research study conducted in the world that has met all of these important criteria. It represents a remarkable accomplishment by the authors and collaborators. With this study, Ireland has become the international leader in developing a model programme for comprehensive and collaborative quality research on clerical sexual abuse.

What makes this project so remarkable? First, the Catholic Church in Ireland made the bold step to both support and fund a comprehensive research study on clerical sexual abuse, teaming with quality academic researchers at the Royal College of Surgeons in Ireland who are independent from the Church. Giving these lay researchers access to Church personnel, and those abused and abusers, was a bold but necessary step. These researchers recently completed the first national Irish lifetime survey of sexual abuse — *The SAVI Report: Sexual Abuse and Violence in Ireland*[3] — and were thus uniquely qualified to complete this important study on clerical sexual abuse. Second, the scope of the project is huge: studying over 1,000 people from the general public via telephone interviews, conducting about 50 face-to-face interviews with victims and perpetrators of clerical sexual abuse, family members of both victims and perpetrators and general non-abusing clergy. The response rates among the general public and clergy were impressive.

I will not discuss the remarkable findings in this Foreword in order to allow the authors of the project to do so in the body of their work. However, it is clear that this study represents exactly what other Church officials and academics should collaboratively do in countries around the world. With this research study, Ireland has become the first country to develop an outstanding and comprehensive model research project on clerical sexual abuse. The findings have enormous implications to better understand and deal with clerical sexual abuse. What is learned from the study has important implications for the victims, perpetrators, rank-and-file Catholics and the Church in general. A serious problem like clerical sexual abuse cannot be understood and adequately dealt with unless solid comprehensive and collaborative research is conducted with full participation and co-operation between the Church, the research community and appropriate state agencies. Hats off to Ireland, and most specifically the Irish Catholic Church officials and the researchers Helen Goode, Professor McGee and Professor O'Boyle, for leading the rest of the world in this area. Let us hope and pray that other countries will follow Ireland's lead. Only then can we truly prevent and recover from the tragedy of clerical sexual abuse in the Roman Catholic Church.

Thomas G. Plante, PhD, ABPP
Professor of Psychology, Santa Clara University
Adjunct Clinical Associate Professor of Psychiatry
and Behavioural Sciences
Stanford University School of Medicine

References

[1] Loftus, J.A. (2004). "What have we learned: Implications for future research and formation" in T.G. Plante (ed.). *Sin against the Innocents: Sexual Abuse by Priests and the Role of the Catholic Church*. Westport, CT: Praeger/Greenwood.

[2] Plante, T.G. (ed.) (1999). *Bless Me Father for I Have Sinned: Perspectives on Sexual Abuse Committed by Roman Catholic Priests*. Westport, CT: Praeger/Greenwood.

[3] McGee, H., Garavan, R., de Barra, M., Byrne, J. and Conroy, R. (2002). *The SAVI Report: Sexual Abuse and Violence in Ireland*. Dublin: The Liffey Press.

PREFACE

This project was conducted by the Health Services Research Centre at the Department of Psychology at the Royal College of Surgeons in Ireland. We were both pleased and challenged by the opportunity to address this important issue for contemporary Irish society and for the Catholic Church in Ireland. The Bishops' Committee on Child Abuse (now known as the Bishops' Committee on Child Protection) commissioned this study in late 2000. The commission followed on from our experience in conducting a separate study, *The SAVI Report: Sexual Abuse and Violence in Ireland*, the first national study of lifetime experiences of sexual abuse in Ireland. We were given the brief to comprehensively examine the issue of clerical child sexual abuse and to develop recommendations for future management — this to be part of the Church's efforts to "undo the harm done" by clerical abuse. Our understanding is that this is the first occasion internationally in which the Catholic Church has commissioned an independent agency to study child sexual abuse by clergy. We commend the Bishops' Committee on this initiative and on their willingness to allow us to work independently.

The study is entitled *Time to Listen* to reflect the sense of wanting to learn from the stories of the many individuals and constituencies affected by clerical sexual abuse who may not have had a forum where they felt able to express their experiences. The word "confronting" is also deliberately chosen in the subtitle of the study. Confronting — to look boldly at — we understood to be the Church's intention in commissioning the work and we understood as our task in completing it.

The project commenced in January 2001. Throughout the project we received assistance from many people. We firstly and particularly wish to acknowledge and thank all of the study participants. Those interviewed gave not only their time but also shared personal, painful and sometimes intimate experiences. We commend their courage and commitment to improving things for the future and we greatly appreciate their willingness to trust us with their stories. Over a thousand members of the general public also gave us their time and their views. We thank them for helping understand the public's perspective.

Several people assisted the project administratively. Particular thanks to the following: Church delegates who assisted in recruiting people for interview; Rape Crisis Centre counsellors throughout Ireland (for agreeing to provide priority appointments for those who required professional help for problems described to us in the study); Ms Ersilia Davidson (Archbishop's House, Dublin); Fr Paul Murphy OFM Cap and Mary Farrelly (Child Protection Office, Conference of Religious of Ireland); Ms Colma McEvoy (Child Protection Office, Irish Bishops' Conference, Maynooth); Mr John Carroll at Eircom (for technical assistance with the public telephone survey); secretarial staff at the Department of Psychology at the Royal College of Surgeons in Ireland (RCSI) — Ms Carole Caetano and Ms Tanya Byrne Ojo.

During the planning stage and throughout the study, academic and research input was obtained. Thanks to all who assisted in this way: Dr James Williams (Survey Unit, Economic and Social Research Institute); Dr Eoin O'Sullivan (Trinity College, Dublin); Mr Bobby Eagar (Solicitor at Garrett Sheehan & Co, Dublin); Dr Alan Carr (University College Dublin); Dr Patrick Walsh (Granada Institute, Dublin); Fr Steve Rossetti (St Luke's Institute, Washington); Professor Thomas Plante (Santa Clara University, California); Professor Patricia Casey (Mater Hospital, Dublin); District Court Judge (name withheld); Senior Counsel (name withheld); Canon Lawyers: Fr Tom Doyle (Germany), Fr Frank Morrisey OMI (Canada), Monsignor John Dolan and Monsignor Alex Stenson (Ireland); Irish Prison Service staff;

members of the print and television media: Mr Chris Moore and Ms Breda O'Brien; research colleagues at RCSI: Ms Rebecca Garavan, Ms Orla Keegan, Ms Colette Leigh, Mr Ronán Conroy and Dr Anne Hickey; library staff at RCSI (for assistance with literature searching), in particular Ms Mary O'Doherty; the Children's Resource Centre, Barnardos, Dublin; Ms Niamh Brennan, Library, Trinity College Dublin; Mr Peter Folan at the Mater Dei Library; and Ms Fiona Keane at the Department of Health and Children Library.

We would also like to acknowledge the contribution of project research assistants: Ms Mary O'Regan, Ms Caitriona Ellis, Ms Joanne Byrne and in particular Ms Aoife O'Riordan who collated and analysed the data from the survey of bishops and delegates.

Finally, we thank the members of the Research Sub-Committee of the Bishops' Committee on Child Protection for their advice throughout the project: Mr John Morgan (Chairperson), Mr Paul Bailey (Executive Director, Child Protection Office, Irish Bishops' Conference, Maynooth), Dr Michael Breen (Media and Communications Studies, Mary Immaculate College, University of Limerick), Fr Frank Buckley (Diocese of Cork and Ross), Ms Rosaleen McElvaney (Principal Clinical Psychologist, St Clare's Unit, The Children's University Hospital, Temple Street, Dublin), Bishop Eamon Walsh (while serving as auxiliary bishop in the Archdiocese of Dublin) and Rev Dr Liam Ryan (St Patrick's College, Maynooth).

We have endeavoured to fairly represent the perspectives of all who participated in the study and to describe the broad social, legal and ecclesial context in which clerical child sexual abuse occurred. It is important to note that most abused persons and abusers offered the opportunity to participate in the study chose not to — this is a pattern often seen in research on very sensitive issues. The account here thus necessarily describes the experiences of the relatively small number of individuals who were willing to participate in the study. It is nonetheless a uniquely representative group in terms of the size and range of individuals invited to participate. What emerged from our research is a very complex story — a story of deep hurt and trust betrayed for many people throughout the Church and Irish society more generally. It is a story that has taken a long time to come to the surface. We hope that this report can be a useful part of the telling of the story. Moreover, we hope that telling the story to date will assist those who must now continue the story and ensure that the next chapters are about healing and reconciliation.

Helen Goode
Hannah McGee
Ciarán O'Boyle

September 2003
Royal College of Surgeons in Ireland

LIST OF TABLES AND FIGURES

List of Tables

List of Figures

Executive Summary

Background

- Almost all of the available information on child sexual abuse by priests and religious in Ireland is generated by media sources (through radio, television and newspaper coverage) or by individual accounts (usually as books written by or with the assistance of journalists). These have portrayed the grave consequences of child sexual abuse by clergy for those abused and their families, and to a lesser extent the impact on families and colleagues of abusers and on the wider Church community. The issue has not been the subject of systematic research to date.

- In January 2001, the Bishops' Committee on Child Abuse (now known as the Bishops' Committee on Child Protection) of the Irish Roman Catholic Church commissioned an independent research study on child sexual abuse by clergy. The Health Services Research Centre at the Department of Psychology, Royal College of Surgeons in Ireland conducted the study.

- The overall aim of the study was twofold. Firstly, since this is an issue with international relevance, an important aim was to extend scientific knowledge about the impact of child sexual abuse by clergy beyond the individual in order to assess its impact on all of those likely to be affected. These range from the family of the abused, convicted members of clergy and their families and colleagues, clergy and Church personnel and the wider Church community. The second broad aim was to understand clerical child sexual abuse in the Irish context — what were the salient factors concerning its occurrence and management and how can this information be used to inform practice in the future.

STUDY OBJECTIVES

There were three specific study objectives:

- To examine the psychological and social impact, and the impact on faith, of child sexual abuse by clergy

- To examine the experience of disclosure and response in relation to child sexual abuse by clergy from the perspectives of all those included in the study

- To inform recommendations for future Church policy.

METHOD

Study Phases

- The study was conducted in three phases, using different research methodologies. In the first phase, a telephone survey was conducted to examine the attitudes and opinions of the Irish general public concerning clerical child sexual abuse. Participants were randomly selected from the general population in order to obtain the broadest representation of views of the wider Church community in the Republic of Ireland. Interviews were conducted during the period January to May 2002.

- The second phase involved qualitative interviews. Face-to-face in-depth interviews were conducted with individuals who had experienced child sexual abuse and their families, with convicted clergy and their families and colleagues, and with general clergy and Church personnel. Interviews were conducted during the period February 2002 to March 2003.

- The third phase of the study was a postal survey of Church personnel with responsibility for the management of complaints concerning clerical child sexual abuse, i.e. Church delegates,[a] members of the Episcopal Conference and retired bishops. The survey was completed over a six-month period (July to December 2002).

STUDY POPULATION

- Over 1,000 randomly selected Irish adults took part in the telephone survey of the Irish general public (N = 1,081). This represented a 76 per cent response rate — a high participation rate for a telephone survey.

- A total of 48 people were interviewed face-to-face. Of these, seven[b] were individuals who had experienced child sexual abuse and three were family members. Eight convicted clergy and five members of their families were interviewed. Twenty-four Church personnel were interviewed; of these, four were colleagues of clerical abusers and the remaining 20 were general members of the clergy and lay persons who work for the Church. Response rates for these groups were very low. For instance, 95 individuals who had been abused and 26 convicted clergy were invited to participate. Even for those who did participate, just over half (9 of 16 participants) were willing to ask family members to participate. Reluctance to participate in an interview study of such a highly sensitive topic is not unusual. While it means that interview results must be generalised with caution, and it is possible that more distressed individuals chose not to participate, the process still provided a wide range of those involved with an equal oppor-

---

[a] Delegates are members of clergy (i.e. priests and religious) in each diocese and religious order who have been charged with responsibility for receiving allegations of clerical child sexual abuse.

[b] In addition to the seven individuals who experienced child sexual abuse, one individual, who experienced clerical sexual abuse as an adult, was interviewed.

tunity to represent their experiences. In this way it furthers the evidence already available from individual accounts of abuse.

- The individuals who experienced abuse were contacted through Church personnel and were known to Church authorities. However, many individuals will not have reported their abuse to Church authorities and must be identified through other means. A large national survey on the prevalence of sexual abuse and violence, conducted in 2001, provided the opportunity to identify individuals who had been sexually abused by clergy but had not reported their abuse to Church authorities. Thirty individuals reported child sexual abuse by clergy in the prevalence study. Of these, 25 gave permission to be re-contacted for future research. Fourteen (out of 25) of these individuals were interviewed by phone.

- All 153 diocesan and religious delegates and all 44 Episcopal Conference members and retired bishops in Ireland (Republic and Northern Ireland) were surveyed. From the total group, 102 delegates (a response rate of 67 per cent) and 35 bishops (80 per cent response rate) took part. The overall response rate of 70 per cent was much higher than general population postal surveys.

RESEARCH FINDINGS

Awareness of Child Sexual Abuse

Clergy

- Most participating clergy reported that their initial awareness of clerical sexual abuse was raised through the media. Knowledge of the effects of abuse on individuals was limited and had evolved over time to an appreciation of the extensive and long-term adverse effects of such experiences on the individual.

General Public

- Similar to clergy, members of the public surveyed knew about child sexual abuse in general and child sexual abuse by clergy from the media (95 per cent and 94 per cent respectively).

- Concerning the prevalence of child sexual abuse by clergy, the Irish public overestimated the proportion of all child sexual abuse which is perpetrated by clergy. They also underestimated the number of clergy convicted for sexual offences against children. However, the majority felt that clergy were as likely to sexually abuse children as other men in society.

- The majority of the public believed that child sexual abuse by clergy should be made public and felt that the media served a useful role in highlighting the issue.

Impact of Child Sexual Abuse by Clergy

Those Abused and Their Families

- Disclosure was described as an ongoing process, rather than a once-off event, by those who had experienced child sexual abuse.

- · Persistent psychological effects including depression, anxiety, suicidal ideation and relationship and intimacy difficulties were reported by some of those who had been abused.

- Other effects included a decline in confidence in the Catholic Church as an institution and in Catholic clergy. Some described having lost their religious faith. This was attributed to the overall response they received from Church personnel when they reported their abuse rather than to the experience of abuse *per se*.

- Some of those abused had regained their trust in clergy and/or their religious faith while others had not done so.

- Family members of those abused described major negative consequences of the abuse, particularly if disclosure occurred when the person was still a child. The impact of abuse extended to all immediate family members. For some, family relationships continued to be strained.

- Family members found the process of officially reporting the abuse to Church personnel to be a very difficult experience.

- In retrospect, both those abused and their family members described a great sense of guilt because they had chosen to report the abuse to the Church rather than to civil authorities. Many felt that other children may have been protected from abuse if they had chosen to report it to civil authorities instead.

Family Members of Abusers

- Family members of convicted clergy also described major negative consequences on discovering that a member of their family had sexually abused children. A major struggle for these family members concerned how to balance providing some support for their relative with their own and others' sense of condemnation of his actions. Tensions existed within families as some family members wanted no further involvement with their convicted relative while others wanted to remain supportive.

Colleagues of Convicted Clergy and General Clergy

- Colleagues of convicted clergy reported a sense of shame, disillusionment and abandonment. Their commentaries indicated that this impact had more to do with Church management than with the occurrence of abuse itself. Most felt they were not provided with information or guidance or otherwise supported by Church leaders when a colleague in their parish or community was accused of sexually abusing children. Instead, they felt they had to face their congregations alone and to continue with increased workloads and personal pressures without assistance.

- Many members of the clergy described feeling shame as a consequence of Church-related child sexual abuse. Some reported attempts to conceal their identity in public to avoid being identified as clergy as a consequence of the issue. They reported a loss of public credibility and trust and a sense of low morale. Fear of a false allegation of abuse was also a concern.

- Overall, clergy who participated in the study reported a significant loss of confidence in Church leadership as a result of mismanagement of child sexual abuse by Church authorities.

General Public

- According to the public survey, child sexual abuse by clergy has affected religious practices to some extent with 36 per cent reporting an effect (e.g. on Mass attendance and time spent praying). It has also had an impact on willingness to trust Church personnel, i.e. 41 per cent unwilling to automatically trust a priest on first arrival in their community.

- Faith in God was strong among the public with 93 per cent believing in a God and the majority also reporting a personal relationship with God.

- The public (72 per cent) believed that priests in general had been unfairly judged as a result of clerical child sexual abuse. About half (54 per cent) reported satisfaction with priests today and 47 per cent judged the quality of priests to be better today compared to the past.

- Compared to the satisfaction level with individual priests, satisfaction with the Church more generally was lower (44 per cent vs. 54 per cent). The quality of today's Church was judged to be better than the Church in the past by 39 per cent of those expressing views, the same by 45 per cent and worse by 16 per cent.

- Two-thirds (66 per cent) of the public said that they looked to priests to provide general moral guidance while only one-third (32 per cent) looked to the Church for guidance on human sexuality. Almost two-thirds (65 per cent) of the public were positive about the prospect of their child becoming or being an altar server and just over half (56 per cent) were positive about the prospect of their son becoming a priest.

Initial Response and Ongoing Management of Child Sexual Abuse by Clergy

Those Abused and Their Families

- Most individuals who experienced abuse reported that Church personnel lacked awareness of the effects of child sexual abuse and did not always show compassion or sensitivity.

- Those who had experienced child sexual abuse and their family members also reported that Church personnel did not keep them informed and did not make themselves easily available to deal with the complaint.

- Legal concerns were seen by abused individuals and their families as taking precedence over a pastoral response by Church personnel.

Convicted Clergy

- All of the convicted clergy interviewed were sent for psychological treatment following an allegation of child sexual abuse. Treatment was usually experienced as very difficult but beneficial.

- Some convicted clergy reported that Church authorities made little attempt to understand them and treated them in a business-like manner. They also reported that Church personnel had inconsistent approaches to the management of convicted clergy, e.g. while none returned to ministry, some but not all have been laicised. Decisions about management of convicted clergy by dioceses/religious orders were seen by these men to focus on factors such as financial considerations rather than on the merits of individual cases.

- Convicted clergy reported mixed feelings about the support received from Church personnel during legal proceedings and time spent in prison.

Family Members of Convicted Clergy

- Some family members of convicted clergy were grateful for any support of their relative by Church personnel. They felt that any assistance should be regarded as positive given the crime that their relative had committed. However, others were critical, particularly in relation to what was perceived to be a lack of "brotherhood" and forgiveness.

Colleagues of Convicted Clergy

- Colleagues of convicted clergy felt that the Church's management approach was more concerned with institutional protection than concern for the individuals abused or Church colleagues affected by the abuse.

General Clergy

- In the postal survey of bishops and delegates, fewer bishops than delegates (45 per cent versus 80 per cent) reported being satisfied with their handling of past allegations of child sexual abuse.

- Similar to colleagues of convicted clergy, other Church personnel interviewed described the Church's overall management strategy in relation to child sexual abuse as an attempt to prevent scandal and protect the Church as an institution.

- Ineffective leadership and poor communication were regarded as factors contributing to ineffective management. Other factors such as unfamiliarity with the issue, lack of procedures and conflicting external advice were also identified as challenges to effective management.

General Public

- Public perceptions of the Church's overall management of child sexual abuse were critical. The majority (77 per cent) felt that the Church was not dealing with the problem adequately. Only 42 per cent believed that the Catholic Church would safeguard children entrusted to its care while 40 per cent trusted the Church to handle problems with its own clergy.

- Most (70 per cent) of the Irish public surveyed believed that the individual abuser was responsible for the *occurrence* of child sexual abuse while 39 per cent saw the Church hierarchy as having responsibility for its *management* with 41 per cent considering civil authorities as the ones responsible for management.

- There was little public awareness of actions the Church has taken in recent years to address the issue of child sexual abuse by clergy. In the public survey, very few (10 per cent) had heard of the *Framework Document,* the Catholic Church's policy document for responding to complaints of child sexual abuse by priests and religious.

CONCLUSIONS

Child sexual abuse is a major international problem. As recently as 2002, the first national prevalence figures on lifetime sexual abuse became available in Ireland. The high levels of child sexual abuse reported and the undisclosed nature of much of this abuse signal child sexual abuse as an important Irish social problem. A very small percentage of those reporting child sexual abuse as children identified their abusers as priests or religious. However, as a component of child sexual abuse more generally, child sexual abuse by clergy is seen as particularly reprehensible. Much has been written on the subject through individual accounts and media coverage. This study provides the first international profile of the overall impact of child sexual abuse by clergy on an entire community — from those abused to the wider Church community. Over 1,200 people (N=1,280) contributed to the development of this holistic account of the impact of such abuse on Irish society. The occurrence, and more importantly the mismanagement, of clerical sexual abuse represents a loss throughout Irish society rather than an isolated problem for an unfortunate few. The problem, and public responses to it, means that truly effective management by the Church is absolutely necessary. The path to restoration of confidence has to be a systematic and transparent one. It is by necessity going to be a slow process where trust, to be reinstated, will have to be earned.

RECOMMENDATIONS

Prevention of Child Sexual Abuse by Church Personnel

1. The Church, as an organisation, should study the systems being put in place in other organisations to identify and manage various types of risk and to respond in a prompt and effective manner to crises.

2. Child sexual abuse is a society-wide issue and the remit for child protection is broader than the Church. The Church should actively seek to work in co-operation with other agencies in this area in the interest of the best possible protection of children.

3. Prevention strategies should be informed by relevant research as conducted by the Church or other agencies and should be communicated to all Church personnel, to the wider Church community and to the general public.

4. The Catholic Church in Ireland should seek to develop a model of best practice for child protection based on ongoing review of current guidelines.

5. Church procedures for prevention should be audited at appropriate intervals. This could be done by the Church or by an external agency using a quality assurance approach.

Management of Complaints of Sexual Abuse by Clergy

6. A clearly defined protocol for managing complaints,[c] based on a standardised approach, should be put in place with due regard for the role of the bishop/superior in a diocese/congregation. This standardised approach could be facilitated by a national Child Protection Office (CPO) or similar national central body and should be widely communicated to the general public. Such a protocol would facilitate those who do not wish to approach clergy, would broaden the categories of Church personnel against whom complaints could be made and would improve accountability for the management of complaints.

7. The protocol should provide, *inter alia*, clear and practical instructions for responding to disclosures of child sexual abuse for all Church personnel. The protocol should also provide information on onward referral of the complaint to the national central body/CPO. Training in complaints procedures should be mandatory for all Church personnel and should be audited at appropriate intervals to ensure adherence. Both training and audit might be best undertaken by an external agency.

8. As per the *Framework Document* (Church Guidelines on Child Sexual Abuse), complaints of child sexual abuse by clergy should be referred promptly to the Garda Síochána. This should be coordinated by the national central body/CPO.

9. The national central body/CPO should notify the bishop, in the diocese where the abuse is alleged to have occurred, of complaints received. This notification should initiate a pastoral response from the local clergy/bishop in liaison with the national central body/CPO.

---

[c] In this context, a complaint is defined as an official accusation by the person abused or a person acting on their behalf. Third-party reports, anonymous claims or hearsay do not constitute an official complaint.

10. Complaints procedures should be widened in scope so that they facilitate complaints against all clergy and lay personnel who work for the Church.

11. Church policies regarding the prevention and management of child sexual abuse should be extended to include inappropriate sexual behaviour of clergy with those who have learning disabilities and mental health problems.

12. All dioceses should have an advisory panel to deal with complaints of clerical child sexual abuse.

13. The *Framework Document* states that "adequate positive steps should be taken to restore the good name and reputation of a priest or religious who has been wrongly accused" (p. 19) but it does not describe the steps required. Policies for re-establishing the person's good name and the procedures to be followed should be developed.

Professional Development of Clergy

14. A code of professional conduct should be developed, in consultation with clergy and laity, to clarify roles and boundaries in relationships, to assist clergy in managing these boundaries and to underpin the professionalism of the Church as an organisation.

15. The personal and professional development of clergy, both those in training and those already in ministry, should be upgraded and should continue throughout their careers.

16. Support structures for clergy should be reviewed with a view to making support available on an ongoing basis. Personal development and spiritual support should be facilitated by these structures.

17. Those in leadership roles in the Church should receive professional training in management and leadership.

18. A programme of ongoing support and supervision for convicted clergy (including relapse prevention and preparation

for life without ministry) should be developed. The programme should facilitate cooperation with clergy who have
abused. Such a programme should be developed in conjunction with professionals working with sex offenders.

19. Professional development procedures for clergy should be
    audited at appropriate intervals. This could be done by the
    Church or by an external agency using a quality assurance
    approach.

Chapter 1

BACKGROUND AND INTRODUCTION

INTRODUCTION

Child sexual abuse is recognised internationally as a major social problem with long-term implications for individuals and families. It poses significant challenges for criminal justice, mental health and child protection agencies. In the Irish context, a recent first national survey on lifetime sexual abuse and violence revealed a high prevalence of child sexual abuse in Ireland.[1] Over time and with increasing awareness of child sexual abuse in general, the problem of child sexual abuse by Catholic clergy[a] has emerged as a significant challenge to the Church and civil authorities. Child sexual abuse by Catholic clergy has been revealed and widely reported in the media as a scandal, a crisis, a betrayal and a cover-up. One of the major issues to emerge is that most cases occurred long before they were made public and, although Church authorities were often aware of allegations of child sexual abuse, they did not respond

---

Note: Numbers used in the text refer to book or journal references which are listed in full at the end of the report. Alphabetical letters used in the text refer to footnotes providing additional information at the end of the same page.

[a] In the interests of brevity in this book, the term "clergy" is used throughout to refer to bishops, priests, religious and deacons. In the context of child sexual abuse, the term "clergy" is widely understood by the public to include both priests and religious. The technically correct meaning of the term "clergy" refers to diocesan priests (who are under the authority of a bishop) and male members of religious orders who have been ordained. It does not refer to other religious members of congregations such as Christian Brothers and nuns. The term "Church" as used in the book refers to the Catholic Church.

expeditiously or effectively. Many Superiors did not report abusers to civil authorities. Abusers often remained in ministry and continued to perpetrate abuse. These revelations, both in Ireland and internationally, have created a high level of public awareness of child sexual abuse by clergy and are generally regarded as having done serious damage to the Catholic Church. While child sexual abuse by clergy has received extensive media attention, it has not been the subject of scientific research to date in Ireland.

STUDY OUTLINE

In 2001, the Bishops' Committee on Child Abuse (now known as the Bishops' Committee on Child Protection) of the Roman Catholic Church in Ireland commissioned the Health Services Research Centre at the Department of Psychology, Royal College of Surgeons in Ireland, to conduct an in-depth independent study of the impact of child sexual abuse by clergy in Ireland. The overall aim of the study was to examine the impact of child sexual abuse by clergy on a wide range of individuals:

1. Individuals who experienced child sexual abuse by clergy

2. Family members of abused individuals

3. Clergy convicted of sexual offences against children

4. Family members of convicted clergy

5. Church colleagues of convicted clergy

6. Church personnel (including lay persons who work for the Church)

7. The wider Church community.

The research did not aim to audit all allegations of child sexual abuse by clergy, as this was the remit of other groups. Instead, the purpose of this research was to provide a broader perspective on the impact of clerical child sexual abuse on those abused and on significant others by documenting the experiences of those involved in or affected by child sexual abuse by clergy.

Research Objectives

The main research objectives were:

1. To examine the psychological and social impact, and the impact on faith, of child sexual abuse by clergy

2. To examine the experience of disclosure and response from the perspectives of those involved

3. To inform recommendations for future Church policy.

Study Phases

The project consisted of three studies:

1. A national telephone survey of the general public

2. An in-depth interview study of individuals directly affected by clerical abuse

3. A postal questionnaire survey of delegates and bishops involved in managing complaints of abuse.

General Public Survey

The first study was a telephone survey of a stratified random sample of 1,081 members of the general population (76 per cent response rate). It was designed to explore the knowledge, perceptions and attitudes of the wider Church community and the general public.[b] The specific objectives of the survey were to evaluate:

- Public estimates of the prevalence of child sexual abuse by clergy

- Public tolerance towards clergy who have sexually abused children

- Public opinions about the Church's response to child sexual abuse by clergy and their level of trust for the future

---

[b] Detailed results of this telephone survey were published in *The Irish Times*, 6 November 2002.

- Public awareness of recent actions taken by the Church to address the issue of child sexual abuse

- Effects of Church-related child sexual abuse on religious practices of the public

- Public opinion on media coverage of Church-related child sexual abuse

- Public sources of knowledge on child sexual abuse

- Public satisfaction with the Catholic Church and clergy

- Public idealisation of priests and commitment to Church leadership

- Level of trust in and relationship with a God.

Personal Experience Study

This study consisted of qualitative in-depth face-to-face interviews. Forty-eight people were interviewed. This study sample consisted of:

- Seven people who had experienced child sexual abuse by clergy[c]

- Three family members of individuals who had experienced abuse

- Eight clergy who were convicted of sexual offences against children

- Five family members of convicted clergy

---

[c] In addition to the seven individuals who experienced child sexual abuse, one individual, who experienced clerical sexual abuse as an adult, was inadvertently asked to participate in the study. Since she had taken significant steps to be available for interview, her experiences, particularly relating to disclosure, were documented. Because most participants reported their experience of child sexual abuse as adults, it was felt that her contribution could usefully be included as part of the overall perspective on management of sexual abuse by Church personnel (Chapter 5).

- Three colleagues of convicted clergy and one priest advisor[d]

- Twenty additional clergy[e] and lay persons who work for the Church.

In addition, the research team were able to obtain a random sample of individuals from the general population who had been sexually abused by clergy. This sample had already taken part in a national prevalence study on sexual abuse and violence (SAVI).[1] Of the 3,120 members of the public interviewed as part of this prevalence study in 2001, 39 reported experiencing sexual abuse by clergy with 30 reporting this abuse as children. Twenty-five gave consent to be re-contacted for further research purposes and of these, 14 were surveyed for this study (see Appendix II, p. 10).

The study was designed to evaluate:

- The psychological and social impact of the abuse on each of the groups described

- The impact of abuse on the spiritual life of these groups

- Their experiences of disclosure and the response of the Church

- Their views on how the Church has managed complaints of clerical child sexual abuse.

Church Management Survey

This was a postal survey of delegates and bishops (including auxiliary and retired bishops). These are the main clerical personnel charged with implementing Church policy on child sexual abuse and with managing allegations of child sexual abuse. The delegate

---

[d] Priests interviewed as colleagues had worked with priests who had been convicted for sexual offences against children. Priest advisor refers to a priest who is appointed as a support person for priests under investigation for child sexual abuse. This was recommended by the 1996 *Framework Document* (Catholic Church guidelines on child sexual abuse).

[e] The clergy interviewed in this group included bishops, retired bishops, provincials of religious orders, priests (including delegates), members of religious orders/congregations and non-clerical Church employees.

role was created as part of the Irish Catholic Church's response to clerical child sexual abuse in 1996. Delegates play a central role in co-ordinating the Church's response to allegations of child sexual abuse while bishops are responsible for its overall management. At least one delegate is appointed per diocese or religious congregation. There were 153 diocesan and religious delegates at the time of the survey and 102 participated, giving a response rate of 67 per cent. Thirty-five of a possible 44 bishops participated, giving a response rate of 80 per cent. The survey was designed to examine:

- Attitudes towards designated roles and organisational structures in the Church

- Challenges and support needs in managing child sexual abuse by clergy

- Personal impact of, and future concerns about, clerical child sexual abuse

- Perceptions of the current and preferred organisational culture in the Catholic Church.

The various study methodologies used are described in more detail in Appendix II.

FACTORS INFLUENCING PUBLIC AWARENESS OF CLERICAL CHILD SEXUAL ABUSE IN IRELAND: MILESTONES

1994: The Fr Brendan Smyth Case

Widespread public awareness of child sexual abuse by clergy in Ireland began with media coverage of the Fr Brendan Smyth case in 1994. Fr Smyth pleaded guilty to 74 charges of indecent and sexual assault and was sentenced to 12 years in prison. There was unprecedented controversy over the failure to extradite Fr Smyth from the Republic of Ireland to answer to similar charges of abuse in Northern Ireland. At the time, the mismanagement of this case "brought down a government in circumstances heavy with suspicions of corruption . . .".[f] Both the then Taoiseach, Mr Albert Reynolds, and the President of the High Court, Justice Harry Whelehan, who had been appointed five days earlier, resigned. The case focused public attention on the relationship between the Catholic Church and the State and on the protection seen to be afforded to the Church when one of its representatives was accused of serious crimes.

1995: First Irish Person Sexually Abused by a Priest to Speak Publicly about it

In 1995, Andrew Madden wrote an article for the *Sunday Times* about his experience of child sexual abuse by a priest in Dublin. His story had already been reported anonymously in the Irish media. Controversy surrounded his case because initial reports that he had received financial compensation from the priest were denied by Church spokespersons in 1994. He decided to waive his anonymity in the 1995 article and to confirm that he had received financial compensation because of sexual abuse. He was the first person in Ireland to go public about being abused as a child by a priest.[g]

1996 and 1999: The *Dear Daughter* and *States of Fear* Television Documentaries

In 1996, the story of Christine Buckley, a woman who was abandoned at three weeks old and subsequently brought up in Goldenbridge Orphanage, was told in an Irish television documentary entitled *Dear Daughter*. She recounted life as a child growing up in the orphanage as one of cruelty and abuse. Her story exposed a regime of cruelty that existed in the fifties and sixties in some orphanages run by religious orders. In 1999, an Irish television series called

---

[f] The case is described in detail in Chris Moore's (1995) *Betrayal of Trust: The Father Brendan Smyth Affair and the Catholic Church*, Dublin: Marino Books.

[g] His story is described in a book, A. Madden (2003). *Altar Boy: A Story of Life after Abuse*. Dublin: Penguin Ireland.

States of Fear broadcast the personal accounts of individuals who
had experienced child abuse in industrial schools in Ireland. These
were subsequently published as a book, *Suffer the Little Children*.[2]
The series had such a significant impact that the government offered a public apology to all those who had experienced abuse in
institutions and made funds available to create a national counselling service for those affected. The Laffoy Commission (Commission to Inquire into Child Abuse) was established in 2000 to investigate the charges and to hear the testimonies of those abused. (See
Appendix III for more on the Laffoy Commission.) Although the
Irish public had been aware of serious individual child sexual
abuse cases such as the "X" case, the Kilkenny Incest Case and the
McColgan case during the 1990s,[h] *States of Fear* provided a disturbing account of widespread abuse within institutional settings. Children under the care of the State in industrial and reformatory
schools run by religious orders had been subjected to widespread
and serious abuse. This was not confined to single instances, isolated perpetrators or a few children but was reported as a pervasive
experience of those children seen as most vulnerable in Irish society
and placed "in care" for their own protection. These revelations
challenged views of recent Irish social history as they created an
image of the Catholic Church in Ireland as punitive and the State as
opting out of child welfare and protection.[3]

2002: The *Suing the Pope* Documentary

On 19 March 2002, British television (BBC 2) screened a documentary entitled *Suing the Pope*, which described experiences of several men who had been sexually abused as children by Fr Sean
Fortune, a priest of the Ferns diocese in County Wexford. The
programme criticised the Church's handling of the cases and alleged that the local bishop had failed to deal adequately with Fr
Fortune. Irish television (RTÉ) televised the documentary in April
2002. The overriding public concern was with the apparently

---

[h] These cases are described in Chapter 3.

inadequate management of these cases at the time they were originally reported and with the current accountability of those in authority. Brendan Comiskey, Bishop of the diocese of Ferns, subsequently resigned. Throughout this period, several other cases of child sexual abuse by clergy were revisited by the media and there was significant public debate about clerical sexual abuse of children. The Church was accused of being interested only in protecting its reputation, power and influence and of hiding behind canon law (the law of the Catholic Church).

Mr Micheál Martin, the Irish Minister for Health and Children, met with the men who were abused as children by Fr Sean Fortune in April 2002. Following this meeting, he announced the appointment of a barrister, Mr George Bermingham, to recommend the type of inquiry to be conducted into the management of cases of child sexual abuse by priests in the Ferns diocese by the Catholic Church and other authorities. In March 2003, the terms of reference of this inquiry were published and Justice Frank Murphy (retired Supreme Court judge) was appointed as chairperson of the inquiry. The Murphy inquiry is non-statutory and held in private. The inquiry will establish the number of complaints made to the diocese of Ferns prior to 10 April 2002 and examine the adequacy of responses to these complaints.

2002: The *Cardinal Secrets* Television Documentary

In November 2002, a documentary entitled *Cardinal Secrets* was broadcast by Irish television (RTÉ). This focused on the Dublin diocese and contended that a number of complaints of child sexual abuse by priests had been mismanaged by the diocese. There were graphic and disturbing accounts of the sexual abuse experienced by some individuals as children. Evidence was provided that Church leaders in the Dublin diocese were not only aware of the abuse perpetrated by some of its priests, but also that they failed to protect other children by allowing these priests to continue in ministry. As with the *Suing the Pope* documentary several months previously, this programme was a major stimulus for media examination of child sexual abuse by clergy.

2002: Launch of the SAVI (Sexual Abuse and Violence in Ireland) Report

In April 2002, the first national prevalence study of lifetime sexual abuse and violence in Ireland was launched by President Mary McAleese at a national conference. This study provided shocking figures concerning the prevalence of sexual abuse in Irish society. Findings indicated that 30 per cent of women and 24 per cent of men had experienced some form of sexual abuse as children and 5.6 per cent of women and 2.7 per cent of men were raped as children or adolescents. Forty-one per cent of these had *never* told another person (not family, friend or professional) about their abuse. The abusers about whom society appear to be most concerned (i.e. strangers, fathers and clergy) constituted a minority of all abusers. They accounted for 27 per cent of all cases of child sexual abuse (21 per cent of abuse was by strangers, 3.2 per cent by clergy and 2.5 per cent by fathers). Response to the findings was muted. International researchers in this area had advised that high prevalence figures would be met with denial or criticism of the research methods used. Instead the findings appeared to have a resonance with the public and professionals and seem to have been accepted as unpalatable but realistic. The SAVI study is discussed in further detail as relevant throughout the book.

International Revelations

Revelations of child sexual abuse by clergy are not unique to Ireland. During the late 1980s, reports began to emerge in the US and Canada and later in Australia, the UK and Europe. Throughout Spring 2002, there were reports from the US concerning the Archbishop of Boston (Cardinal Law) who was criticised for his handling of cases of child sexual abuse by priests. Between 1995 and 1999, 21 priests in England and Wales were convicted for sexual offences against children. In Belgium and France, bishops have been criticised for mishandling cases and an archbishop in Poland resigned when he himself was accused of sexual misconduct. In May 2002, the Catholic Church in Hong Kong confirmed that complaints of child sexual abuse had been made against some priests. Africa and Latin America are currently notable for the absence of reports of child sexual abuse by clergy.

IRISH CATHOLIC CHURCH'S RESPONSE TO CHILD SEXUAL ABUSE: MILESTONES

1994: The Advisory Committee on Child Sexual Abuse

In 1994, the Irish Bishops' Conference established an Advisory Committee to advise on appropriate Church responses where there was an accusation, suspicion or knowledge of clergy having sexually abused a child. The Committee was also asked to generate guidelines for Church policy with procedures to be followed in responding to complaints.

1995: CORI Child Protection Task Force and Child Protection Office

The Conference of Religious in Ireland[i] (CORI) established a Child Protection Task Force and a Child Protection Office in 1995 to train personnel, to offer advice on the assessment and treatment of abusers and to assist religious congregations in drawing up their own guidelines and child protection policies.

1996: Church Guidelines on Child Sexual Abuse

Church guidelines entitled *Child Sexual Abuse: Framework for a Church Response* were published in January 1996.[4] One of the most significant aspects of these guidelines was the recommendation that allegations of child sexual abuse, known or suspected, against priests and religious, should be reported to the civil authorities. It was also recommended that each diocese and religious congregation adopt a protocol for responding to complaints and circulate

---

[i] Umbrella organisation for approximately 140 male and female religious congregations based in Ireland.

this protocol to all priests and religious in dioceses or religious congregations. In addition, each bishop or religious superior was advised to appoint a number of personnel: a delegate to implement the protocol; a support person who would be available to those making complaints and their families; a priest advisor for each person accused; and an advisory panel to review complaints and offer advice to the bishop/religious superior. The guidelines also provided for the assessment, treatment and pastoral care of the abuser and advised on the selection and formation of candidates for priesthood and religious life. In relation to the parish and local community where a priest had been accused, the bishop was advised to make a public statement about the matter, while having due regard for the privacy of the accused and the possibility of interfering with the course of justice. Furthermore, a pastoral visit to the parish by the bishop was advised along with a programme of pastoral support and spiritual renewal.

1996: The National Resource Group

Following the publication of the Church's guidelines, a National Resource Group was established to facilitate the implementation of the guidelines and to act as a resource for the Catholic Church in Ireland in responding to the issue of child sexual abuse by clergy. It was also to provide training programmes for personnel (such as delegates and support persons) as appointed by dioceses.

1997: Counselling Service for Church-related Abuse

In 1997, CORI set up a confidential telephone counselling service called *Faoiseamh*[j] to listen to and, if required, arrange face-to-face counselling (by independent counsellors at a convenient location) for people abused by members of religious orders. This service is offered for those affected both in Ireland and those now living

---

[j] The Irish word meaning respite or relief.

abroad.[k] Several dioceses also contribute financially to this service and refer individuals who require counselling.

1999: The Bishops' Committee on Child Abuse

In 1999, the Irish Bishops' Conference established the Bishops' Committee on Child Abuse. A key concern was to ensure a comprehensive approach by the Irish Bishops' Conference to the work of the Government's Commission to Inquire into Child Abuse (Laffoy Commission). The Committee on Child Abuse made a submission to the Irish Bishops' Conference in September 2000 recommending the establishment of one national committee on child protection to advise bishops and to be resourced by a secretariat and executive head. This recommendation was endorsed by the Irish Bishops' Conference in November 2000.

2001: The Bishops' Committee on Child Protection and the Child Protection Office

In 2001, the Bishops' Committee on Child Abuse was replaced by the Bishops' Committee on Child Protection, an umbrella group to incorporate the work of the National Resource Group. A national Child Protection Office was also established in 2001. The Child Protection Office works in conjunction with the Committee on Child Protection and assists the Committee in several ways such as: providing information and advice to bishops, diocesan personnel and others to help them meet the therapeutic and/or pastoral needs of those affected by clerical abuse; promoting best practice among diocesan personnel who have responsibility for dealing with complaints about child abuse and assisting in the provision of ongoing training and development for such personnel; and advising Church personnel and institutions on best prac-

---

[k] Since February 1997 (to 31 January 2003) the Faoiseamh Helpline has responded to over 11,375 calls and offered face-to-face counselling to 2,452 people (of whom 1,923 have accepted). There are currently 648 people in counselling with the service.

tice policies and national guidelines in relation to the prevention of child abuse.

2001: Scientific Study of Clerical Child Sexual Abuse

In January 2001, the Bishops' Committee on Child Abuse (now known as the Bishops' Committee on Child Protection) commissioned an independent scientific study on the impact of clerical child sexual abuse in Ireland. The Health Services Research Centre at the Department of Psychology, Royal College of Surgeons in Ireland was employed to conduct the study. Internationally,[1] this was the first such study to be commissioned from an independent organisation by the Catholic Church. Its aims were to increase understanding of the problem of child sexual abuse by clergy and to identify changes needed for the future. In June 2001, the Irish Bishops' Conference publicly announced the study.

2002: Independent Commission on Child Sexual Abuse

In June 2002, the Catholic Church announced the terms of reference for an Independent Commission on Child Sex Abuse with (retired) Judge Gillian Hussey as chairperson. It was set up jointly by the Irish Bishops' Conference, the Conference of Religious in Ireland and the Irish Missionary Union. It began in September 2002 and was due to publish a final report in February 2004. However, in December 2002 the Commission was disbanded. The decision by the Commission members not to proceed with the inquiry was taken in light of the Minister for Justice's announcement of his intention to introduce legislation for a new procedure which would enable a detailed and focused investigation into how Church authorities dealt with allegations of child sexual abuse by clergy. It was felt that the proposed legislation for statu-

---

[1] In March 2003, a committee appointed by the Catholic bishops in the US commissioned researchers at the John Jay College of Criminal Justice in New York to study the extent of child sexual abuse in the Catholic Church in the US. The study will survey bishops and representatives of religious orders asking them to provide details about child sexual abuse cases.

tory investigations could duplicate the intended work of the Commission.

2003: Child Protection Policy Group

Following the disbandment of the Hussey Commission, the Irish Bishops' Conference decided to develop a comprehensive and integrated Child Protection Policy for application throughout Ireland and extending to all priests, religious, Church personnel, employees and volunteers. A group of experts in education, health, child protection, social work, law enforcement, victims' rights and theology was established by the Bishops' Conference, the Conference of Religious in Ireland (CORI) and the Irish Missionary Union (IMU) to develop this policy. In June 2003, the group held its first meeting and it is expected that by early 2004 a central policy will be presented to the Bishops' Conference, CORI and the IMU for adoption.[m]

There is no way of knowing how the Church initiatives outlined are being implemented by dioceses and religious congregations as there are currently no national audit systems in place to oversee the implementation of Church policy.

---

[m] Appendix I outlines the structure of the Catholic Church in Ireland.

Chapter 2

THE EPIDEMIOLOGY OF CHILD SEXUAL ABUSE

SUMMARY

o By its very nature, child sexual abuse is hidden and difficult to study.

o Prevalence estimates are hampered by the stigma of child sexual abuse and by differing definitions, methods, samples, age categories and locations of research.

o One of the main findings from prevalence studies is the low rate of reporting of child sexual abuse to authorities such as police or child protection agencies.

o High prevalence rates are reported in psychiatric populations. This may provide some indication of the negative long-term effects of child sexual abuse.

o The number of cases of child sexual abuse reported in Ireland increased through the 1990s and has now begun to decrease. This may reflect a reduction in the number of historical or contemporary cases being reported, or both.

o The prevalence of child sexual abuse in Ireland has been documented at 20 per cent for women and 16 per cent for men (for child sexual abuse involving physical contact) and 10 per cent for women and 7 per cent for men (for non-contact abuse).

o   The reported prevalence of child sexual abuse by clergy in Ire-
    land is 3.2 per cent of all cases of child sexual abuse. It is
    higher for abused boys (5.8 per cent of men abused as children
    reported their abuser to be a member of the clergy) than
    abused girls (1.4 per cent).

DEFINING CHILD SEXUAL ABUSE

There is no universally accepted definition of child sexual abuse.
The term has evolved from other descriptive terms such as "the battered-child syndrome", "non-accidental injury to children" and
"child abuse". Published literature on child sexual abuse contains
considerable variation and inconsistency in descriptions and definitions used. These include molestation, child-rape and sexual victimisation.[5] Irish criminal law enables prosecution for sexual
offences against children.[a] However, child sexual abuse is not in itself a specified criminal offence under Irish law and there is no legal
definition of child sexual abuse in Ireland. A report by the Law Reform Commission on Child Sexual Abuse in 1990,[6] recommended
the creation of a new criminal offence "child sexual abuse" or "sexual exploitation" and outlined a definition of child sexual abuse.

Definitions of child sexual abuse vary on several dimensions:
whether physical contact is involved, the age of the abused individual and abuser, the age difference between the person abused
and abuser and whether only unwanted experiences are considered.[7] Some acts are clearly viewed as abusive. However, there is
less agreement about other acts, such as exhibitionism, that do not
involve physical contact with the child. The intent of the adult is
often considered when deciding whether an act is sexually abusive or not but intent is not always easy to establish.

Some commentators have argued that any sexual act with a
child is abusive.[8] This means that a broad range of acts can come

---

[a] Those convicted of sexual offences against children are charged under laws
such as the Criminal Law Amendment Act 1935, Criminal Law (Rape) (Amendment) Act, 1990, Criminal Law (Sexual Offences) Act, 1993 or the Criminal Law
(Incest Proceedings) Act, 1995.

under the definition of abuse. Legal and research definitions of child sexual abuse usually require two elements. Firstly, there must be sexual activities involving a child and secondly there must be an "abusive condition" such as coercion or a large age gap between participants, in which consent is absent or compromised.[9]

Definitions used for research purposes have tended to be broad. Within this, a wide variety of activities from indecent exposure to rape can be included. These activities are usually divided into two categories: non-contact abuse and contact abuse. However, using broad definitions may be unhelpful in determining the likely impact of abuse on individuals. Thus, it cannot be assumed that "non-contact" forms of child sexual abuse are always less traumatic for the abused than "contact" child sexual abuse.

It is difficult to achieve a commonly accepted definition of child sexual abuse given that the term is used in diverse ways in legal, clinical and social contexts. Each context has its own set of priorities and functions when dealing with child sexual abuse. Thus, one definition may not suffice. It may be appropriate to have the term vary across contexts but to promote uniformity within settings, i.e. narrower (e.g. behaviourally specific) definitions to be used in research and broader (e.g. self-evaluation) definitions to be used in child protection and clinical contexts.[10] In the Irish context, the definition recommended by the 1990 Law Reform Commission Report on Child Sexual Abuse and subsequently outlined in *Children First* (National Guidelines for the Protection and Welfare of Children, 1999)[11] is the most common definition used. According to this definition (page 33), examples of child sexual abuse include:

- Exposure of the sexual organs or any sexual act intentionally performed in the presence of a child

- Intentional touching or molesting of the body of the child whether by a person or an object for the purpose of sexual arousal or sexual gratification

- Masturbation in the presence of the child or the involvement of the child in an act of masturbation

- Sexual intercourse with the child whether oral, vaginal or anal

- Sexual exploitation of a child includes inciting, encouraging, propositioning, requiring or permitting a child to solicit for, or to engage in, prostitution or other sexual acts. Sexual exploitation also occurs when a child is involved in the exhibition, modelling or posing for the purpose of sexual arousal, gratification or sexual act, including its recording (on film, video tape or other media) or the manipulation, for those purposes, of the image by computer or other means. It may also include showing sexually explicit material to children which is often a feature of the "grooming" process by perpetrators of abuse.

- Consensual sexual activity involving an adult and an underage person. In relation to child sexual abuse, it should be noted that for the purposes of criminal law, the age of consent to sexual intercourse is 17 years. This means, for example, that sexual intercourse between a 16-year-old girl and her 17-year-old boyfriend is illegal, although it may not be regarded as constituting child sexual abuse.

THE INCIDENCE AND PREVALENCE OF CHILD SEXUAL ABUSE

Incidence

"Incidence" refers to the number of new cases identified in a fixed period of time, often a year, while "prevalence" refers to the total number of cases that exist in a population. In relation to child sexual abuse, "incidence" usually refers to the number of new cases reported in a year to child protection and law enforcement agencies. The number of reported cases is usually believed to be significantly lower than the actual number of cases. The level of reporting may vary considerably and in part reflects both a community's awareness of the problem of child sexual abuse[12] and its willingness to promote disclosure, detection, support and treatment.

Prevalence

"Prevalence" concerns the cumulative score, i.e. a count of all individuals who have experienced a particular phenomenon. There are many different prevalence estimates of child sexual abuse. These may be influenced by the time (year) the information was obtained and the country being studied. Lack of uniformity in the type of definitions of child sexual abuse among researchers also contributes to discrepancies in reported prevalence rates. The most popular and often cited prevalence rate is "1 in 4 girls and 1 in 9 boys" and these figures are credited to the seminal research on human sexuality by Kinsey in 1953. Since then there have been numerous international studies on the prevalence of child sexual abuse. Community, college and clinical samples have also been assessed. Prevalence rates for child sexual abuse have been reported to range from 6 per cent to 54 per cent for girls and 4 per cent to 16 per cent for boys among international community samples while higher rates for women (up to 90 per cent) have been reported among adult clinical (psychiatric) samples.[12] Researchers have cautioned that prevalence rates found in most studies underestimate the true level of child sexual abuse. Furthermore, very few studies have obtained information on sexual abuse directly from children.[b]

Irish Statistics on Child Sexual Abuse

Irish statistics on child sexual abuse come from a range of sources: the annual reports of agencies providing counselling services, official government statistics on reports to health boards and general population prevalence surveys. A substantial proportion of clients using Irish rape crisis centres (RCC) in 1996 were adults

---

[b] Finkelhor and Dziuba-Leatherman[190] conducted the first study of this kind in 1992 using a telephone survey. Two thousand children aged 10 to 16 years were surveyed (1,042 were boys and 958 were girls). Experiences of attempted or completed sexual abuse were reported by 10.5 per cent of the sample. Of those who experienced sexual abuse, 60 per cent reported it to someone but only 3 per cent reported it to the police.

who had experienced sexual abuse as children.[13] Annual statistics for the year 2000 showed that 51 per cent of all telephone calls to the RCC crisis line (N = 8,150) related to child sexual abuse.[14] Regarding government statistics, the most recent national childcare statistics in Ireland show that almost 6,000 cases of child abuse were reported to the Irish health boards in 2001.[15] Of these, 31 per cent were cases of child sexual abuse (see Table 2.1 for an overview of reported cases and their status at the time of the report).

*Table 2.1: Number of Reported, Confirmed, Unfounded, Inconclusive and Ongoing Cases of Child Abuse for 2001 by Type of Abuse for all Health Boards in the Republic of Ireland**

	Type of Abuse				
	Physical	*Sexual*	*Emotional*	*Neglect*	*Total*
Reported	1,252	1,842	814	2,086	5,994
(N)	(21%)	(31%)	(13%)	(35%)	
Confirmed	419	397	270	774	1,860
	(33%)	(22%)	(33%)	(37%)	(31%)
Unfounded	130	170	72	232	604
	(11%)	(9%)	(9%)	(11%)	(10%)

*Statistics as reported were provisional. Some cases were still under investigation or had decisions pending

There were fewer (22 per cent) confirmed cases of sexual abuse and a higher number of inconclusive and ongoing cases (69 per cent) compared to other types of abuse. The majority of both reported and confirmed abuse cases involved neglect.[c] The provisional figures for 2001 showed a significant decrease in the

---

[c] Despite the high rate of reported child neglect, a recent review of the trends in child maltreatment literature (Behl et al., 2003)[191] over a 22-year period showed that published literature on child neglect (CN) has remained consistently low compared to an increase in the annual percentage of published literature on child sexual abuse and a decrease in literature on physical abuse. The authors concluded that CN was still in the initial stages of scientific inquiry and that this gap in child maltreatment literature should be addressed to further enhance the understanding of CN.

number of reported cases of child abuse compared to the two previous years.[d] Reasons for this are not known. They may reflect a
tapering-off following disclosure of a large number of historical
cases or reduction in incidence (contemporary cases of abuse) or
both.

In a study of cases reported to the Eastern Health Board in
1988, 512 confirmed cases of child sexual abuse were examined.[16]
Three-quarters of the children abused were girls and in a third of
cases the children abused were aged 6 years or under. The average age at time of abuse was 9.2 years for girls and 7.9 years for
boys. In 30 per cent of cases, at least one other sibling was also involved in a suspected or confirmed case. The main type of abuse
was non-penetrative sexual abuse. Violence was used in over a
quarter of cases and abuse generally occurred in the child's home.
The abuser was male in 90 per cent of confirmed cases. Fathers
constituted the largest single category of offenders (29 per cent)
followed by neighbours (16 per cent), brothers (12 per cent), uncles (11 per cent) and strangers (3 per cent).[e] A parallel study reported on the incidence of child sexual abuse in Northern Ireland
based on reports to professionals during 1987.[17] This study
showed a similar pattern of child sexual abuse in Northern Ireland. The majority of children abused were girls; children were on
average under 10 years of age when abused and boys typically
experienced abuse at a younger age than girls. The abuse was
mainly intrafamilial, was perpetrated by males and occurred in
the child's own home.

Some general population studies have also been conducted
that give an indication of the prevalence of child sexual abuse in
Ireland. The Market Research Bureau of Ireland (MRBI)[18] con-

---

[d] In 2000, 8,269 cases of child abuse (2,104 or 26 per cent were child sexual abuse)
were reported to the health boards. In 1999, 10,031 cases were reported (2,530 or
25 per cent were child sexual abuse). This contrasts with 3,856 reported cases in
1991 and 1,646 in 1987.

[e] Information on the abuser was not available for all reported cases.

ducted the first survey in 1987.[f] Seven per cent of women and 5 per cent of men reported being sexually abused as children. All of the alleged abusers were male and one-third were close relatives of the person abused. In 1993, Irish Marketing Surveys (IMS)[19] conducted a survey on behalf of the Irish Society for the Prevention of Cruelty to Children (ISPCC). The study involved face-to-face interviews with the general public. While the main focus was on experiences of, and attitudes towards, child discipline and punishment, some questions on child sexual abuse were asked. A total of 160 (16 per cent) of those surveyed (N=1,001) reported having experienced child sexual abuse;[g] 12 per cent had experienced contact abuse (15 per cent of girls and 9 per cent of boys). This rate was significantly higher than that reported in the MRBI study in 1987.

The most recent and most extensive sexual abuse prevalence study in Ireland, the Sexual Abuse and Violence in Ireland (SAVI) Study, was commissioned by the Dublin Rape Crisis Centre with government support and conducted by this research group in 2001.[1] It involved over 3,000 anonymous telephone interviews with adult members of the general public about their experiences, beliefs and attitudes concerning sexual violence. The response rate was high at 71 per cent (N= 3,120). In relation to child sexual abuse, the study reported that 20 per cent of women and 16 per cent of men experienced sexual abuse involving physical contact in childhood while a further 10 per cent of women and 7 per cent of men experienced non-contact sexual abuse as children. Most child sexual abuse reported in the study occurred under the age of 12 years. Forty per cent of participants reporting childhood abuse experienced ongoing abuse rather than a single episode of abuse. For

---

[f] A total of 500 people, aged 18–44 years, were surveyed in the Dublin area about sexually abusive experiences under the age of 16. The survey used a self-administered confidential questionnaire. The sample was representative of the age-specific general population for gender and socio-economic status.

[g] To maximise response rates and participant confidentiality, they were asked to complete a short written questionnaire, without discussion with the researcher and to return this in a sealed envelope to the researcher.

many of these, the duration of abuse was longer than one year. The majority (89 per cent) of the perpetrators of child sexual abuse were male. For girls, these perpetrators were persons known to them but unrelated (52 per cent), family members (24 per cent) and strangers (24 per cent) while for boys perpetrators were persons known to them but unrelated (66 per cent), strangers (20 per cent) and family members (14 per cent). Disclosure to professionals was low among those who had experienced child sexual abuse (i.e. 5 per cent to police, 4 per cent to medical professionals and 10 per cent to counsellors). Almost half of those who reported experiences of child sexual abuse (41 per cent) said that they had not disclosed their abuse to any other person prior to their participation in the study. The SAVI study also provided some preliminary indicators that the prevalence of child sexual abuse was decreasing — the youngest (adult) participants in SAVI reported lower levels of child sexual abuse than previous generations. Similar trends showing a decline in reported cases of child sexual abuse have been reported recently in the US[20] and Australia.[21]

The Prevalence of Child Sexual Abuse by Clergy in Ireland

While many individual cases of child sexual abuse by clergy have been publicised in Ireland over the last decade, they cannot accurately reflect the prevalence of child sexual abuse by clergy. The SAVI study[1] found that 3.2 per cent of those reporting sexual abuse as children identified their perpetrator as a religious minister or religious teacher (i.e. clergy). Clergy were more likely to have abused boys (5.8 per cent of boys and 1.4 per cent of girls abused who reported child sexual abuse were abused by clergy). In absolute numbers, three times as many boys were abused by clergy. Abusers were categorised into family, non-family and stranger types of perpetrator. Non-family abusers were further defined as neighbours, friends, authority figures and brief acquaintances. Twenty-two per cent of boys and 16 per cent of girls abused were abused by authority figures. Clergy constituted the largest category of authority figures who abused boys, i.e. 27 per cent of authority figure abusers of boys were clergy (compared with 8 per cent for girls). Two-thirds of those abused by clergy in SAVI reported that their abusers were priests with the other one-third reporting that their abusers were male members of religious orders. Overall, the SAVI study showed that a very small proportion (3.2 per cent) of those reporting child sexual abuse identified clergy as their abusers. This compared with 2.5 per cent for fathers, 3.7 per cent for male siblings and 6.2 per cent for uncles. While the percentages of abusers of children identified as clerical are very low in SAVI, there is little consolation in this percentage since it represents a large number of individuals throughout Ireland.

One proposition sometimes forwarded about clerical child sexual abuse is that it is mostly homosexual. Figures from the SAVI study do not support this view. A total of 39 people (25 men and 14 women) reported abuse by clergy at some point in their lifetime. Most of the men (19 or 76 per cent) reported abuse as children and were aged 13 years or younger. Of the 14 women reporting abuse by clergy, 6 were abused at 13 years or younger, 3 were aged 10 years or younger, 3 were aged 14–17 years and 5 women were in their twenties. Thus 25 of 39 cases (64 per cent) involved children under 13 years of age, 8 (20 per cent) involved female teenagers or adults, 5 (13 per cent) involved males aged 14-17 and there was one case involving a male over 17 years of age. These figures show that most acts of clerical sexual abuse in Ireland are paedophile in nature and that only a small number of cases could be classed as ephebophile (abuse of male adolescents) or adult homosexual in nature.

The broader message from the SAVI study was that no one group could be identified as the "typical abuser". Images of fathers and clergy as primary abusers may come to mind when people ask "Who abuses children?" The small proportion of child sexual abuse which was attributable to clergy and fathers is an important reminder of how media representations can create stereotypes of the typical abuser which have little basis in fact. The role of the media is discussed further in Chapter 3.

The differences in profiles of abuse and abusers when comparing reported cases and general population prevalence is important. General population evidence gives the most representative profile and illustrates differences between those reporting and not reporting abuse to authorities. For instance, in SAVI those availing of counselling for abuse were more likely to have experienced penetrative abuse within the family and ongoing (rather than a single incident) abuse than those who did not present for counselling.

In conclusion, prevalence estimates for child sexual abuse are difficult to determine. Recent Irish evidence indicates that a substantial minority of Irish men and women have experienced sexual abuse in childhood. Approximately 3 per cent of those abused identified clergy as their abuser with three times more boys than girls being abused by clergy. Thus, in epidemiological terms, clerical abuse constitutes a very small proportion of child sexual abuse in Ireland.

Chapter 3

SOCIAL AWARENESS OF CHILD SEXUAL ABUSE

SUMMARY

o The Society for the Prevention of Cruelty to Children was established as a voluntary organisation in the US, the UK and Ireland in the late nineteenth century. It provided the first major international focus on child abuse and neglect.

o Social policies and laws to protect children from abuse and neglect have developed slowly over the twentieth century.

o The history of child sexual abuse is characterised by periods of denial and failure to recognise the seriousness of the problem.

o The 1962 publication of a paper entitled "The battered-child syndrome" by US paediatricians highlighted the physical abuse of children and is credited with the "discovery" of child abuse *per se*.

o Assessment and treatment of sex offenders developed from the late 1970s. Treatment has evolved from psychoanalytic approaches to behavioural modification through to cognitive behavioural therapy. There is now increased emphasis on controlling behaviour and addressing interpersonal deficits. It was not until the 1990s that specific treatment facilities for sex offenders were established in Ireland.

o In the 1970s, the feminist movement linked child sexual abuse with the abuse of women. Its campaigns for tougher penalties for sex offenders were instrumental in securing a place for child sexual abuse on contemporary social and political agendas.

o   Throughout the 1990s, several highly publicised cases of child sexual abuse in Ireland raised public awareness and instigated social policy and criminal law reform.

o   Studies of public awareness and knowledge of child sexual abuse show a progression in awareness and knowledge over the past 20 years. For instance, the public are now more likely to recognise that children are at more risk of abuse by persons known to them than by strangers.

o   The media are the main source of information on social problems for the general public. Analysis of media coverage shows that it reports the most sensational cases of child sexual abuse and over-emphasises "stranger danger". However, the role of the media is vital in creating general public awareness of the issue.

o   Management of convicted child sexual offenders may involve rehabilitation efforts. In some countries, it also involves surveillance once released from prison into the community. Such surveillance may be seen as a punitive rather than a restorative process for integrating the offender with the wider community.

INTRODUCTION

The sexual abuse of children by people in positions of trust has long been considered a serious crime[22] but the formal protection of children's sexual integrity has emerged more slowly in both criminal law and in social services.[23] Child protection has been a focus of serious public and professional concern in two distinct periods in the last two centuries: from the 1880s to World War I and from the 1960s to the present. The abuse of children occurs across all countries and cultures.[24] Society's reaction to the abuse of children has evolved over the last century from one of incredulity and disbelief to one of belief accompanied by intolerance and horror. The current level of awareness of child sexual abuse has not always existed. In the first section of this chapter, a short historical overview is outlined which illustrates that although child sexual abuse has existed for centuries, its existence was sometimes denied or ignored. Public awareness of and attitudes to child sexual abuse are discussed in the next section. The role of the media in constructing child sexual abuse as a social problem and creating public awareness is the subject of the subsequent section. The media have also been influential in demanding new or updated policies on child protection and welfare. Combined with increased public awareness, this has increased demands on policy makers and agencies responsible for childcare. Developments in this domain are outlined. Societal views of sex offenders, in particular concerning the long-term management of convicted sex offenders following custodial sentences, are outlined in the final section.

HISTORICAL OVERVIEW[a]

The sexual abuse of children gained widespread attention in the United States in the 1970s followed by Europe during the 1980s. Exactly what was responsible for the recognition of child sexual abuse as a major social problem is not easily explained. It is most likely due to a combination of factors. The problem of child abuse must be analysed as a social construction, which has relied on a history of recognition, identification and labelling by expert systems.[25]

Throughout history, child sexual abuse is documented but it is not always referred to by this name. In the 1800s, papers on child sexual abuse appeared in medical journals. They were written in the context of establishing medical evidence where there was an allegation of rape. A paper by Lyons (1997)[26] provides a comprehensive review of medical involvement in cases of child sexual

---

[a] As far back as the Roman era (455 AD) and during the medieval era and Renaissance years there are documented cases of child sexual abuse and of concerns being expressed about the protection of children and the prevention of child sexual abuse. For example, in England in 1548, a law was passed protecting boys from forced sodomy and protecting girls under 10 years of age from forcible rape (c.f. Schultz, 1982).[23]

abuse in nineteenth-century Ireland. It was suggested, for instance, that sexual intercourse was anatomically impossible between an adult and a child. In these Victorian times there was a sense of sexual prudery. For instance, details given by a nine-year-old girl of her rape were described as "too disgusting to be quoted". In 1862, Ambroise Tardieu, a French professor of legal medicine, documented 515 sexual offences, of which 420 were against children.[27] Although the emphasis at that time was establishing medical evidence, Tardieu argued that children do not always have physical signs of sexual assault. He acknowledged the potential psychological consequences of such assault and was the first to write on the sexual abuse of children as a social problem. Tardieu's concerns were ignored and the existence of child sexual abuse was denied. It is argued that this established a pattern of denial for many years that followed[28] and that Tardieu's plea for medical recognition and action had still not been heard a hundred years later.[29] Freud began formulating the "seduction theory" in 1896. According to this theory, hysteria and other neurotic psychological problems were caused by premature sexual experiences. The trauma of these sexual experiences was seen to be carried into adult life and manifested through hysteria. This process was thought to be unconscious. Freud proposed that most premature sexual experiences involved family members (i.e. incest).[30] The seduction theory not only drew attention to child sexual abuse but also described the psychological effects that were likely to be carried into adulthood. This proposition was shocking in Victorian society and was met with much resistance. In 1900, Freud retracted his seduction theory claiming instead that his patients' reports were constructed from fantasies and dreams.

Early twentieth-century medical literature discussed venereal diseases in children. One of the most respected medical journals, the *Lancet*, published an article in 1925 on venereal diseases in young girls.[31] Venereal diseases were known to be sexually transmitted at this time but among children transmission was described as "innocent" or "accidental", i.e. non-sexual. The source of infection was usually attributed to lavatories or baths or to poverty and overcrowding and there was rarely a suspicion of sexual assault. It is suggested that it was as late as the 1980s before physicians became aware of the fact that venereal diseases in children should be treated as an indication of sexual abuse.[31] However, in 1909 Dr Flora Pollack described how men raped children to rid themselves of venereal diseases — a practice described as the "infectionist theory".[31] Pollack claimed that it was rare for gonorrhoea to be transmitted from lavatories and viewed this explanation as a way of protecting the perpetrators of abuse and impeding justice.

In 1937, a study of children aged 5–12 years who had been sexually abused concluded that there was a possibility that in many cases the child was the active seducer rather than the one "innocently seduced".[32] Similar claims were made regarding children who had been sexually abused in studies published in the 1950s and 1970s.[33, 34] Around the same time, Kinsey et al. (1953) published a survey which reported that 24 per cent of their female survey participants were sexually abused as children. Kinsey and colleagues were surprised that these women reported being frightened by this experience. Similar surveys reporting the prevalence of child sexual abuse followed but the results were largely ignored by the professional community.[27]

From the 1930s to the 1950s, and in a separate medical context, radiologists began to associate infant fractures with trauma. There was some resistance to this proposition, particularly to the suggestion that parents were deliberately causing physical harm to their children. In 1946, Caffey suggested that some fractures among children were of "traumatic origin".[35] Against the backdrop of Caffey's work, Kempe et al. (US paediatricians) published a paper in 1962 describing "the battered-child syndrome".[36] The paper is credited with successfully bringing child abuse to professional attention.[37–40]

Since the 1980s, a significant body of empirical research on the nature, prevalence and effects of child abuse, including child sexual abuse, has emerged. Dissemination of information on child abuse was international. In the 1970s, the Irish Department of Health issued official guidelines on the identification and management of non-accidental injury to children for professionals

working with children. In 1983, Irish government guidelines referred to injuries resulting from sexual abuse[41] and in 1987, guidelines were issued on the identification, investigation and
management of sexual, physical and emotional child abuse and
neglect.[42] In 1965, child abuse was added to *Index Medicus*[b] as a
subject heading. The first journal article on child sexual abuse was
indexed in 1973 and in 1987 child sexual abuse appeared as a
separate subject heading in *Index Medicus.*[43]

There are several theories on what caused the resurgence in interest in child (sexual) abuse and why it remained on the professional and public agenda from the late 1960s. The feminist
movement has been credited with increasing and sustaining public
awareness of child sexual abuse. In the 1970s, the feminist movement incorporated child abuse into their cause. Feminist writers
were among the first to focus on extra-familial abuse rather than
incest. They explained sexual abuse as a function of the inferior
status of women and children combined with male predatory attitudes as perpetrated by the media and pornography. Feminist theory adopted a "victim-advocacy" approach to treatment and
intervention based on the model of rape crisis counselling. Femi-
nists have campaigned for more vigorous criminal justice sanctions for offenders as a deterrent against re-offending and as a
means of reinforcing appropriate sexual conduct.[44] Alongside the
contribution of the feminist movement, the prevalence and effects
of child sexual abuse were established through community surveys by the end of the 1980s.[27] As a result, there were demands on
professionals to treat and prevent such abuse.

In light of the current knowledge on the prevalence and effects
of child sexual abuse, it is interesting to note that "earlier discov-

---

[b] The record of current medical literature of the world from the 1800s to present
date. It is now called *Medline,* is available in electronic form and holds a record of
medical literature from 1960 to the present date. New terms are listed in the "vo-
cabulary" of *Index Medicus* when it becomes apparent that the term is being increasingly used in clinical and research reports. Thus, listing of terms as separate
subject headings does not signal the origin of the phenomenon but rather indicates growing attention to the topic.

eries of this abuse were suppressed".[45] Furthermore, when examining the history of child abuse, it is important to recognise that
"sporadic records do not necessarily indicate sporadic incidence".[46] It is argued that there has been a historic tradition of
avoidance in relation to child sexual abuse and a trend in discred-
iting each revelation.[47] Tardieu was discredited by his academic
contemporaries, Freud's theory was also rejected and Kempe was
criticised by many of his colleagues for creating "hysteria with
unprecedented speculation about his so-called battered children".[47] It is evident that child sexual abuse is not a recent phe-
nomena but that its widespread recognition and attempts to
respond to it are quite "modern". The most outstanding feature in
reviewing the literature on child (sexual) abuse is that the literature is characterised by cycles of "discovery and suppression".[45]
While both professional and public awareness has waxed and
waned throughout history, current public concern shows no immediate signs of diminishing.

CHILD SEXUAL ABUSE: PUBLIC AWARENESS AND ATTITUDES

> Child sexual abuse went unnoticed for centuries, it is only by
> highlighting it that we can undo the consequences of its invisibil-
> ity. Public awareness is essential. To the extent that public
> awareness exists we treat the problem and find resources to deal
> with it.[48]

Awareness of child abuse varies from one society to the next and
depends on the political, social, economic and cultural milieu of
the country at a particular time.[49] As child sexual abuse has become a major media topic over the last 20 years, public awareness
has "gone from slumber to preoccupation"[50] while public attitudes have evolved from "shocked disbelief to shocked acceptance".[51] Although child sexual abuse has been recognised as a
problem over time and across cultures, societies have varied in
their level of commitment to addressing it. Responses vary once
abuse is revealed. There can be a tendency to ignore abuse, to

deny how common it is or to see it as happening only in selected sub-groups such as those with low income. Conversely, the public may respond with outrage and may condemn abuse with no compassion for the abusers.[52] The increase in numbers of disclosures of child sexual abuse in recent decades has helped to bring the size and significance of the problem to public awareness.[53]

Early Public Awareness

In the late nineteenth century, child abuse and neglect were seen to be associated with the poorer sections of society. State support for single parents, "broken families" and families in difficult circumstances was inadequate and governments struggled to establish ways of dealing with unwanted and neglected children.[54] The Society for the Prevention of Cruelty to Children (SPCC) was set up in New York in 1875 and then later in the UK. Ireland had its own branch of the society from 1889. Societies were run by middle-class concerned citizens who confined their efforts to protecting the children of the poor. They created and supported custodial institutions, which are now often documented as worse than the situation from which the child had been rescued.[52] In the early twentieth century, the SPCC was referred to as "The Cruelty" because of the threat of children being taken from their families.[55] It has been argued that the primary objective of these societies at the time was not to save children from abuse but to save society from future delinquents.[56] Whatever the historical view of their interventions, the efforts of such groups have been credited with bringing the issue of child abuse to public attention. Alongside the public awareness they created, they also did much to make such abuse socially unacceptable in the absence of State intervention.

Events Influencing Public Awareness of Child Sexual Abuse in Ireland

In Chapter 1, the case of Fr Brendan Smyth was described briefly as the landmark case that brought child sexual abuse by clergy to widespread public attention in Ireland in 1994. In 1999, the television programme *States of Fear* and its associated book *Suffer the Little Children*, revealed the extent of both physical and sexual abuse experienced by many children in institutions run by religious orders with State funding (the actual number of children abused in institutions is difficult to ascertain but the potential figure could be somewhere in the region of several thousand). Before this, other notable individual cases (of child sexual abuse) helped to create awareness among the general public. In 1993, the Kilkenny incest case (the prosecution of a man for the sexual abuse of his daughter) provided the first high-profile and shocking illustration of child sexual abuse for Irish society.[c] This case led to an official government inquiry which received much media attention and was instrumental in securing a place for child sexual abuse on public and political agendas. The government inquiry considered not only management issues for individual professionals but also issues of public accountability and the status of child sexual abuse as a social problem. The report of the inquiry acknowledged that the public often remained passive in situations of abuse because of ambivalence in Irish society about abuse itself and because of a concern about the rights of outsiders to interfere in family matters.[57]

In 1995, the McColgan case came to public attention.[d] This involved a man who had sexually and physically abused four of his children over a number of years. Following his conviction, the siblings successfully sued the health board and the general practitioner involved in their case, for failing to protect them from continuous abuse. This was the first case of its kind in Ireland. Although these cases are usually held in private to protect those abused, the siblings waived confidentiality and their story received detailed media coverage. For this they received huge public support. Their case greatly increased public awareness of child sexual

---

[c] The "X" case in 1992 (the sexual abuse of a 14-year-old girl) was also a case of child sexual abuse. However, media attention was focused on the resultant unwanted pregnancy and questions over whether a termination of pregnancy was permissible because of the risk of suicide. Little attention was given to the issue of child sexual abuse in this case.

[d] Their story is told by Susan McKay (1998).[192]

abuse.[58] The McColgans also publicly urged other people who had been abused not to be afraid or ashamed to report their abuse.

Research on Public Knowledge and Attitudes: Prevalence and Profiles of Child Sexual Abuse

Research in this area must be considered with reference to the time, location and samples included in the study.[e] Little research has been conducted in Ireland. One of the first major studies was conducted in Boston in 1981, with parents[f] of children aged 6 to 14 years.[44] The study examined many myths and misconceptions about child sexual abuse as well as the effects of abuse on children, perceptions of perpetrators and reporting patterns. Here, the focus is on the questions relating to how informed the public were about child sexual abuse at that time.

Almost all of the parents had been exposed to a discussion of child sexual abuse, had read something about it in a newspaper or had seen something on television in the year prior to the study. Parents rated child sexual abuse as the most serious and traumatic event that could happen to a child, whether male or female. They estimated a high prevalence of child sexual abuse, with 19 per cent estimating that sexual abuse occurred in 1 in 4 girls and 17 per cent estimating the same occurrence for boys. Thirty per cent estimated that it occurred in 1 in 10 girls with 23 per cent estimating the same for boys. Thus, half (49 per cent) the parents thought that at least 1

---

[e] In 1969, an early national US survey (N=1,520) was conducted on public knowledge, attitudes and opinions on the *physical* abuse of children in the US following the "battered-child syndrome" paper.[193] Over 80 per cent of participants had recent knowledge of child abuse and only 17 per cent of the participants had not heard or read about the problem during the year preceding the survey. Main sources of information were newspapers (69 per cent) and radio and television (48 per cent). Over half of the participants thought anybody could be capable of injuring a child in "his" care. The majority favoured treatment over punishment for the perpetrator.

[f] The sample (N=251 parents) was drawn from the total population of parents in Boston who had children aged between 6 and 14 years. Participants were interviewed face-to-face.

in 10 girls had been sexually abused while 40 per cent thought that 1 in 10 boys had been abused. The majority estimated that abuse typically occurs before 11 years of age (this matched available evidence at the time). However, most parents did not consider that children under 5 years of age were at risk, an opinion contrary to the evidence available at that time. Parents were also aware that children do not readily report abusive experiences.

When given a hypothetical scenario involving a neighbour sexually abusing their daughter and then asked what they would do about it, the majority of parents said they would report the abuse to the police. Hypothetical situations were also used to determine how the public defined child sexual abuse. The most important characteristics in determining the seriousness of child sexual abuse were the age of the perpetrator and the type of abusive act. Once it was clear that the perpetrator was an adult, and that the abusive act was sexual intercourse or attempted sexual intercourse, the situation was rated as abusive. In cases where the child was described as passive, the scenarios were rated as less abusive than if the child protested.

A survey of adults in the US (in the state of Kentucky)[8] in 1986 assessed public knowledge of and attitudes to child abuse in general.[59] The public's ability to recognise child abuse, to identify characteristics of child abusers and abused children, to outline the effects of abuse and to know the procedures for reporting suspected cases of abuse were assessed. The majority of respondents had a good understanding of what constitutes physical, emotional and sexual abuse and child neglect through their ratings of different hypothetical scenarios. Similarly, respondents were well informed about the characteristics of abused children. The majority (72 per cent) knew that they were required by their State law to report suspected cases of child abuse to the authorities. However, only 30 per cent of those who knew of a case of physical abuse in the past had actually made an official report.

---

[8] This study was a telephone survey (N=742).

Another US study (in the state of Oregon),[h] conducted in 1998, examined public opinion and knowledge about child sexual abuse in a rural community.[60] Almost two-thirds of the sample thought that physical signs would be evident if a child was sexually abused. This is contrary to the available evidence — most sexually abused children have no physical signs of the abuse. The majority (72 per cent) thought that sexually abused children would always show behavioural changes and believed that children would tell the truth about child sexual abuse (86 per cent). About half thought that children would wait for several years before disclosing the abuse. Respondents were asked how they thought they would react if a child told them about sexual abuse — the majority (76 per cent) said they would support the child. They were also asked to whom they would report child sexual abuse: 35 per cent said a physician, 33 per cent said police and 21 per cent said a Child Protection Agency/Evaluation Unit. Overall, the Oregon study found that men were less knowledgeable about child sexual abuse than women. The greatest deficiencies in knowledge were found among single, less-educated and lower-income groups.

Public perceptions of sexual violence in Ireland were assessed by the SAVI study.[1] With regard to the prevalence of abuse by different types of perpetrators, participants significantly overestimated the prevalence of incest perpetrated against girls and boys and underestimated the prevalence of child sexual abuse by non-family members. When asked about education and awareness, the majority (88 per cent) said that they had not been told about the risk of child sexual abuse themselves as children. However, over half of those who had children themselves had spoken to their children about the risk of child sexual abuse.[i] Participants were also asked if they agreed or disagreed with statements concerning

---

[h] In this survey respondents were approached by researchers in public areas such as shopping malls and asked to self-complete a questionnaire (N=246).

[i] A recent Swedish study[194] found that parents talked less to their preschool children (aged 3 to 6 years) about sexual matters than did teachers and that mothers spoke more to their children about sexual matters than did fathers.

general beliefs and myths about sexual abuse and violence. The majority (79 per cent) disagreed with the statement "accusations about having been sexually abused as a child are often false". Thus the Irish public are broadly sympathetic towards those abused.

Research on Public Knowledge and Attitudes: Perceptions of Perpetrators

In the 1981 Boston study,[44] strangers were identified as the most probable offenders by 35 per cent of parents. Parents and step-parents were rated as the next most likely offenders in the Boston study. Most parents felt that elderly people would not abuse children and indicated that children were more likely to be abused by adults aged 30 to 40 years of age. Most parents were also in no doubt that the offender would most likely be male. The majority surveyed thought that sex offenders were mentally ill and favoured treatment over punishment. In cases of incest, they recommended removing the father from the home rather than the child. Emphasis on cautioning children about the danger of "talking to strangers" may place children at risk, as evidence shows that most sexual abuse is perpetrated by people known to the child. This is not to suggest that children should not be cautioned against the danger of interacting with strangers. Instead, the concern is that the public may believe that child abusers and the children they abuse fit a stereotypic profile; a profile that research in Ireland as elsewhere has not been able to identify. When research shows findings that contradict stereotypes (for example, that most child sexual abuse is perpetrated by family members rather than being perpetrated by strangers), the public may be sceptical of the results.[61]

In the 1986 Kentucky study,[59] most (85 per cent) respondents thought that child abusers had been abused themselves as children. Almost a third of respondents thought that child abusers were mentally ill, over half (55 per cent) thought that abusers would want help to stop their abusive behaviour while the majority (73 per cent) also felt that abusers are ashamed of their behaviour. Most (76 per cent) respondents were aware that abusers come from all socio-economic backgrounds.

Only 18 per cent of those who participated in the 1998 Oregon study[60] identified "a stranger" as the most likely perpetrator of child sexual abuse. This is significantly lower than the estimate (35 per cent) by parents in the 1981 Boston study and may indicate a significant increase in knowledge during the intervening period. Most (76 per cent) respondents in the Oregon study identified a person known to and trusted by the child as the most likely perpetrator of child sexual abuse. Similarly, in the SAVI study[1] the majority (91 per cent) disagreed with the statement "child abuse is mostly committed by strangers" and agreed with the statement "women sometimes sexually abuse children" (73 per cent). This demonstrates a less stereotypical view of child sexual abuse perpetrators among the Irish public at present.

Research on Public Knowledge and Attitudes: Attributions of Blame for Child Sexual Abuse

This issue has been considered in a number of studies, usually involving college students. Perceptions about blame in cases of abuse may be an important factor in determining whether abuse is reported or not. In a US study[62] of college students in the 1980s, participants were asked to read a description of child sexual abuse where the child's sex, age and relationship to the offender varied.[j] Most (61 per cent) attributed no blame to the child. The age of the child was significant as older (15-year-old) children were blamed more than 7- and 11-year-olds. Men attributed more blame to 15-year-olds than did women. Men also attributed more blame to 15-year-old boys than 15-year-old girls. Participants who indicated a personal history of child sexual abuse were less likely to blame the child than non-abused participants. Least blame was attributed to children when the offender was a parent.

In a similar study in the US,[63] college students were asked to rate the amount of responsibility attributable to an adult and child

---

[j] Children were described as aged 7, 11 or 15 years. Offenders were described as parent, acquaintance or stranger.

(aged 15 years)[k] in descriptions of sexual activity. The amount of responsibility attributed to children was associated with the response of the child in the description. When children were described as encouraging and passive, they were rated more "responsible" than children described as resisting. Notably, in both of these 1980s studies, some responsibility was attributed to the child. A more recent study (1998) asked undergraduate students to indicate the degree to which they believed sexually abused children (aged 6 or 13 years) and parents were responsible and to blame in extrafamilial child sexual abuse vignettes.[64] As with the earlier studies, greater responsibility was assigned to older children. Parents were ascribed more responsibility when the child was younger.

Promoting Public Awareness

Prevention of child sexual abuse and child abuse generally depends on public awareness and concern because this increases the likelihood of suspected abuse being reported.[59] Public awareness campaigns about child sexual abuse should promote the message that child abuse is everyone's responsibility.[65] In the UK, The National Commission of Inquiry into the Prevention of Child Abuse (1996)[66] recommended the need to create "child friendly communities" in which children and young people feel valued and listened to and where their needs are met. This type of community is believed to be essential for the prevention of child abuse because children will more likely feel supported enough to disclose abuse. A society where abuse is denied or hidden is seen as facilitating abuse. The UK's National Commission of Inquiry into the Prevention of Child Abuse sought views on its work and received over 1,000 written submissions from individuals who were abused. Many expressed the view that society kept abuse hidden and denied its existence. Professionals, organisations and members of the general public who wrote to the Commission also endorsed this view.

---

[k] This age was selected as a result of the previous study which reported that significantly more responsibility was attributed to 15-year-olds rather than younger children.

It is interesting to consider the dramatic changes in perceptions of child sexual abuse over the past thirty years. While the
changes can be seen as overwhelmingly positive, some negative
consequences may occur as a result of an increased awareness of
child sexual abuse, particularly if it escalates into a type of moral
panic. West (2000)[67] outlined some adverse consequences such as:

- Vigilante attacks on suspected and convicted paedophiles

- An emphasis on "stranger danger" which places children at
  risk because they should be taught to report all sexual ad-
  vances, not just those from strangers

- Fewer male applicants for teacher training

- Fewer people willing to work as volunteers with, or in sports
  with, children

- "Dangers" for academics who publish politically unacceptable
  conclusions about abuse.[1]

Such consequences need to be monitored in order that the benefits
of increased awareness of child sexual abuse do not create other
difficulties.

AWARENESS OF CHILD SEXUAL ABUSE: THE ROLE OF THE MEDIA

Social problems usually "emerge" through the media.[68] Media
representations of social problems influence public attitudes because the media are the main source of information about such

---

[1] This is illustrated by responses to a paper published by Rind et al. (1998)[195] in
the journal *Psychological Bulletin*. The authors summarised previous research and
concluded that child sexual abuse had resulted in minimal negative long-term
consequences. Academics, the media and politicians attacked the report and the
journal's decision to publish it. A motion was passed in the United States House
of Representatives condemning the study. Some argued that even if the conclusions were accurate, the possibly negative consequences of the study meant it
should not have been published.

problems.[69] The "battered-child-syndrome" paper, published in 1962, is generally credited with the "discovery" of child abuse. While serving to increase professional awareness, Kempe's ideas were also described in the popular press and this coverage was important in highlighting the problem of child abuse.[70]

Moral Panic

Much of the research on media reporting of child abuse describes the media as taking a "moral panic"[m] approach. An essential component of moral panic is the proposal that traditional values and social institutions are under attack from "folk devils". There is a sense of social crisis. The media create and sustain this crisis by identifying "folk devils" and reaffirming traditional social values perceived to be under threat.[71] The media are seen to "create" what becomes publicly recognised and understood as a social problem. Moral panic can be created by the media despite evidence of any real threat or increase in the rate of a particular crime. In relation to child sexual abuse, newly reported cases provide opportunities to revisit previous cases and reinvigorate panic.[69]

In the context of child sexual abuse, the folk devils are often not the actual abusers. Press reporting of child sexual abuse is often less concerned with sexual abuse as a crime and more with the accountability of those in social services and others in positions of authority who appear to have dealt inadequately with particular cases. This mismanagement by authorities is usually represented as worse than the actual crime of abuse itself. It seems that "no degree of power can substitute for a lack of judgement".[71]

It has been argued by one author that rather than creating "moral panic", the media break political silences, create social

---

[m] The term was first used in the 1970s by Cohen to explain the rapid increase in press reporting of "mods and rockers". Moral panic is described as: ". . . the feeling, held by a substantial number of the members of a given society, that evil-doers pose a threat to the society and to the moral order as a consequence of their behaviour and, therefore, something should be done about them and their behaviour".[196]

resistance and moral action and document social realities which differ from the official version of events.[72] Regarding child sexual abuse by clergy in Australia, this author speculated that Church leaders relied on the moral panic approach in their response to allegations of child sexual abuse by clergy and "attempted to portray the impression that there was no social reality underlying the allegations". Furthermore, they publicly remained "calm in the face of what was construed as an unfounded and exaggerated attack on churches".

Research on Media Reporting of Child (Sexual) Abuse

Representation of Abuse Risks

An examination of how journalists represent child sexual abuse risks showed that they rarely focused on the sexual abuse of children within families but instead focused on more dramatic abductions by strangers and on paedophile rings.[73] Intra-familial child sexual abuse coverage provided a profile of false accusations by children or inappropriate intervention by professionals. This gave the impression that parents were more at risk than their children. Media over-emphasis on the message that children need protection from strangers was seen as failing to acknowledge that children may also be at risk and need protection from those well known to them.[74]

Use of Language

An analysis of print media describing child sexual abuse found that the language used often reduced the seriousness of such abuse.[75] Words such as "relationship" and "affair" were sometimes used to describe the sexual abuse of a child by an adult. In addition, abused or neglected children were often objectified in newspaper or magazine articles with the word "it". On the other hand, the media, notably the tabloid press, regularly use terms such as "beast", "monster" and "sex fiend" when describing the perpetrators of abuse.[67]

Types of Reporting

Researchers examined 1,302 media reports of child maltreatment in "quality" (broadsheet) and tabloid press in Australia during 1995.[76] They found that child abuse stories were either represented as "hard news" or "soft news". Hard news stories on child sexual abuse focused on individual cases[n] and tended to be of a "hit and run" nature, that is, describing only the most immediate and sensationalistic details of the case. Soft news stories were characterised by human interest or research-related stories. Many of the human interest stories were "victim success" stories, usually a celebrity who had been abused but had "made a success of their lives". The authors proposed that the stories reflected a stereotypical perception that those abused as children are likely to develop serious problems (thus, this was not really newsworthy). Instead, success in life following abuse is seen as unexpected and therefore newsworthy. Research-related stories reporting the findings from professional research in the area of child abuse received less media attention than did hard news sensationalist stories and rarely ever made front-page news. Disproportionate coverage was given to more severe and/or atypical forms of abuse in both the quality and tabloid press. The press were seen to over-report sexual assault and extra-familial abuse that occurred outside the home and to under-report emotional abuse, neglect and abuse perpetrated by family members. Abusers were usually portrayed as "mad", "bad" or "sad", i.e., mentally disturbed, evil or inadequate.

Stories about "respectable" abusers in non-familial positions of authority were also popular, with disproportionate coverage compared to their prevalence as understood by official statistics. Crimes committed by those in authority are newsworthy since they are unexpected and because of public expectations that these individuals should be trustworthy given their role in society.[77]

---

[n] McDevitt (1998)[83] compared media trends in reporting child abuse in the US and the Republic of Ireland, using a sample of articles from *The Irish Times* and *The New York Times* in 1997. Both newspapers emphasised the sensationalistic aspects of child abuse while neglecting other aspects of the issue. The most common type of story was the individual case.

Increased media attention to these types of offenders means that attention is diverted from abuse that occurs within the home (the most common form of abuse). However, it does create awareness that individuals of any status in society can perpetrate abuse. There is a concern that "respectable" people are less susceptible to allegations of abuse because typically they have less contact with professional childcare agencies and greater abilities to resist intervention. Persons "in authority" represented 47 per cent of all offenders in the study of Australian newspaper articles on child sexual abuse.[76] They featured priests, teachers, police officers, scoutmasters and politicians. A similar newspaper analysis[o] of child abuse reports in the US found that accounts were generally unrepresentative of child abuse in general.[78] This distorted focus may represent the challenge to the media to consistently have "new" or "news" items: there may be little "news value" in another abuse story unless something unusual occurs or the status of the perpetrator is noteworthy.

In the Irish context, analysis of the language used to describe offenders has shown an interesting pattern concerning clerical abuse. In an analysis of one quality national newspaper (*The Irish Times*), the term "paedophile priest" was used 332 times between August 1993 and August 2000.[79] Apart from the term "paedophile farmer", which was used 5 times, no other occupation was linked with paedophilia in the reports.[79, 80] It has been argued that such reporting misleads people into thinking that Catholic clergy are the predominant perpetrators of child sexual abuse.[79]

Criticisms of Media Reporting of Child Sexual Abuse

Several analyses of British media reports have shown that the coverage of child abuse is often used as an opportunity to criticise social workers.[69, 71] UK media have also been accused of generating fear about the proximity of paedophiles. In 1998, a UK newspaper

---

[o] In this analysis, 8 major US newspapers were reviewed for the first 9 months in 1995 along with CD-Rom and Internet searches for over 30 newspapers during 1989 and 1995.

(the *Daily Mail*) reported that a seaside resort was harbouring more than 600 "child sex perverts" who were "walking freely around".[67] This type of reporting can lead to vigilante attacks, often with fatal consequences involving people other than those being targeted. For example, vigilantes burned down the house of a suspected paedophile in the UK in 1997 resulting in the death of a 14-year-old girl.

In 2000, following major publicity about a case, the main tabloid newspapers in the UK set up what they called a "name and shame" campaign in memory of Sarah Payne, a 9-year-old girl who was sexually assaulted and murdered. The campaign involved publishing photographs, names and locations of convicted sex offenders.[P] There are a number of serious problems with such campaigns.[81] Firstly, there is considerable concern about how the public responds to this sort of information. Secondly, there are cases of false identity, whereby people without previous charges or convictions are attacked. Thirdly, there is also the risk that this sort of action could drive sex offenders "underground". Thus, whatever co-operation the authorities have with such offenders, e.g. checking in regularly with authorities or notifying them of a change of address, could be damaged as a result of such a campaign. Finally, this sort of campaign may divert attention from other dangers and risks to children. For instance, heightened awareness of "stranger danger", means that time and resources may be needed to remind people that it is not just strangers who abuse children. It has been argued that media attention has transformed child abuse from a social problem to a "social spectacle" with the primary interests of the children themselves being lost in the public debate.[82]

Advantages of Media Reporting of Child Sexual Abuse

In defence of the role of the media, child sexual abuse "scandals" may not have come to public attention were it not for media

---

[P] The decision of the newspaper editors was criticised by the British police, the government and children's charities. The sex offender register in the UK was never meant to be a public document although the police are empowered to disclose the identity of a convicted sex offender.

persistence and reporting.[69] Media sources have increased public awareness, which in turn can prompt governments to introduce or update policies to deal with the problem of child sexual abuse. Even sensationalist coverage may be beneficial, since children may have to rely on journalists and whistleblowers for protection from abuse.[69] The power of the media on this issue is substantial. Research has established that the image portrayed by the media becomes the image that those in the general population (those without personal information on an issue) have of that issue.[83]

SEX OFFENDERS: DEVELOPMENT OF THEORIES AND TREATMENT

Understanding of paedophilia has developed significantly over the past 20 years. Although there are written references to child sexual abuse and sex offenders as far back as the Roman era, no published research was found in a search of the psychological and psychiatric research literature prior to 1965. The first journal specifically dedicated to research on sex offenders was launched in 1988.[84] Paedophilia is now considered a psychiatric disorder affecting "a portion of individuals who sexually abuse children".[85] As a psychiatric diagnosis,[q] paedophilia describes a person who is sexually attracted to and/or aroused by children aged 13 years or younger, whether or not this attraction is acted upon. Although paedophilia was listed in the first major international classification system — the *Diagnostic and Statistical Manual* of the American Psychiatric Association (DSM) — in 1952, it came under the heading of "psychopathic personality with pathologic sexuality". In the third edition of the DSM in 1980, paedophilia was first included under a new term "paraphilia"[r] which was categorised under the broad category of psychosexual disorders.

---

[q] Some authors/clinicians argue against classifying and treating paedophilia as a disease.

[r] Other paraphilias listed in the DSM-IV-TR (2000) are: exhibitionism, fetishism, frotteurism, sexual masochism and sadism and voyeurism.

Theoretical formulations have been developed to explain the motives and orientation of those who sexually abuse children. Many have focused on a single dimension and so cannot explain the diversity of behaviour seen in perpetrators of child sexual abuse. In 1986, Finkelhor,[86] a leading expert on child sexual abuse, organised the various types of explanation into a four-factor model. The factors are as follows:

- *Emotional congruence:* some theories suggest a "fit" between the emotional needs of the adult and characteristics of the child. Male socialisation promotes dominance, power and the initiator role in sexual relationships. For men with psychological problems such as low self-esteem, relating to a child may provide a feeling of power, omnipotence and control. This explanation is similar to some psychoanalytic theories which see those who abuse children as having arrested psychological development and also to feminist theories which suggest that power rather than sex is the driving force in abuse.

- *Sexual arousal to children:* some theories focus on explaining how adults become sexually attracted to children. Learning theories have been evoked to explain this as has the possibility that critical experiences in their own development, most particularly the experience of sexual victimisation during their own childhood. While some theories try to explain this sexual attraction, the view that paedophilia was not really a sexual orientation was fashionable in the early 1980s.

- *Blockage:* these theories seek to explain why some people are blocked in their ability to have their sexual and emotional needs met in adult relationships. The view is that the preference is to have adult relationships but that sexual interest in children develops because of a block to this preference. In some cases this may be because of the person's poor social skills or because significant relationships have broken down. This type of reasoning has often been used to explain father–daughter incest, e.g. the father's marital relationship breaks down and for a variety of reasons he chooses to seek sexual gratification within rather than outside the family.

- **Disinhibition:** this describes a set of theories that seek to explain why conventional inhibitions against having sex with children are overcome or not present in some adults. Factors such as alcohol, bereavement and stress have been outlined as causes.

The four-factor model was useful in providing structure to the many theories in existence. It did not, however, offer guidance as to which was the best fit for the research evidence or which had the most potential for the development of treatments. To date no one theoretical position has emerged as dominant.

Treatment of sex offenders is recognised as one of the most crucial issues in the prevention of child sexual abuse.[87] It is important to note when considering treatment of those who sexually abuse children that almost all treatment occurs within the context of the criminal justice system. Treatment recommendations have changed significantly over time. It has been suggested that since the 1930s, the treatment of sex offenders, like treatment for those with psychiatric problems more generally, has been subject to various "fashions".[88]

Prior to the late 1970s, very few treatment facilities were available. Furthermore, few psychiatrists and psychologists trained specifically to treat paedophilia and/or sex offenders were available. However, because sex offenders were originally diagnosed as "sexual psychopaths" (according to the early DSM classification), they were viewed as appropriate candidates for medical treatment and cure. Psychiatry offered the promise to legislators in the US that diagnosis, treatment and potentially cure was achievable for sex offenders.[89] Psychiatrists originally used psychoanalytic/ psychodynamic psychotherapy. Based on Freudian theory, the assumption was that paedophilia was the manifestation of underlying conflicts that developed during a maladaptive childhood. It was thought that paedophilia could be "cured" by resolving these conflicts and that the person would no longer be sexually attracted to children. This led many of those treating paedophilia to believe that paedophiles could be returned to their environment with minimal or no risk of repeating their behaviour.[85] However, the predictive accuracy of the clinical judgement of professionals on re-offending has been recently reported as only slightly better than chance.[90] A recent overview of the area suggests that psychiatrists have had little success in the diagnosis and treatment of sex offenders.[89] Rather than a progressive advancement in the psychiatric understanding of sex offenders, psychiatry is seen as having broadly withdrawn from this area of work.[89] Up to the 1960s, the leading documents on sex offenders were written by psychiatrists. Today they are more likely to be written by psychologists or criminologists who specialise in assessing and treating sex offenders. Furthermore, psychoanalytic theory has not had a major influence on current treatment approaches for sex offenders.[91]

Since the 1970s, the aim of treatment has been on "control" rather than "cure", i.e. stopping the behaviour and preventing its recurrence. Initial attempts in the US and Canada to treat sex offenders were based on a behaviour modification approach, i.e. aversion therapy. This involved providing electrical shocks (punishment) to offenders when viewing "deviant stimuli" (such as sexually explicit photographs of children) as a way of reducing "deviant arousal".[84] However, it became clear that reducing deviant arousal was not enough and that treatment should involve ways to enhance arousal or interest in other more appropriate sexual behaviour and partners.[84] Cognitive psychology approaches then began to influence behavioural methods. This combination, known as cognitive behavioural therapy (CBT), targeted cognitive processes such as beliefs, attitudes and other thoughts, as well as modifying behaviour. This is seen as a significant advancement in the psychological treatment of sex offenders and CBT strategies have continued to develop since the 1980s.[92] Overall there has been a shift in treatment from response suppression techniques (aversion therapy) to CBT with greater attention paid to interpersonal deficits, victim awareness, social skills training and relapse prevention.[92, 93] The 1990s have been described as a decade "characterised by an explosion" of broader treatment programmes and research articles.[84] In addition (since clinical judgements of dangerousness were shown to be inaccurate),[84] formal measures to predict risk were developed to guide decisions about the release of sex offenders and about how sex offenders should be managed in the community

Developments in assessment and treatment in the US and Canada followed in Ireland in the late 1980s and early 1990s, as reflected in the establishment of treatment facilities and programmes for sex offenders. The history of official treatment of sex offenders in Ireland is a short one. In 1966, the Commission of Enquiry on Mental Illness recommended that ". . . psychiatric treatment is likely to be more effective for sexual deviates than imprisonment".[94] However, no agency existed in Ireland for the specific treatment of sex offenders prior to 1985. A treatment programme was set up in 1985 in Donegal by a multidisciplinary team which was concerned with the number of child sexual abuse cases under investigation by the area health board at the time. In 1999 it became a full-time service. For the last two years, a similar service has been piloted for adolescents who sexually offend. In 1989, a sex offender treatment programme was established at the Central Mental Hospital (Dublin) and ran for some years. The programme was initially for incest offenders but in 1993 a group therapy programme began for non-incest offenders. These Central Mental Hospital programmes are no longer in existence. The Department of Justice established a psychological treatment programme for sex offenders in Arbour Hill Prison (Dublin) in 1994 and in the Curragh Prison (Kildare) in 2000. These are group programmes based on a cognitive behavioural model. Programmes are lengthy (taking approximately one year to complete) and, at present, there are ten places per programme in Dublin and eight in Kildare.[5] The Granada Institute, an organisation established by the St John of God Order in 1994, provides assessment and treatment services for those who have experienced sexual abuse, for those who have perpetrated sexual abuse and for the families of both. Services are

---

[5] In August 2002 there were 406 sex offenders in Irish prisons.

also offered to others affected by abuse, e.g. the relatives, friends and colleagues of those who have experienced abuse or who have abused. There are also services for adolescent sex offenders in Dublin, Kilkenny and the North Eastern Health Board. A service for adolescent offenders was set up in Cork in 2002 but is not currently running because of lack of referrals. The Irish Probation and Welfare Service, in conjunction with the Granada Institute established a programme in 2003 for sex offenders who have been processed by the criminal justice system. This programme is located in Dublin. Plans for a similar project in Cork are in the initial stages.

SOCIAL POLICY: CHILD PROTECTION AND CHILD SEXUAL ABUSE

For most of the twentieth century, Irish childcare legislation was based on the 1908 Children's Act. The 1991 Child Care Act superseded this at the end of the century. Many of the changes in relation to social policy have come about as a result of increased professional and public awareness of child sexual abuse. Increased awareness of child sexual abuse increased the demands on professionals responsible for the protection and welfare of children.[16] There are now policies on the reporting and management of child sexual abuse in many professions and institutions. These are based on recent official guidelines as issued by the government (i.e. *Children First: National Guidelines for the Protection and Welfare of Children*, 1999).[11]

The Development of Social Policy in Ireland[t]

In the UK, the post-war welfare State shifted responsibility for child welfare and protection from voluntary organisations such as the National Society for the Prevention of Cruelty to Children to government departments. This shift occurred much later in Ireland through the Health Act (1970).

---

[t] Appendix III provides a chronological outline of Irish childcare policy and legislation on sexual offences.

The Irish State has been accused of taking a "back seat" in terms of direct provision for childcare[95] and of being reluctant, until recently, to protect children through legislative reform.[96] It has been argued that the family-centred ideology of Irish society originally led to unwillingness by the Irish State to problematise childcare.[97] Thus, childcare has "struggled" to become a political issue. Traditionally, the Irish State did not have a "managerial" or "social democratic" ideology.[98] Many issues relating to the establishment of the Irish Republic — the struggle for legitimacy of the State following political independence in 1922, the "political power" of the Roman Catholic Church in a predominantly Catholic society, and the economic problems facing a young country — have been seen to take priority over tackling social problems.[95] The new State has been seen as preserving and extending the influence of the Catholic Church, particularly in areas of moral significance in twentieth-century Ireland.[95] In parallel, the State availed of services such as hospitals and schools, which were run by the Church. This interaction of Church and State is important in understanding the evolution of social policy in Ireland and in considering the Catholic Church's influence on social policy.

Up to the 1950s, economic problems and high unemployment rates also meant that Irish government spending was curtailed. As a result, social policy was not always a priority. In the more liberal 1960s, social developments in Ireland challenged more conservative attitudes and the State became more willing to address social problems. Economic growth, a decline in emigration and a national television service were some of the factors responsible for these developments. Social problems were revealed to the public via the media. It has been suggested that media reporting of child abuse can have more influence[u] on child protection policies than

---

[u] Australian media has been shown to have influenced child protection policies positively and negatively.[197] On the positive side, media campaigns helped to produce more effective child protection policies and practices while on the negative side much of the media coverage, particularly in the tabloid press, tended to be sensationalist and simplistic.

professionals working in the field. This is referred to as "legislation by tabloid".[69]

During the 1970s, the Irish State began to employ social workers for two newly developing services: community health care and probation. Prior to the 1980s, the Irish Society for the Prevention of Cruelty to Children championed child protection. In the 1980s, emerging awareness of child sexual abuse was evident from the actions of the government. The Department of Health, responsible for policy and service provision for children, issued a number of initiatives during this decade (these guidelines are outlined in Appendix III). These initiatives were influenced by international events, by pressure from women's groups in the voluntary sector and by increases in confirmed and suspected cases of child sexual abuse as reported to the health boards.[16] As a result, a number of policies were issued which included guidelines for professionals, the development of assessment services and the inclusion of child sexual abuse in childcare legislation. In addition, specific Irish court cases concerning child sexual abuse have drawn attention to inadequacies in the legal system and in the laws pertaining to sexual offences.

Socio-legal Policy on Sex Offenders

Treatment and management of convicted sex offenders is aimed at contributing to the protection of children. A punitive socio-legal policy towards sex offenders has been driven by public outrage and demands for harsh punishment.[67] This has been influenced by sensationalist media coverage, which often implies that the sexual abuse of children is increasing.

The crime of child sexual abuse provokes strong reactions from the general public, with almost unanimous repugnance. Hence, it is not difficult to imagine the reaction to convicted sex offenders, especially those who have served their sentences and are released into the community. In many countries, sex offenders are required to register and to notify local police about where they are living. Community notification is a separate requirement. This informs residents that a convicted sex offender is living in their community. This form of notification is widely used in the US. The specifics of notification vary between states; for example some states inform the entire community while others make the information available upon request. Community notification originated in the 1980s in the US as part of a community justice initiative, i.e. the right of people to protect themselves. Modern punishment has been judged as utilitarian and humanitarian, with an emphasis on rehabilitation and reducing recidivism. However, community notification appears to be based on surveillance. The requirements of community notification have been described as a "new punitiveness".[99]

Some critics have argued that community notification is not a form of restorative community justice[v] because it does not seek to prevent crime and there is no opportunity for offender–victim mediation.[100] Some community notification programmes and requirements have been judged as counterproductive because vigilante attacks, often the product of community notification, force the offender to go into hiding rather than integrating into society.

There is little research on the impact of community notification on those who are informed or on offenders. One US study showed that, contrary to popular belief, recidivism rates for sex offenders subject to community notification and sex offenders not subject to community notification (because their conviction predated the law) were not significantly different.[101] In this study, the sex offenders subjected to community notification requirements reported being ostracised by their neighbours and expressed concern for their personal safety. They criticised the media for treating all sex offenders as a homogeneous group and for sensationalising their offences. On the other hand, the public may feel safer having information on the location of offenders. For instance, a telephone survey of residents in Washington State found that an overwhelming majority felt safer having been informed that a convicted sex offender was living in their community.[102]

---

[v] Restorative justice is a development of the community justice movement. Restorative justice aims to repair the harm caused by crime and to unite those offended against, offenders and communities through activities such as victim–offender mediation, family group conferences and sentencing circles. All of these involve healing dialogue and communal participation.

In conclusion, social awareness of child sexual abuse has increased significantly over the twentieth century. Changes in social policy and legal changes have followed this change in awareness. The media have served a valuable, if at times controversial, role in these changes. Management of sexual offenders is informed by both rehabilitative and ongoing surveillance perspectives.

AWARENESS OF CHILD SEXUAL ABUSE: FINDINGS FROM THE PRESENT STUDY

Summary

- Most clergy interviewed for this study reported only recent awareness of the problem of child sexual abuse and this was based on media reports.

- Issues relating to child sexual abuse and child protection were not typically addressed in training, according to the clergy interviewed.

- Most of the public overestimated the percentage of all child sexual abuse that is perpetrated by clergy. However, they typically underestimated the number of clergy actually convicted of sexual offences against children in Ireland.

- The media were reported as the main source of information on child sexual abuse for the public. Overall, media coverage was judged as beneficial but media coverage of clerical child sexual abuse was seen as more damaging, particularly to the Catholic Church, than coverage of child sexual abuse in general. The majority of those surveyed felt that media coverage of clerical child sexual abuse was fair.

- During the public survey, reports of child sexual abuse in one Irish diocese became a major source of public debate with extensive media coverage. Those interviewed as part of the public survey following this high-profile coverage were more critical of the Church's handling of child sexual abuse by clergy than those interviewed prior to its coverage. Thus, media coverage can significantly alter public attitudes even within a short timeframe.

Awareness among Clergy

Child sexual abuse by clergy has occurred over an extended period. Therefore, some awareness of the problem must have existed among clergy, most likely senior members of the Church, for some time.[w] However, the way in which inappropriate sexual behaviour was interpreted by senior Church personnel varied. Anecdotally, sexual contact with male children was sometimes understood as homosexual behaviour rather than child sexual abuse *per se*. The emphasis was on the moral implications for the offending cleric and a confessional approach was used. In the present study, most clergy, particularly "front-line" priests and religious, reported becoming aware of the problem quite recently, just as the general public did, through media reports.

Rumour and Media Reports

Church personnel interviewed typically recalled first hearing about child sexual abuse in the late 1980s or the early 1990s. Media sources provided the first indication of child sexual abuse by clergy for most, in particular reports from the US during the late 1980s. A small number said that they had heard rumours about priests in Ireland during that time. Some of the bishops interviewed had received complaints of child sexual abuse by clergy in the 1980s. A significant milestone for most participants in terms of awareness of the issue was the case of Fr Brendan Smyth in 1994.

---

[w] For instance, media coverage in February 2003 indicated that 24 of 26 Catholic dioceses across Ireland took out insurance policies from 1987 to cover lawsuits concerning cases of child sexual abuse by clergy. According to a press statement issued by the Irish Catholic Communications Office on 4 February 2003, most dioceses obtained insurance policies between 1987 and 1990 against the eventuality of legal liability accruing to a diocese from acts of child sexual abuse by priests (www.catholiccommunications.ie/Pressrel/4-february-2003.html).

Knowledge of Child Sexual Abuse

Most participating clergy said they had never heard of child sexual abuse prior to the 1980s. As a result, they reported a very limited initial understanding of what was involved and of the prevalence and impact of such abuse. Others noted it was not covered in their seminary training:

> ". . . that was in the '80s. It came in the paper that there was something about paedophiles and we were asking each other what a paedophile meant and nobody knew . . . we just didn't know what it involved . . . it was unknown, it was something we had no experience of and we didn't know what to think. It was a complete puzzle that anyone should interfere with children . . . and that priests should do that . . . we didn't use the word paedophile, we didn't have the language."

> "I had no idea of the nature of the problem, the deep level of denial, of compulsive and repetitive behaviour, the minimisation, how it thrived on secrecy and the impaired normality of the accused. I had no idea of any of these at the time."

> "When I was a student there would have been no mention of the term child sexual abuse. We weren't spoken to about it, we didn't read anything about it, so it just wasn't in the consciousness at all."

When initially dealing with allegations in the 1970s and 1980s, many senior clergy were not made aware of the potential long-term traumatic effects child sexual abuse may have on abused individuals by mental health professionals consulted at that time. As a result, many did not anticipate that it would become a major issue within the Church:

> ". . . did I have the sense that this was going to show significant numbers of priests and religious having abused? That didn't occur to me. I didn't have awareness that that was going to emerge or the specific emphasis on priests and religious that has emerged. I didn't foresee that . . ."

Participants reported that there was now a greater and growing awareness among clergy about the impact of child sexual abuse and the needs of those reporting abuse:

> "I never realised before just how awful the experience is, the damage it does to their relationships in terms of marriage, trust in other people, just anything to do with sexuality and pride of life, how it's constantly there, although it happened maybe thirty or forty years ago and how over a period of time they never told anyone, or how they struggle with counselling."

> "It is or certainly was in the past, a big jump for somebody who has been abused to approach the bishop, it is a significant jump for them. While we might say we are available it is still a big step for them to take."

> ". . . the main difference is the realisation of the harm that abuse may cause the victim. In the past there wasn't that awareness. Our priority was that he [abuser] wouldn't do it again. . . ."

PUBLIC AWARENESS: VIEWS OF THE
GENERAL PUBLIC IN IRELAND

The public survey (N=1,081), representing the views of the wider Church community,[x] examined public awareness of child sexual abuse by clergy. Survey participants estimated the prevalence of child sexual abuse by clergy. This question was asked in a number of ways: comparing clergy to other men, considering the percentage of clergy involved in abuse and considering the percentage of abuse attributed to clergy. Participants were also asked to estimate the number of clergy convicted of sexual offences against children in Ireland. In addition, participants were asked about sources of knowledge concerning child sexual abuse in general and by clergy and to judge the fairness or balance of media coverage of child sexual abuse by clergy.

---

[x] Ninety per cent of respondents said they were a member of a particular religious denomination and of these, 94 per cent were Roman Catholic. Thus, overall the survey results were taken as broadly representative of "wider Church community" views.

Prevalence Estimates for Clerical Child Sexual Abuse

Regarding the prevalence of child sexual abuse by clergy, those surveyed were asked whether they thought that the level of child sexual abuse by male clergy was more, less or about the same compared with other men in society (Figure 3.1).

Figure 3.1. Public Perception of Levels of Child Sexual Abuse Perpetrated by Catholic Clergy Compared with Other Men

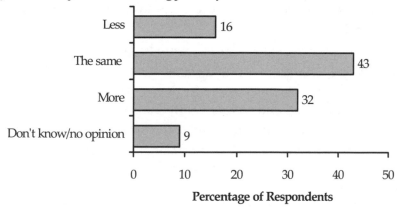

Figure 3.1 shows that over half thought that the level of child sexual abuse by clergy was the same (43 per cent) or lower (16 per cent) compared to other men in Irish society. However, a third (32 per cent) felt that clergy abused children more frequently than did other men. Participants were also asked to estimate the prevalence of abusers among members of the clergy (Figure 3.2).

Figure 3.2: Public Estimates of Catholic Clergy Involved in the Sexual Abuse of Children

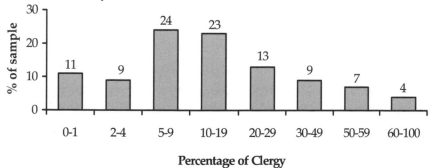

As Figure 3.2 shows, 20 per cent thought that less than 5 per cent of clergy sexually abuse children with 47 per cent estimating the level to be between 5 per cent and 19 per cent. Therefore, two-thirds of those surveyed believed that less than 20 per cent of all clergy have sexually abused children. Eleven per cent of those interviewed felt that abuse was so endemic that over 50 per cent of clergy sexually abused children. There are no comprehensive statistics to indicate the actual percentages. It has been suggested that 2–5 per cent of priests in the US are involved in the sexual abuse of children.[103]

Participants were then asked to estimate the percentage of all sexually abused children who have been abused by clergy (Figure 3.3). Over a third of participants (36 per cent) thought that less than 10 per cent (of all children sexually abused) were abused by clergy with 26 per cent estimating between 10 per cent and 19 per cent. Thirteen per cent estimated that clergy perpetrated over 50 per cent of all sexual abuse against children.

Figure 3.3: Public Estimates of Percentage of Child Sexual Abuse Perpetrated by Clergy

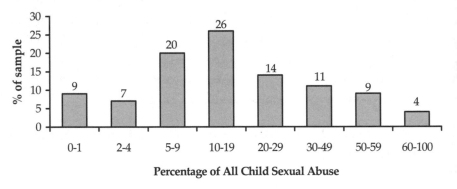

Based on evidence from the SAVI study,[1] 3.2 per cent of those reporting sexual abuse as children identified a member of the clergy as the perpetrator. Therefore, most of those surveyed in this study significantly overestimated the percentage of child sexual abuse that is perpetrated by clergy. Only 16 per cent came close to correctly estimating the percentage found in SAVI (i.e. less than 5 per cent of abuse is perpetrated by clergy).

Estimates of the number of clergy convicted of child sexual abuse in Ireland in the last ten years were also sought. The average estimate was 31 convictions whereas the actual number (obtained from the Child Protection Office of the Irish Bishop's Conference) was 49 (from 1992 to March 2002).[y] Twenty-four percent felt unable to answer the question. Of those who did estimate, 62 per cent estimated the number as less than half the actual number (i.e. fewer than 24 convictions) while 8 per cent estimated it to be greater than double the actual number (i.e. 99 or above). Only 11 per cent estimated the numbers to be within 10 above or below the actual number (i.e. 40–58). Thus most of those surveyed underestimated the number of clergy convicted for sexual offences against children over the last decade.

Sources of Knowledge about Child Sexual Abuse

The majority (95 per cent) surveyed reported the media as their main source of knowledge about child sexual abuse in general. Seventeen per cent (n=179) stated they had more personal experience of the issue, i.e. that they knew someone who had experienced child sexual abuse. Similarly, with regard to child sexual abuse by clergy, almost all (94 per cent) cited non-religious sources, mainly television and print media, with 5 per cent obtaining knowledge from both religious and non-religious sources.

Attitudes to Media Coverage of Child Sexual Abuse

Participants were asked their views about media coverage of child sexual abuse in general and of abuse by clergy. More specifically, they were asked whether they thought media coverage was beneficial or damaging (Figure 3.4).

---

[y] Approximately 55 priests and religious have been convicted of sexual offences against children since 1983 in Ireland.

Figure 3.4: Public Evaluation of Media Coverage of Child Sexual Abuse in General and Child Sexual Abuse by Clergy

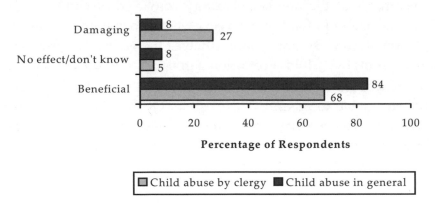

As Figure 3.4 shows, differences emerged between the responses to media coverage of child sexual abuse in general and by clergy. Participants judged media coverage of child sexual abuse by clergy to be more damaging and less beneficial than media coverage of the issue in general. Eighty-four per cent of participants thought that the coverage of child sexual abuse in general was beneficial, while 68 per cent believed this about media coverage of clerical child sexual abuse. The main reasons cited were related to increasing public awareness by highlighting the issue. In relation to clerical child sexual abuse, the general consensus was that without media coverage the public would be unaware of the issue. Media coverage of child sexual abuse by clergy was regarded as more damaging than coverage of the issue more generally — particularly to the Catholic Church. The media were seen by many as "destroying the Catholic Church's reputation in Ireland" and creating a situation where "stigma is attached to priesthood and people are suspicious of all priests". Overall, the results show that while the public generally viewed media coverage of child sexual abuse favourably, they were more convinced about its benefits in relation to coverage of the topic in general than to coverage of clerical child sexual abuse.

Survey participants were asked to evaluate the "fairness" or balance of media treatment of child sexual abuse by clergy. Over two-thirds believed that media coverage was fair with 22 per cent rating coverage as unfair. Those who thought coverage was fair were generally of the opinion that the media brought the issue of clerical child abuse "out in the open", that the media were just "doing their job" and "telling the truth". Some believed that the Catholic Church "deserves" the negative media attention: "the Church did wrong and now deserve all they get" and "guilty priests deserve the bad publicity". Of those who believed that media coverage was unfair (22 per cent), some thought the media sensationalised the reporting of child sexual abuse by clergy: "the issue is blown out of proportion" and "stories are grossly exaggerated by the press". Others believed that the media was biased and had an agenda against the Catholic Church.

The study provided an opportunity to examine a "natural experiment" in terms of the impact of specific revelations of child sexual abuse by clergy on public attitudes. At about the mid-point in the four-month data collection period (22 April 2002 — Easter weekend), UK television (BBC) screened a documentary called *Suing the Pope*. This programme detailed complaints of child sexual abuse made to the authorities in the diocese of Ferns (County Wexford) by a number of families concerning a priest of that diocese, Fr Sean Fortune. These reports were allegedly not investigated appropriately by Church authorities. Many Irish viewers watched this television programme. Media coverage of the issue in Ireland was extensive (including re-showing the programme on an Irish television channel some weeks later). Survey responses before and after this date were examined to see if coverage of the issue had any influence on public views.

Six hundred people were surveyed before, and 481 were surveyed after the television programme. Significant differences in attitudes were found on a number of questions. There were significant differences between pre- and post-event groups. Those surveyed after the programme was broadcast were:

- More critical of the Catholic Church's management of child sexual abuse

- Less willing to trust a priest on first arrival in their community

- Less trusting that the Church could take care of problems with its own clergy

- More likely to estimate higher prevalence rates for child sexual abuse by clergy

- More suspicious that joining the priesthood was an indication of sexual problems

- More personally affected by child sexual abuse by clergy in terms of their religious practices

- Less willing to look to priests for moral guidance

- Less willing to encourage their children's participation in the Church

- Less tolerant of having clergy convicted of sexual offences return to ministry.

Thus, specific coverage of clerical child sexual abuse was associated with more negative public attitudes to the Church and to priests (issues listed here will be discussed further in Chapters 4 and 5).

In conclusion, most clergy and the public became aware of clerical child sexual abuse through media coverage. The public mostly overestimated the proportion of child sexual abuse which could be linked to clergy. Extensive media attention to disclosure on specific complaints of clerical child sexual abuse during the survey was associated with significantly more critical public views of the Church's handling of clerical child sexual abuse.

Chapter 4

THE IMPACT OF CHILD SEXUAL ABUSE

SUMMARY

o   Child sexual abuse has been associated with a range of adverse long-term effects such as depression, anxiety, post-traumatic stress disorder and relationship problems.

o   These effects have been established through general population studies and prevalence rates among psychiatric populations.

o   Characteristics of child sexual abuse such as the type of abusive act, duration of abuse and amount of force used influence the severity of effects.

o   Religious beliefs have been shown to assist in coping with traumatic events.

o   Child sexual abuse has been associated with both alienation from religion and God and an increase in religious practices.

o   Those who have experienced child sexual abuse by clergy have been shown to experience a loss of faith in their religion, clergy and Church.

o   The effects of child sexual abuse extend well beyond the abused individual and can have significant impact on "secondary victims" such as family members of the abused and the abuser.

o   Parents of sexually abused children often feel guilty because of a perceived failure to protect their child — they may also find it difficult to accept help without feeling judged.

o   Family members of abusers may feel guilty or stigmatised by association with their relative and may risk being criticised if they are seen to support their relative.

o   In relation to clerical child sexual abuse, non-offending clergy and the wider Church community could also be considered "secondary victims".

INTRODUCTION

This chapter describes the impact of child sexual abuse by clergy on those who have been abused and on others affected by the abuse. The other people affected, sometimes referred to as "secondary victims", include the families of those abused, family members of the abuser, non-offending clergy and the wider Church community.

THE IMPACT OF CHILD SEXUAL ABUSE: INDIVIDUALS WHO HAVE EXPERIENCED ABUSE

The Impact of Child Sexual Abuse

There is a large body of evidence linking childhood sexual abuse with a variety of adverse long-term outcomes such as depression, anxiety, low self-esteem, substance abuse, post-traumatic stress disorder (PTSD), suicidal behaviour, relationship difficulties and sexual disorders.[104–108] However, research also indicates that effects are highly variable with some children showing no detectable negative effects and others showing severe adverse effects with psychiatric symptomatology.[109] Thus, there does not appear to be a unique pattern or a specific post-abuse syndrome.[39, 107, 109–112] There is no reliable way to predict who will experience which symptoms and what intervention will be necessary. In fact, child sexual abuse may be best understood as a risk factor for a wide range of subsequent problems.[111]

In the short term, sexually abused children and adolescents have shown behavioural and academic problems in school, depression, low self-esteem, suicidal ideation and behaviour and substance abuse.[113, 114] Some evidence has indicated that older children and teenagers exhibit greater disturbance as a consequence of abuse than younger children.[115]

The effects of child sexual abuse may not manifest until much later in life. Depression is the most common long-term effect reported[116, 117]. Other reported effects include relationship problems, parenting problems, anxiety, PTSD, alcohol abuse, and intimacy and sexual problems. It is estimated that at least 20 per cent of sexually abused children suffer serious and long-term psychological effects.[118] In parallel, longitudinal studies have found that some children can recover from the effects of sexual abuse.[117] Long-term effects are evident from general population studies and studies of psychiatric populations. Several general population studies have found that those who report experiencing child sexual abuse also report more depression, PTSD, anxiety, substance abuse and suicidal behaviour compared to non-abused persons.[119–122] It has also been shown in some of these studies that child sexual abuse directly contributes to adult mental health problems.[119] In the Irish context, the SAVI study[1] found that those who had experienced sexual abuse in their lifetime were more likely to have received psychiatric care, i.e. they were eight times more likely to have been an inpatient in a psychiatric hospital than those with no experience of sexual abuse. Another way to assess impact is to examine levels of child sexual abuse in psychiatric populations. Prevalence rates for child sexual abuse have been found to be higher among adult psychiatric populations than in the general population. One study has estimated that 50 per cent to 60 per cent of adult psychiatric inpatients have experienced childhood sexual or physical abuse[123] and a review of epidemiological studies found childhood sexual abuse prevalence rates from 3 per cent to 90 per cent among psychiatric populations.[124] Thus, child sexual abuse may play a significant role in the development of psychiatric disorders in the general population.

The effects of child sexual abuse depend not only on the nature of the traumatic event itself, but also on characteristics of the child and the type of abuse. The impact may be influenced by the child's pre-abuse functioning and by the presence of risk and protective factors such as the social, emotional and financial resources available to the child.[109] The impact may also be influenced by characteristics of the abuse such as age at onset, frequency, duration, force used, number of abusers, relationship to abuser and the nature of the abusive act. Repeated abuse has been found to cause the most significant detrimental effects.[1, 125]

Child Sexual Abuse and Religious Beliefs

Religious beliefs and practices have been associated with better mental health, enhanced coping and higher levels of happiness and life satisfaction in the general population.[126, 127] This positive effect on mental health may be explained by the meaning, purpose and hope that religious faith provides in people's lives. In addition, most religions promote a worldview that is forgiving, compassionate and caring and a God that responds to pleas for assistance.[126] People with strong spiritual beliefs have been shown to resolve grief following the loss of a close friend or relative more rapidly and completely than those with lower levels of spiritual belief.[128]

Children who are being sexually abused may pray to God and ask God for help.[129] Similarly, adults who have experienced child sexual abuse may turn to their faith and spirituality for support.[130] While the benefits of a religious orientation in dealing with child sexual abuse have been reported, one study found that adults sexually abused as children were less likely to describe themselves as practising religion than non-abused adults.[131] In a separate US study, women sexually abused as children were found to express more anger with, and distance from, God than non-abused women.[132] Many of these abused women had left the religious faith of their family of origin but for some spirituality remained important to them. Similarly, men abused as children[a]

---

[a] Abuse in this study included sexual, physical and emotional abuse.

have reported negative effects on their religious behaviour as adults.[133] Researchers described the effects collectively as "spiritual injury" (i.e. feelings of guilt, anger, meaninglessness and less stability in religious belief, practice and experience). They concluded that rather than a simple alienation from religion and God, child abuse resulted in a "multidimensional" reaction towards religion and God. Overall, these studies suggest some polarisation of the effects of abuse on religious experience with some becoming more orientated to the spiritual and religious dimensions of their lives and others becoming more alienated from them because of their experiences.

The Impact of Child Sexual Abuse by Clergy

For many people, members of the clergy represent God and the Church. Thus, to experience abuse by clergy may result in feeling violated by God and the Church.[134] Catholics abused by Catholic clergy are thought to be at particular risk for permanent separation from the Church and religious practices.[135] A study on the impact of sexual abuse by clergy in the US in 1994 found that Catholics (more than non-Catholics) experienced profound spiritual loss as a direct result of abuse and that those sexually abused as children were more negatively affected than those abused as adults.[136] Church attendance was also affected. The institutional Church was not seen as helpful in bringing individuals abused by clergy closer to God. Instead, therapy and friends provided more help in finding peace and getting closer to God. In a separate US study, Rossetti reported on "spiritual damage" caused as a result of child sexual abuse by priests.[137] Three groups were compared in this study: those with no experience of child sexual abuse (N=1376), those who were sexually abused as children by priests (N=40) and those sexually abused as children by non-clerical abusers (N=307). Adults sexually abused by Catholic priests reported less trust in the Catholic priesthood and Church and in their relationship with God than those sexually abused by non-clerical abusers and those with no experience of child sexual abuse.

It has been proposed that sexual abuse by clergy is different in nature rather than worse than other forms of abuse because it creates unique trauma characteristics.[138] One such trauma characteristic is the use of "God" as a silencing strategy by the abuser. For example, some of those abused by clergy have described how their abuser told them that God would punish them if they told anyone about the abuse. Others have described how the abuser heard their confession or said Mass following the abuse. Thus, aspects of religious belief or practice may be deliberately used to facilitate the abuse itself or to maintain secrecy. The spiritual or religious support that may help in recovery from abuse may be "desecrated" when the abuse is perpetrated by clergy.[135] Hence, child sexual abuse by clergy may be facilitated by the use of God as a threat, appeasement or explanation for the abuser's actions while recovery from the abuse may be hindered by the weakening or removal of religious or spiritual convictions as sources of meaning and solace in times of difficulty.

THE IMPACT OF CHILD SEXUAL ABUSE ON THE ABUSED: FINDINGS FROM THE PRESENT STUDY

Summary

Individuals Who Had Experienced Abuse and Reported it to Church Authorities: Face-to-Face Interviews

- Seven people who experienced child sexual abuse by clergy were interviewed.

- The impact was described by those abused in terms of both the impact of the abuse itself and the impact of disclosure and/or non-disclosure.

- Initial effects such as fear, anxiety and depression were described. The fear of not being believed was particularly potent and this was sometimes sustained through manipulation by the abuser.

- Depression and anxiety were also described as persistent effects. Women described experiencing significant difficulty with intimacy and trust in relationships.

- Six of seven people interviewed face-to-face had received some form of counselling and three received psychiatric in-patient treatment.

- Religious faith was also affected with all those interviewed describing some loss regarding faith in the Church or clergy. However, belief in God and relationship with God was not affected.

- Six of the seven people interviewed face-to-face did not disclose their abuse until they were adults. Some reported a sense of guilt as they believed earlier disclosure could have protected others from abuse.

- Responses to disclosure varied — in one case a negative response by Church personnel meant the person waited a further ten years before disclosing to the Church again.

- The findings indicate that disclosure is a process rather than a once-off event.

- Feelings of sympathy and pity were expressed towards the abuser.

Individuals Who Had Experienced Clerical Abuse in a General Population Survey: Telephone Interviews

- Most of those experiencing clerical child sexual abuse were boys and were abused in school settings.

- Two-thirds did not report the abuse at the time with over 40 per cent never disclosing it to others until asked in the SAVI research study.

- In a small number of cases, local Church or school-based religious personnel were informed. Only one person went to civil authorities. This was 25 years after the abuse.

- Participants noted a collective awareness of clerical child sexual abuse in the wider community. Thus, while it was hidden it was not unknown.

- There was a view that individual members of the clergy, but not the institution, were responsible for the abuse. However, the Church as an institution was seen as having mismanaged the issue.

- Abuse experiences had little impact on faith in God.

- None of those interviewed now intended to report their experiences to civil authorities and only one intended to report them to Church authorities. Thus, public record through the various Church and civil mechanisms established to hear complaints will be a reflection of only a portion of the abuse perpetrated by clergy.

The Impact of Child Sexual Abuse on the Abused: Findings from Face-to-Face Interviews

The personal impact of child sexual abuse as reported by study participants focused on two themes: the impact of child sexual abuse itself and the impact of non-disclosure and/or disclosure. All of those interviewed for this study experienced sexual abuse involving physical contact. The duration of abuse ranged from a single experience to ten years of abuse by the same abuser. Two participants were abused at age 16; the remaining participants were aged between 5 and 13 years of age. Of the seven participants, two were sexually abused in institutions by religious brothers and five were abused by priests (three of these were abused in the context of ministry, e.g. giving sacraments). The priest was not previously known to three of the participants but for the remaining two participants, the priest was local and well-known to their family. Six of the seven participants have received professional counselling as a result of their abuse and in addition, three have had treatment in a psychiatric hospital.

Initial and Persistent Effects: Psychological and Social Impact

Participants described initial and persistent psychological and social effects of their abuse. The experience initially caused fear, self-blame, anxiety and depression. This led to problems at school for some. Depression and anxiety typically remained throughout life along with suicidal ideation, relationship and intimacy problems and a sense of guilt as a result of non-disclosure of the abuse as a child.

In terms of initial effects, the fear experienced by those who were abused manifested in different ways. There was a fear that they would not be believed, fear of possible repercussions if they told anyone about the abuse, and fear that they themselves would be blamed. Contributing to this fear was the culture at the time when clergy and the Catholic Church in Ireland were feared and held in high esteem:

> ". . . I probably wouldn't have been believed . . . I was too scared because I mean I knew it was wrong . . . this was a priest . . . and who would have believed you at that time."

> ". . . I think I was afraid that they [parents] wouldn't believe me or they'd blame me."

Some participants felt that they were actually to blame. This prevented them from telling anyone about the abuse and they worried about the repercussions of telling:

> "I always wanted to tell somebody but I couldn't . . . I thought it was me. That it was my fault and that once I let anyone know . . . no one would talk to me or I'd be banished forever . . . I thought it was my fault."

> ". . . I always felt that it was me. I was the one that had tempted him . . . the Devil tempts people so if you do wrong the Devil was tempting you . . . I took it that a priest could do no wrong . . . I was the temptress, the Devil, I was responsible."

> "I had done something wrong . . . I felt I was damned for eternity . . ."

There were two main reasons why participants blamed themselves for the abuse. Firstly, they were abused at a time when
clergy were figures of unquestioned authority and were sometimes feared:

> ". . . for most people of my age we did think if we didn't go to
> mass we'd go to Hell . . . you did things for your parents be-
> cause you were afraid of what might happen if you didn't . . ."

> "I remember my grandmother saying don't ever fall out with a
> priest or say anything bad about a priest because they can put
> horns on you. They really believed these myths that priests
> had power over you."

Secondly, some abusers manipulated the children into thinking
that the abuse was part of his role as a priest and that as a priest
he could not do anything wrong. One participant described how
the abuser told her that he had to teach her how to love:

> ". . . his line was that I had nobody to teach me anything and
> his mission was to teach me how to love . . . a child is looking
> for love and security . . . he conned me into thinking that he
> was loving me . . . of course it wasn't love but it confused
> everything for me . . ."

Another participant wanted to tell someone about the abuse but
her abuser repeatedly told her that as a priest he could do nothing
wrong:

> ". . . every time I objected he would say, 'Well, I'm a priest, I
> can't do anything wrong' . . . he said, 'You're looking at things
> oddly because you know that a priest can't do anything
> wrong' and the more he argued with me the more I thought
> he had to be right . . ."

The fear created by the abuse and the self-blame acted as barriers
to disclosure for six of the seven participants. The greatest barrier
was the feeling that they would not be believed. Some also
reported experiencing anxiety and depression as children. This
sometimes affected their family and school life:

"I had gone from a happy child to extremely angry . . . I rebelled against both parents. A more awkward child you couldn't find . . . during adolescence . . . it couldn't have come at a worse time . . . she [mother] was afraid that I'd take my own life. She absolutely meant that. Her biggest fear was suicide . . ."

"I was so frantic with anxiety. I just blocked it all out because during that year at school I used to be popular and I thought that everyone knew and my whole life changed . . . I began having panic attacks and suffered depression."

Persistent effects experienced by study participants included relationship problems and problems with intimacy and trust. A range of mental health problems such as depression, anxiety and suicidal ideation were also reported:

"I'm grateful to be here today. There were times when I felt so, so low that I thought I'd be better off dead."

". . . over my life I'd suffered from a number of psychiatric illnesses, the basic one being depression but I also suffered from agoraphobia, panic attacks and anxiety, some more severe than others. I was hospitalised eight or nine times over the years. The abuse affected my mental health for thirty-five years. It affected my relationships, my view of myself, everything."

"I was in a terrible state. I was having nightmares and I couldn't sleep and I'd break down. I was on tablets and everything . . . I'm thinking about it all the time."

The women interviewed described how they had experienced difficulties in trusting men and difficulties with intimacy:

"The main effect it had was in the relationship with my husband and in our sexual relationship . . . a big fear was trusting him and that he said he loved me because he wanted to use me. I know that came from the abuse."

". . . it [abuse] does affect my ability to be intimate with somebody. It frightens the life out of me and although I'm married . . . it still frightens me. That's the biggest area that I'm having

difficulty with but I'm getting there slowly . . . if someone tells
me they love me I'm frightened of it. That love thing is uncertain and makes me afraid because he approached it from a
loving manner. I hate being told I'm loved even from my husband . . . it has taken me years to realise that I am a worthy
person . . . the abuse is in my skin. I feel it in my skin, it crawls
when I have to go into it."

"I never thought that I deserved a nice guy. I always went for
the other type. I never thought I deserved to be treated well . . .
it affected . . . my relationships."

". . . I wouldn't even be comfortable around men in general. I
was never comfortable with the intimate side of it [relation-
ships] or the physical side of it."

Six participants have received some form of counselling or treatment. For some, a considerable amount of time had been spent in
counselling or treatment and some participants felt that this time
has been stolen from their lives. However, attitudes towards
counselling were positive overall and for some, counselling
helped them to face disclosing their abuse to Church and other
authorities. Most of the participants interviewed described being
content in the present and optimistic about the future. For some
this began when they became part of an intimate relationship or
had children. Many qualified this by pointing out that they had
gone through a lot of counselling and treatment to reach this
stage. However, some participants reported still feeling fragile.
Some also hoped they would regain their faith in the Church in
the future. Disclosure of their abuse was a difficult but liberating
experience for most. This finding from a small number of qualitative interviews in this study is echoed in a recent large quantita-
tive study of experiences of counselling for those abused as children in institutional care in Ireland.[139] Of 268 participants, the majority reported very positive effects from counselling: 83 per cent
felt it helped them deal with their difficulties, 80 per cent became
more confident and 81 per cent reported improved ability to make
life choices.

Effects of Non-disclosure and Disclosure of Child Sexual Abuse

The process and timing of disclosure of abuse for study participants is outlined in Table 4.1.

Table 4.1: Process and Timing of Disclosure for Study Participants

Participant	Year of Onset of Abuse	Year of Disclosure	Made Disclosure to:
1	1960s	1990s	Priest friend
2	1960	1985	Psychiatrist
3	1970s	1970s	Parents
4	1978	1990s	Spouse
5	1952	1990	Spouse
6	1974	1990s	Social worker
7	1970*	1973	Spouse

* This person was aged 16 when abused

As Table 4.1 shows, most of the participants did not disclose their abuse until they were adults. Some reported feeling a great sense of guilt later in life because of this. There was a sense that they might have prevented others from being abused if they had reported earlier. Reciprocally, there was a more positive sense that disclosure when it did happen could prevent further abuse from happening. Hence, guilt was paralleled by a motivation to ensure change:

". . . the thing that bothers me now is that he went on and abused further which maybe I could have prevented . . ."

"I could be sparing other people from having to go through what I went through because the more cases that come forward the less chance of it happening to other people . . . why should I leave somebody at risk because I hadn't the guts to do something about it?"

". . . I began to think . . . that he may have done it to others . . . that maybe there were others and maybe he was still around . . .

this man is an abuser and he shouldn't have access to children
and I want to make sure he doesn't."

Other precursors to disclosing their abuse were the establishment
of an intimate relationship and/or getting married. Some felt they
had reached a stage in their life where they felt secure and had the
personal strength to deal with disclosing the abuse they had experienced. The fear associated with abuse ceased to exist or no
longer acted as a barrier to disclosure. This progress was sometimes facilitated through counselling:

> "I thought . . . until I tell the truth about this I will never be
> free . . . thankfully I am not intimidated by priests and bishops
> or anybody . . ."

> "I wanted to build up my confidence and it has taken me a
> good few years to build up my confidence into knowing that
> I'm fine rather than feeling low because I wouldn't be able to
> do it otherwise. I wouldn't have been able to do it a few years
> ago. I feel very well now through counselling and now I have
> no fears . . ."

With support and encouragement from family and friends, and/or
through counselling, some felt able to make an official report. The
process of disclosure was typically described as very difficult:

> "I went into a state of total anxiety. I was so anxious I began to
> feel frantic when the doorbell rang. . . . I didn't know why but
> suddenly I realised that I was afraid that he [abuser] would
> call to the door and he was coming after me for having told on
> him . . ."

The initial response to disclosure determined whether disclosure
had a positive or negative impact on participants. Some described
a sense of relief following disclosure. They felt that a burden had
been lifted from them:

> "It was the best and the worst day of my life. . . . It was won-
> derful from the point of view . . . of his [friend's] reaction . . .
> all those years I blamed myself but that was a great day. It
> really, really was."

> ". . . it does help definitely to get it out because I think I had dragged this big black cross behind me for years . . ."

Everyone did not experience this sense of relief. One woman reported her abuse to a priest and he minimised her experience, was unwilling to listen and told her she was "forgiven". His reaction was such that she did not pursue the matter further for another ten years. Consequently she felt a sense of guilt because she had "wasted" ten years before pursuing the matter again:

> "Going to a priest was enormous. I had to psych myself up for it . . . I was shattered by his [priest's] response . . . I wasn't really sure if I was doing the right or wrong thing. I was all over the place."

Negative reactions did not always deter participants. Another woman went to a solicitor and asked for advice on whether she should report her experience of abuse to the bishop. He advised her to see a psychiatrist instead. However, with the support of her family, she ignored this advice and pursued the matter. Almost all participants were positive about their experience of reporting their abuse to the Gardaí[b] and other officials. They found them to be helpful, supportive, informative and understanding. For some, this was very different from the response they received from Church officials.

A positive Church response had particular salience in terms of healing. One woman described how understanding and compassion from two priests has counteracted some of the harm experienced as a result of her abuse:

> ". . . there are individuals in the Church that are very good and very caring and I've been lucky to meet two of them and through me meeting these two priests . . . the harm . . . has been balanced by the two . . . it was important for me to meet a Church person to wipe out the badness of the other Church person [abuser] . . ."

---

[b] Refers to members of the Irish police force, An Garda Síochána.

The Process of Disclosure

It has been suggested that the term "disclosure" in relation to child sexual abuse is a simplification and distillation of a very complicated series of events. Rather than being a singular event, it is more usefully seen as an intersection of many factors with several consequences.[140] In this study, disclosure of child sexual abuse was not a once-off event. Participants in this study disclosed their experience of child sexual abuse to several people for different reasons. Some disclosures were to authorities, civil or Church, in an official capacity, while other disclosures were of a more personal nature to family, friends and children at different stages in their lives — for instance, telling partners as relationships developed, telling children as they got older or telling extended family and friends if the case was to become public. Three of the seven participants reported that the response to their first disclosure was unhelpful. Where the response received was negative, participants either tried to suppress thoughts of their experience or delayed telling others. A positive reaction to disclosure was reported as being therapeutic, in the sense of affording reassurance, support and understanding to the person.

Feelings about the Abuser

Most of those interviewed expressed pity and sympathy for the abuser. They recounted not being angry with the abuser at the present time. Instead, most were angry with the Church as an organisation because they felt that it did not do enough to protect children from abuse. For some, whatever anger they had felt about the abuser had shifted to anger with the Church. Counselling was reported as helping some to address their feelings towards the abuser. While some felt that the abuser should not be punished on an ongoing basis, but should instead be treated and monitored to reduce the risk of re-offending, others felt that justice would only be served if the abuser remained in prison.

It was important for some participants that the abuser admitted to the abuse. Three participants had met their abuser as adults following their disclosure. A bishop, at one women's request, set up a meeting with the abuser as she wanted an apology from him. However, the meeting was unsatisfactory. She felt that the apology given was insincere and that the abuser had just repeated what he had been told to say. In retrospect, her view was that abusers in general are not capable of feeling guilt but she was glad that she had asked to meet her abuser and that she had the "strength" to do it. Another woman who met her abuser as an adult also felt that his apology was "meaningless" because she felt that he was unaware of the damage that he had caused. For those who had not met their abuser as adults, the general view was that they would like an explanation from the abuser and an opportunity to describe to him how the abuse had affected their lives:

> "... there is not even anger with the priest. I feel sorry for him more than anything else and part of me would like to meet him and say these are the effects of what you did on me all my life, why did you do it? They are the questions."

"Spiritual Injury"

Some of the effects of child sexual abuse as described by participants related to clergy and the Catholic faith and Church more generally. Alongside the particular effects of child sexual abuse by a member of the clergy there were effects resulting from the response they received from Church personnel upon initial disclosure and from subsequent management of their complaint. Overall, the effects were described in terms of loss. Inability to trust priests was described as an initial and persistent effect of abuse:

> "I remember meeting a priest . . . one day. I didn't know him and he walked past me very close to me and my reaction to him frightened me . . . my body language towards him wasn't very nice. I wouldn't risk being in a place with a priest on my own . . . as the mother of sons I know I wouldn't encourage either of them to become priests."

> "I would have avoided priests and my kids would have been minded from priests and although we brought them to mass I wouldn't allow them serve mass."

> ". . . it did have an effect on my life from the day it happened
> because I was never comfortable with confession again. I was
> never comfortable with priests again, I wouldn't like to be
> around priests . . ."

However, for some the ability to trust priests was somewhat re-
stored by Church responses to disclosure by Church personnel:

> "Meeting the delegate has helped me trust priests again . . . the
> feeling that they are not all the same."

> "I judged them all the same as him and I was so angry because
> he was a priest but now I can individualise them but . . . I
> won't trust him [a new priest] until he proves that he is trust-
> worthy. I was trying to meet these priests saying, 'Prove to me
> that I can trust you'."

For some, the experience of abuse had a negative effect on their
trust in the Catholic Church. This was directly related to their experience of reporting their abuse to Church officials. Most reported having no confidence in the Catholic Church or no longer
being part of the Catholic Church:

> "I really have no time for institutional Church and all the rules
> and regulations."

> "I lost my religion but not my faith."

> "I had no outlook in life but now I have faith in God but I
> don't have any religion."

> "I'm a Christian more than a Catholic."

> "I suppose trust . . . trust is a big word in my life. I think the
> thing I lost the most was trust . . ."

Effects on faith were complex. One woman described that because
of her abuse she felt that she had to be a more devout Catholic:

> "I was a very ardent Catholic . . . I was very conscious about
> practising . . . from the time of the abuse I became very black
> and white about religion. I had to do things right. I stuck by

the rules. That was the way it had affected me. I have to be ten times better than everyone else because I have a lot to make up for so I was a very conscientious Catholic."

However, once she reported her experience of abuse to the Church her perspective changed:

". . . the more I had contact with the Church and the workings of the Church the less belief I had in their word. In the beginning I believed everything they told me. As time went on I began to realise that everything they were telling me was not true . . . in my mind the Church was trying to protect the priest and I felt worse because instead of feeling that the Church was behind me I felt that they were on the other side. It looked to me like they were protecting him [abuser] and it shattered any illusions I had about the Church . . . I'm no longer a practising Catholic."

Despite problems with Church officials, all participants reported that they believed in a God and that their relationship with God remains important to them. What emerged from interviews was that alongside losing their Catholic faith, some felt that their relationship with God had also changed, but for the better, because of their experiences:

"I still believe there is a God. I believe God visits me in some shape or form."

". . . old enough to separate God from the Church . . ."

For some participants, an important routine in their life, e.g. going to mass and participating in the Church, was changed because of the abuse. Their perception of the Church and clergy was damaged. As a result they have experienced a sense of loss:

"I'd love to be able to go to mass every Sunday. I'd love to be able to bring myself to mass."

". . . it was an important part of my life. I'm sad at losing it."

The Impact of Child Sexual Abuse on the Abused: Findings from a National Random Sample[c]

A national random sample of those abused as children by clergy was identified from the SAVI Study (see Appendix II for further details). SAVI participants who had given consent to be re-contacted for future studies were included (25 of 30 gave consent).[d] This larger study provided a wider context within which clerical child sexual abuse in Ireland could be understood. Tables 4.2 and 4.3 provide a profile of the 30 SAVI respondents reporting clerical child sexual abuse. Most reported abuse which occurred during the 1960s and 1970s (72 per cent of 22 boys and 50 per cent of the 8 girls). About half of the respondents reported a single instance of abuse (45 per cent of boys and 62 per cent of girls). All abusers were men. All of those abusing girls were priests while almost half of the boys (45 per cent) were abused by religious teachers. Furthermore, 72 per cent of boys, but none of the girls, were abused in schools. This may reflect the different access which male clergy had to boys through the educational system.

In all but two cases, abuse involved physical contact. These two cases (with girls) involved photography and sexual questioning during confession. Regarding disclosure of abuse, nine boys (41 per cent) had never told others (apart from the SAVI interviewer), seven told parents (N=4) or friends (N=3) close to the time and six told some years later (three to family member, three to spouse). Similarly, four (50 per cent) of girls had never told others, two told close to the time (to mother or friend) and two told later (to mother or husband; the latter was told 40 years later.

---

[c] We thank those involved with the SAVI study who facilitated access to the clerical abuse sub-sample. SAVI was commissioned and funded by the Dublin Rape Crisis Centre with additional support from the Department of Health and Children and the Department of Justice, Equality and Law Reform. The original SAVI interviews were conducted in 2001.

[d] To ensure appropriate continuity for those who had given permission to be re-contacted, Professor McGee (director of the SAVI study) conducted all of the follow-on interviews.

Table 4.2: Female SAVI Participants who Reported Sexual Abuse by Clergy when Less than 17 Years (N=8)

Year of Abuse Onset (*Approx*)	Age at Onset	Current Age	Duration of Abuse	Location	Most Serious Type of Abuse	Perpetrator
1948	10	65	Many times	Institution	Penetrative	Priest
1952	10	61	Once	Public place	Contact	Priest
1955	12	60	Once	Own home	Contact	Priest
1964	9	48	2 years	Both homes	Contact	Priest (relative)
1966	5	42	Once	Own home	Non-contact	Priest
1976	16	43	Once	Workplace	Contact	Priest
1976	10	37	Months	Girl-guides	Contact	Priest
1984	16	35	Once	Confession	Non-contact	Priest

Table 4.3: Male SAVI Participants who Reported Sexual Abuse by Clergy when Aged Less than 17 years (N=22)

Year of Abuse Onset (*Approx*)	Age at Onset	Current Age	Duration of Abuse	Location	Most Serious Type of Abuse	Perpetrator
1943	7	67	2 years	School	Contact	Christian Brother
1946	15	72	Once	School	Contact	Religious teacher
1947	11	67	Once	School	Contact	Christian Brother
1957	10	56	Once	Outdoors	Contact	Priest
1957	8	54	Once	Home	Contact	Priest (relative)
1960	8	51	6 weeks	School	Contact	Priest (teacher)
1963	12	52	Once	School	Contact	Priest
1963	10	50	Once	School	Contact	Priest
1964	8	47	Twice	Swimming pool	Contact	Priest
1965	9	47	10 weeks	School	Contact	Christian Brother
1967	13	49	Twice	School	Contact	Religious teacher
1967	6	42	6 years	School	Contact	Priest

Year of Abuse Onset (*Approx*)	Age at Onset	Current Age	Duration of Abuse	Location	Most Serious Type of Abuse	Perpetrator
1967	9	45	Unsure	School	Contact	Priest
1968	11	46	Once	School	Contact	Priest (teacher)
1970	9	42	1 year	School	Contact	Christian Brother
1972	9	40	1 year	School	Contact	Religious teacher
1972	10	41	Twice	School	Contact	Christian Brother
1973	11	41	2 years	Church	Contact	Priest
1973	11	41	6 months	School	Penetrative	Christian Brother
1974	16	45	Once	Car	Contact	Priest
1975	8	36	Once	School	Contact	Religious brother
1985	15	33	Once	Car	Contact	Priest

Of those who told at the time or during the next few years, there were two cases of priests of the parish and four involving priests or religious as teachers. In three of these six cases (all involving schools), parents went to the school to complain. In one case, the offending teacher was moved out of the school and in the other cases the abuse stopped. These figures show that at every level there was reluctance to disclose and act. In summary, 43 per cent of those describing abuse had never disclosed this to others in their lifetime; 27 per cent disclosed later (often many years later) with 30 per cent disclosing at the time. Three cases were brought to the attention of school-based religious authorities. One of these cases went to civil authorities (Gardaí) 25 years later but was not concluded for a variety of reasons (mainly concerning the emotional demands of reporting for the person concerned). Two of the 30 people availed of counselling services as adults. This profile of disclosure to others and contact with authorities is similar to that of child sexual abuse in the overall SAVI study. Thus clerical child sexual abuse does not appear to have been uniquely hidden. Instead it was *as* hidden from society as other forms of child sexual abuse at the time.

When contacted for this study, 14 participated.[e] Only one of the 14 had told his parents about the abuse, who at first did not believe him but subsequently they reported the abuse to a priest friend. The offending priest was immediately moved from the area. Reasons given by others for not telling were: too ashamed/ embarrassed, "wouldn't be believed", too young and experience was "not too upsetting". One person felt there was no one to tell while conversely another felt it was common knowledge and that telling was not going to make people act if they were not already doing so:

> "It was common knowledge . . . the [recreational location] was crawling with them [clergy who might abuse boys] . . . we used to laugh and joke about it."

---

[e] Two respondents were not invited to participate because household contact indicated serious illness/distress; one respondent declined participation and the eight remaining individuals were un-contactable.

Other participants reiterated this sense of a collective awareness of clerical abuse. One man recounted how, as altar boys, they knew that when a boy was given particular duties after Mass, it was because he was likely to be "picked on" by the priest. It was never directly spoken about and the aim of all the other altar boys was to "get away as fast as possible". Another participant said:

> "Everyone knew about the clergy . . . and it's out now . . . the papers have done us a favour."

In terms of the personal impact of abuse experiences, the effect was reported as slight or moderate with three reporting major psychological effects. One of these attended Church-funded counselling as an adult. Regarding effects on faith and views of the Church, the majority said that their faith in God was not affected while one person reported some negative impact. Concerning views of the Church, most said their experiences did not affect their views of the Catholic Church. Two of these pointed out that they were in fact very committed Catholics. For one person it had a moderately negative impact, while two others had very strong negative reactions to the Church as an institution. There was a strong sense however, from most respondents that "one individual is not the Church" and "you can't blame the Church for what individuals did". In parallel, there was a sense that a lot of damage had been caused through abuse and that it was good to have this out in the open. However, Church responses were seen as inadequate:

> " . . . they [Church authorities] have responded very badly from a Christian point of view . . . the lawyers got to them and reminded them that there was property at stake."

Others reflected that exposure of clerical abuse was part of Ireland growing up as a society. Participants were asked if they envisaged taking any of their complaints to Church or civil authorities in the future. One person wanted to do so, he wanted to have abuse experienced as a child by a now deceased religious teacher "on the record" of that Order. None of the participants wanted to take complaints to civil authorities.

Overall, interviews highlighted the hidden but not unknown nature of clerical child sexual abuse in twentieth-century Ireland. The lack of public acknowledgement of this abuse appears to have stemmed from a combination of factors ranging from a genuine naivety about what constitutes inappropriate sexual behaviour through embarrassment abut the issue to a concern about not being believed if one reported such behaviour. The profile of abuse and its impact on these SAVI participants indicates that the abuse experienced was no less serious than that experienced by those interviewed face-to-face who chose to report to Church authorities. It is clear from these participants that most of this unreported abuse will continue to be unreported in the future. Thus, the scale of abuse by clergy needs to be acknowledged as significantly greater than that which will be documented through Church and civil mechanisms investigating this issue in the coming years.

While acknowledging that the primary and most pervasive impact of child sexual abuse is on those who have experienced abuse, the overall impact of such abuse cannot be gauged without reference to the impact on a wide range of other individuals. This wider impact of abuse is discussed next.

THE EXTENDED IMPACT OF CHILD SEXUAL ABUSE: "SECONDARY VICTIMS"

The psychological and social effects of child sexual abuse on those who have been abused are well researched and documented. However, the impact of abuse and its effects on others who are involved, for example, families, has been studied to a lesser extent. The majority of research literature in this area focuses on incest and the non-offending mother. A sexually abusive experience may not just disrupt the life of the person abused but also the lives of several other people. Parents and siblings of the abused child could be described as "secondary victims". Besides this immediate family impact, those close to the child as he or she grows up and develops their own family and friends may be affected by the impact of abuse and its disclosure. Less obvious but also important is the impact on those close to the abuser when allegations are made or legal cases are taken against them. In the case of clerical child sexual abuse, this group includes not only the abuser's immediate family but also his extended work and friendship network. This will mainly be other clergy and those involved in Church work. In the current social climate, all clergy may feel a certain sense of victimisation because their occupation has been associated and linked with the sexual abuse of children. It has been suggested that when Catholic clergy are the perpetrators of child sexual abuse, the psychological and spiritual effects may extend well beyond those abused.[141-143] Evidence on these distinct groups of secondary victims is considered next.

Families of Those Who have been Abused

> Sexual violence can not only affect victims themselves but can cause "fundamental change" in the lives of their families also.[144]

Research has shown that parents of abused children are often overwhelmed with guilt because they feel they failed to protect their child[ren] or recognise signs and symptoms of sexual abuse.[145-148] They may also feel guilty that other children were, or could have been, abused because they were not aware of the problem. Older siblings have also been found to report guilt for not protecting their younger sibling.[146] In most cases of child sexual abuse, family members will know the abuser, hence there is the added shock of discovering that someone they know is capable of sexual abuse. Anger towards the abuser may become all-consuming and disrupt normal family life and relationships.

It has been estimated from research in the US that the sexual abuse of a family member can disrupt family equilibrium and highlight vulnerable areas to such an extent that for every abused individual as many as three or four other family members will seek professional help.[149] Parents of sexually abused children have been shown to experience clinically significant mental health problems over the first year following disclosure of abuse: mothers showed more significant and lasting difficulties than either the children abused or fathers.[150] Other studies have found parents feeling that the crisis would never end and that their family would never recover.[146] Such feelings were exacerbated when their typical support structures were not available. Some families may be criticised by family, friends and their local community for making allegations against people who were regarded as good citizens or neighbours. However, even when support is forthcoming, it may be hard to accept. One study reported that mothers had difficulty accepting help from family and friends because they felt a barrier between themselves and other women who were "good mothers" and had not "failed" their children.[145] Fathers have sometimes been reported as less willing to talk about the abuse because they felt an intense overriding desire for revenge.[149] This lack of communication in itself can lead to other problems within the family.

It has also been found that families worry about the long-term impact of child sexual abuse and feel helpless in anticipation.[146] For instance, parents mourned the loss of their child's innocence, feared that their child was irrevocably damaged, became overprotective and were unable to allow the child freedom to be with others, and worried that their child might become an abuser because of their experience. When abuse was reported officially, police, social workers and legal representatives were seen to "invade" the family. Families felt powerless and re-victimised by the criminal justice system when they were not informed about decisions or when there were delays. With clerical child sexual abuse, families may feel re-victimised by the Church if their complaint is responded to inadequately or not taken seriously.

Families of the Abusers

Perpetrators of sexual abuse often lead double lives; one that appears "normal" and one that is sexually exploitative. The families of offending clergy experience humiliation, grief and loss of reputation and friends.[151] The person they knew who was once well respected becomes a hated and repugnant figure. They may blame themselves for failing to identify indicators of the abuser's offending behaviour and feel that others think that they must have known. Everyday understandings of crime are generally rooted in perceptions of poor parenting and familial socialisation.[152] This "family toxicity"[153] theory of crime may lead the abusers' family members to feel implicated in the crime itself and feel excluded from "normal families". They may use different strategies to cope such as avoiding people or social situations, which can lead to social isolation. They may also avoid discussing issues related to child sexual abuse and struggle between concealing and revealing the nature of their relative's whereabouts and crime.[152] If they are seen to support the abuser, they may be criticised and risk being ostracised by their local community. They may receive little attention or support from the Church and may even be partly blamed for somehow not preventing the abuse.[135] There is a paucity of research on the experience of families when one of their members has been convicted of sexual offences.

Non-offending Clergy

Clergy who take over positions where their predecessor has been removed because of child sexual abuse face a difficult task. In cases where they have not been informed about their predecessor's behaviour and the subsequent dynamics of the situation, e.g. in a parish situation, they are likely to feel angry and "thrown in at the deep end" once they become aware of the situation that preceded them. A number of outcomes are possible for such clergy. New complaints of child sexual abuse may be forthcoming. Members of the congregation may not believe the allegations or charges of child sexual abuse and resent having lost their former priest. They may be hostile to his successor and use him as the target for their anger. The new priest may have to cope with mistrust from the congregation while ministry or contact with children may become a source of fear and anxiety. It has been reported that some priests in the US who succeeded clerical abusers sought therapy or counselling to help them cope with stress, depression, anxiety, isolation and loneliness.[154] These priests also reported adverse effects on health such as fatigue and insomnia. For some, their vocation was strengthened by their experiences while it caused others to struggle with their vocation.

Child sexual abuse has become a common topic for discussion among clergy. Much informal discussion arises from feeling stigmatised and being singled out unfairly for scrutiny and criticism.[155] Faced with regularly publicised reports of child sexual abuse by clergy, and reports of mismanagement of complaints by the Church, the feeling is that they must continue their ministry and represent the Church. They may be confronted by angry members of their congregation or verbally abused by strangers. Most clergy grew up in families and communities where a religious vocation was held in high regard; it was seen as a uniquely trusted and valued role. Clergy now find themselves in a "broad web of suspicion" and many are reluctant to wear clerical dress in public to avoid unwanted attention and to avoid having to explain that they are not child molesters.[155] Some clergy may also feel regret and guilt because of mistakes made in handling complaints or failure to act on suspicions about a colleague. A perception of declining attendance at religious services may indicate a loss of faith by the congregation and may demoralise clergy. Faith in their Church and its leadership may also be tested.

The Wider Church Community

It has been suggested that intervention with the congregation in managing the effects of child sexual abuse by clergy is "as crucial as [intervention] with the primary victims".[156] Reports issued by churches internationally and in Ireland in response to child sexual abuse by clergy have acknowledged that members of the public may experience spiritual damage when clergy perpetrate child sexual abuse. Parish communities from which a priest has been convicted of sex offences may be among the groups most affected.

The public have been horrified by clerical sexual abuse of children in part because people abhor child sexual abuse *per se* but also because child sexual abuse by clergy is seen as a serious abuse of trust and innocence. Clergy, alongside other professionals, command power because of their role, but additionally clergy often "embody the divine" or God for people.[157] Furthermore, priests are allowed significant access to the most important personal experiences of people's lives. They are involved in major life events such as births, deaths, illness and marriages. Child sexual abuse by priests and religious was an unanticipated problem in part because of the clerical vow of celibacy but also because priests and religious are generally regarded as moral, spiritual and ethical members of society. The sexual abuse of children by clergy has been seen as misuse of power and authority and exploitation of a professional position for personal gain when actions should be in the best interest of the congregation.[158] Thus, "child sexual abuse is the polar opposite of what priests and religious are meant to be doing".[159]

Child sexual abuse by clergy violates the public's sense of order, trust and faith.[143] Responses by the public will be influenced by a number of factors such as their relationship with the clergy member concerned and with clergy more generally.[137] The main effects are likely to be loss of trust in priesthood and Church, feelings of anger and betrayal and an inability to look to the Church to provide leadership. As a result people may suffer a crisis of faith. Parents and other parishioners may blame themselves and feel guilty that children were abused in their parish.[143]

The impact on parishioners may be augmented when they do not receive information or intervention from their Church. Parishioners may have to rely on the media to reveal the occurrence of abuse in the first place and to provide information on the fate of the priest where the abuse is confirmed. They may feel exposed or shamed and they may perceive their parish or community as tarnished because of negative media attention.[143] Understandably, Church officials may be legally constrained from commenting on allegations of child sexual abuse. However, poor handling at this stage by those in authority can create as much anger as the abuse itself.[160, 161] Although increased media attention does create awareness, it may also increase fear and anxiety. The public may restrict their activities and contact with clergy because of a perceived threat of sexual misconduct. Awareness of clerical child sexual abuse may increase anxiety about the safety of children more generally. As a result, Catholics may avoid attending Mass and other religious rituals. Alternatively, some parishioners may not believe allegations and instead question the veracity of the complainant.[157] Unresolved conflict may remain in parishes even after a priest is convicted of sexual offences. A congregation can divide according to whether they support or oppose the priest involved.

There is very little research on the impact of child sexual abuse by clergy on the wider Church community. What little research exists is from the US. Recent surveys in the US[f] have consistently found that Catholics felt that they had not been kept adequately informed by the Church on the subject of child sexual abuse. Although the Catholics surveyed in the US were highly critical of how cases of child sexual abuse by clergy had been managed, this had not affected their commitment to the Catholic Church more generally or to religious practices. The Church hierarchy, i.e. the Pope and the national Church leaders, were subject to most criticism for the problem while much less criticism was directed towards local clergy. Even though little tolerance of priest perpetrators of child sexual abuse was expressed, respondents in these US surveys saw child sexual abuse by clergy as part of a larger problem of child sexual abuse. A separate US study reported on the effects of priests being publicly accused of child sexual abuse on the trust of adult Roman Catholics in God, the Church and priests.[141] Those with more experience of priests as perpetrators of child sexual abuse (i.e. those knowing of abuse in their own parish) were less trusting of the priesthood and the Church. However, more experience of priests as perpetrators of child sexual abuse was not associated with less trust in God. The majority of respondents felt that the Church was not dealing directly with the problem, that the Church's response had been inadequate and that the Church had not kept them adequately informed.

---

[f] Two national surveys have been conducted recently in the US. The *Washington Post*, ABC and Beliefnet conducted a poll in March 2002 (N=1,086 adults). In April/May 2002, the *New York Times* and CBS News carried out a national telephone survey of 1,172 randomly selected adults.

In Ireland, Irish Marketing Surveys (IMS) conducted a survey of religious confidence among 1,400 members of the general population in 1997. It found that religious practices such as attendance at Mass had declined significantly compared to figures recorded during the 1970s and 1980s.[8] Almost 25 per cent of Catholics interviewed reported that recent "scandals" involving priests and bishops[h] had affected their religious beliefs and practices.[162]

THE IMPACT OF CHILD SEXUAL ABUSE ON "SECONDARY VICTIMS": FINDINGS FROM THE PRESENT STUDY

Summary

Family Members

- Family members of those abused: The most significant impact on family members of the abused was a loss of faith in the Catholic Church because expectations of a compassionate and caring Church were not met when the abuse was reported to Church personnel. These family members witnessed the effects of abuse as experienced by their relative and felt helpless — this was exacerbated by the perceived failure of Church personnel to respond adequately.

- Family members of the abuser: They reported initial shock and a constant struggle between supporting and condoning their offending relative. Not all these families were united in supporting the abuser and this had caused tension and splits within the family.

---

[8] Catholic mass attendance was recorded at 91 per cent in 1974 and 65 per cent in 1997.

[h] At that time, it is likely that some survey participants were referring to scandals other than child sexual abuse by clergy as one survey question referred only to "scandals" while another question asked, "Would you say the recent scandals involving Bishop Casey and a number of priests in Ireland have affected your religious belief and practice in any way?"

Non-offending Clergy

- The most significant effect experienced was a loss of faith in their leadership. Loss of credibility and trust were also reported while faith in God was not affected. They also reported feeling stigmatised and described attempts to conceal their identity in public to avoid harassment and verbal abuse.

General Public Survey

- Over half of those surveyed said their religious practices had not been affected as a result of child sexual abuse by clergy. Willingness to trust new clergy arriving in a community had been affected.

- The majority felt that priests were not closer to God than other people and thought that people should not be expected to do what a priest tells them to do.

- The majority still felt that a priest's moral conduct should be better than other people's. Two-thirds said that they look towards priests for moral guidance.

- The majority felt that the Catholic Church was damaged and over half of these felt that the damage was permanent — the general consensus was that most priests had been unfairly judged as a consequence of child sexual abuse by some clergy.

- Belief in God was high among the public and most people reported a personal relationship with God.

Family Members of Those Abused

Three family members of two individuals who experienced child sexual abuse by clergy were interviewed (a mother, sibling and husband). These family members described both an emotional impact and an impact on their faith in the Catholic Church and clergy. The impact, however, varied according to whether disclosure of the abuse occurred during childhood or adulthood. For family members where disclosure of the abuse occurred during childhood, the impact was typically long-term and included all family members. One family, before they became aware of the sexual abuse, reported witnessing a dramatic change in the personality and behaviour of their abused family member:

> ". . . his whole personality changed, he was arrogant and screaming the place down and going out and you wouldn't know where he was for hours . . . I would go into his room at 3.00 am and he'd be sitting up in bed and I'd say try to sleep but the aggression he had in him towards me no matter how much I held him or told him I loved him, nothing. The simplest things would set him off . . . he was either leaving [home] or committing suicide. At about 17 years of age I think he reached his worst point."

The mother in this family described this as a "nightmare situation" and wonders how the family "survived it". This particular family tried several times to find out what was wrong and why he was so angry and unhappy. Eventually they established that he was being sexually abused by a priest known to them. They were initially shocked but also angry and determined to report the abuse. Family members were shocked because they believed in the sanctity of priests and were willing to trust clergy without any suspicion at the time:

> ". . . people think it's all strange now but if the abuser had said to me, 'Can I take [son] away for a week' I would have said, 'Yes' because they were gods to us and our mother always told us to genuflect when you see a priest and that's what you did . . ."

Only some family members were aware that the sexual abuse had occurred. This caused initial and ongoing problems as described by a sibling:

> ". . . within the family when something like this happens the whole thing [family] breaks down . . . and from being a complete family we were broken up . . . because of covering up . . . it altered our family from the day it was told and I don't think we'll ever be right. I personally feel that the whole family was

abused and there were bonds broken at that time that will never be repaired."

The process of reporting the abuse to Church officials and subsequent attempts to get help for her son proved extremely difficult and emotionally draining for one mother:

"I was a demented thing back then. I met someone recently and they said they remembered meeting me a few years ago and she said, 'you were demented . . . were you suffering with your nerves?' Because we told no one [about the abuse]."

A sibling reiterated the desperation as experienced by family members:

"At the time, the damage that was done to our family could have been repaired, we were desperate for help . . . and that was never forthcoming . . ."

The type of response from the Church had a significant impact on family outcomes. One mother described how her faith in the Catholic Church has been affected as a result of her dealings with Church officials:

"There is nothing the Church could ever do to make it up to us. I'm a very religious person. I love God, I'd never let them [Church personnel] interfere with me and God. I've no faith in them . . . The Church could never do anything to make it up to us, it's too late."

This mother described a huge sense of guilt. She regretted relying on the Church to deal with the abuse:

"If I could have prevented abuse I wouldn't have the conscience I have now, the burden I feel. If we had handled it differently . . . gone to the police . . . this is the guilt we have to carry . . . I'm riddled with guilt for not going to the police from day one. All of those children that were abused might not have been abused."

Many people who experience child sexual abuse do not disclose their abuse until adulthood. One woman coped with long periods of psychiatric illness and tried to deal with disclosure of child sexual abuse through this time. Her husband described how difficult it was during the official reporting process:

> "It was a bit of a rollercoaster because there were days when she was very positive and determined and other days she felt like giving up the whole thing because of the reaction [from Church officials]. There seemed to be an obstacle at every turn and there were days when she was very down . . . ."

The most significant impact of his wife's abuse on this man was the effect it had on his faith in the Catholic Church:

> "It has rattled it [faith] and that's what I think is the saddest thing about it; people of our generation . . . where the Church was important and very central . . . the very people they should have been looking after but yet they were doing the very opposite. They are actively alienating people through their actions. It's sad really."

Overall he was angry about the way in which Church officials reacted to and handled his wife's report of abuse. He had expected the Church to be more compassionate and also thought that they would be anxious to protect children from sexual abuse in the future. However, he felt that none of his expectations were met. Nonetheless, he was sympathetic towards the abuser:

> "I suppose the man is more in need of a prayer than anything else. His family I would feel sorry for."

Impact on Family Members of the Abuser

Initial Impact

As with the family members of individuals who experienced abuse, the five family members (all siblings) of the abusers who were interviewed reported experiencing an emotional impact and an impact on their faith in the Catholic Church and clergy more generally. Overall, the emotional effect was characterised in terms of crisis and shock. The shock experienced by some family members was described as synonymous with the shock of hearing about the sudden death of a loved one. When they first learned that their brother had sexually abused children, they were "torn" between wanting to care for him because he was distressed and also wanting to vent their anger towards him and condemn his actions. Striking a balance between these opposite reactions was a strain for most of the siblings interviewed.

Ongoing Impact on Families

Not all families were united in extending support towards their brother. This meant that either one or more family member carried the responsibility for keeping in contact with their convicted brother, attending court and in one case visiting him in prison:

> "From that day to this they [other family members] don't want the topic discussed . . . we're still in contact . . . we still talk to one another . . . it should be discussed . . . if you can't support your own family you can't support anyone . . . [some family members] never ask about him, whether he's dead or alive, when he's coming out . . . I find it hard to accept that they can't support their own."

In two cases, the convicted family member was regularly excluded from family occasions or the homes of certain family members. However, the conditions of exclusion and inclusion were not straightforward. Although some family members welcomed their convicted brother into their home, there were still some instances when they were excluded because in-laws or friends were not willing to be in the same room as a convicted sex offender. This has had implications for relationships with friends and in-laws. "Keeping everyone happy" has been an ongoing source of stress for siblings in these family settings. As families extended the tensions were reported to increase as more and more people had to be informed and considered. Most of the siblings interviewed have children of their own. By extending support to their convicted relative, they reported risking judgement from others and being ostracised by their peers who also have children. Another sibling commented that "publicity punishes the family".

All of the family members reported that awareness of their brother's offence had changed relationships within the family. Alongside conflict and tension it has also "exposed other cracks and problems in the family". Some siblings described how their perception of their family had been affected. They no longer felt proud of their family name and felt that family achievements, individually and collectively, had been "tarnished". One woman was having difficulty coming to terms with the fact that she belonged to a family where one of its members had offended in this way. It was feared that some opportunities might no longer be available to them because of the nature of their brother's crime, for example, taking up employment that involved working with children or applying to foster or adopt children.

Family members also expressed a sense of helplessness. They felt caught up in something, obviously abhorrent, with no way to demonstrate that they too found the sexual abuse of a child reprehensible. One sister recalled attending court with her brother and that their exit from the court was shown on television. She subsequently felt that accompanying her brother to court for such an offence signalled to those watching that she condoned the sexual abuse of children: "There is no avenue to say we don't condone this crime."

One woman said that she has "great admiration for the victim" who had the courage to make an official complaint and try to prevent other children from being abused. Some said they would have liked the opportunity to help the "victims" in some way but realised that this was not an option:

> "He has caused a rip in the fabric of society and we would like to be able to repair it somehow."

Managing Information

Some family members described the knowledge of their relative's offence as a burden. They were either asked not to, or felt themselves unable to, talk to anyone about it. As a result, some were "isolated in the knowledge" and felt they had to deceive those closest to them. Once their relative went to court and was convicted, the balance between concealing and revealing this information to others as they thought necessary, continued to be a source of stress. This also led to conflict within the families where those not initially made aware of the abuse felt betrayed. Some of those interviewed noted that they also had to decide about telling their own children. While some were too young to be told as yet, parents worried that someone else might tell them before they decided the time was right. They also reported being unsure about when they should tell other people and worried about the consequences. For example, one woman wondered if she should tell the parents of her children's friends although they are not at any risk. All of the siblings of convicted clergy who had children were concerned that their younger children would be excluded from events such as birthday parties and worried about how they would explain this to a young child. However, one family member reported not feeling ashamed. He has made no attempt to conceal the nature of his brother's whereabouts, i.e. prison, or his reasons for being there:

> "I never tried to cover up or try to hide, if anybody had come
> to talk to me about it I would have spoken to them."

In the context of managing information, most of the siblings explained that they found themselves in a position whereby they could no longer comment on the issue of child sexual abuse by clergy or child sexual abuse in general. Where once they may have been very vocal, particularly as parents, they now felt their right to free speech on this issue was prohibited. They expected reproach from others if they were vocal on the issue. Some said they deliberately avoided the topic while others said they would not be silenced on the issue.

Perceptions of the Church

Perceptions of the Catholic Church were also affected. Some had a prior scepticism confirmed as they observed the Church's management of the allegation against their brother. For example, one man described how his brother was dealt with "ruthlessly" and "administratively" rather than humanely by Church authorities when the abuse was reported. Another woman who practised in the Catholic faith said that she learned that the Catholic Church was not a Christian institution because of the way in which "Church-going people" responded to her brother's conviction.

Future Perspectives

Some siblings reported feeling slightly burdened at the prospect of having to monitor their relative in the future in the interest of preventing further abuse. Some were concerned about their relative's future, his mental health and his ability to cope without religious life/priesthood. Some also felt a responsibility to regularly remind their relative that his actions had not been forgotten:

> "There is pressure on the family to remind him that what he did was wrong. We don't judge him but don't let him rationalise it or think of himself as a victim but it will eat away at him for the rest of his life. He no longer has the status and rewards of being [clergy]. He is excluded because of his own actions."

Overall, the siblings interviewed felt that there was no ending, happy or otherwise, to their experience. The current climate did not help them. Each time child sexual abuse by clergy was reported in the media, this was experienced as a setback for some siblings because they began experiencing the same negative feelings they had when they first learned about their own brother's offence. As a result some reported using avoidance strategies as part of day-to-day coping.

Impact on Non-offending Clergy[i]

Loss of Confidence in Church Leadership

Loss of confidence in Church leadership was reported as the most significant effect of child sexual abuse by clergy. More specifically, the Church's handling of reported abuse was the problem for non-offending clergy. According to the interviewed colleagues and priest advisor to a convicted cleric, lack of support, not being listened to, or not being informed had affected their ability to trust their leadership. They reported feeling isolated, abandoned, betrayed and deceived with consequent feelings of both anger and depression:

> ". . . nobody had made contact with me to see how I was in this situation . . . I went through a period at one stage I would say of terrible depression . . . I was deeply annoyed that I was involved in something and . . . I had to get my own resources and the way I was treated was just abysmal . . . I can't trust what they are saying. I regressed . . . into a numbed state, a depressed state, just doing my job and getting on with it, then I just found the whole thing earth shattering."

Family, friends and parishioners often provided necessary support when it was most needed. As a result of their experiences, colleagues of convicted clergy had lost considerable faith in Church leadership:

> ". . . it was a reality check, you learn that priests lie. You presume that priests and bishops tell the truth but they lie . . . some of it would be covering up but some of it would be lies. They just don't tell you the truth, the covering up is telling you on a need-to-know basis but I think they lost perspective on this."

---

[i] This section presents the findings from two study phases: qualitative face-to-face interviews with clergy and Church personnel (N=24) and findings from the Church management survey of delegates and bishops (N=137). Data from the survey of delegates and bishops was collated and analysed by Ms Aoife O'Riordan.

> "I don't think my faith as in faith in God and so on [was questioned] but maybe faith in various elements of leadership and so on that I question . . . there was incompetence in what I'm doing, not so much what I'm doing but what I represent . . . I would have to rewrite what my faith is, what priesthood is about."

> ". . . I feel that we were hugely let down by the diocese . . . there is a huge problem of leadership."

Other clergy interviewed also described how their confidence in Church leadership has been affected:

> "I got upset the first Mass I read it [letter from bishop] at and then didn't read it again at Mass because it used the phrase 'sexual abuse by priests' six times. I felt the focus of it was wrong. There was no mention of the bishops' response . . . priests were being demonised again, nothing about their cover-up, no taking of responsibility . . . it saddened me that after all we've been through that he could write such a letter."

> ". . . I'd say it does raise questions about the whole system, the manner in which we operate as a Church . . . does it affect your faith [in the organisation], it certainly raises question marks."

Disillusionment and anger with Church hierarchy over their perceived mishandling of clerical abuse cases was also a common theme among the delegates and bishops surveyed. Over half (59 per cent of delegates and 51 per cent of bishops) reported that it had affected their perception of the Church. Disappointment at the "failure of the Church authorities to deal adequately with both the perpetrator and the victim" was voiced. Some delegates reported a cynicism in relation to the Church and a few went so far as to say they would hesitate to suggest religious life/priesthood as a viable option for today. Delegates were also asked if the issue of child sexual abuse had affected their faith and 13 per cent reported that it had. When asked to describe these effects, participants focused mostly on their perception of the Catholic Church as an institution and their faith (i.e. confidence) in it rather than their faith in God. Likewise, a minority of bishops surveyed (20 per cent) reported that their faith had been affected in terms of their confidence in the institutional Church and "some aspects of its teachings". Fifty-one per cent of bishops said their perception of the Catholic Church as an institution had been affected. Mismanagement was seen to be influenced by attitudes such as the preference for the avoidance of scandal, the precedence of the institution over the individual, and insensitivity to the nature and effects of abuse.

Faith in God was not affected among the clergy interviewed or surveyed. Most had relied on their faith in God to help them cope with the issue of clerical child sexual abuse.

Personal Effects

All clergy and Church personnel, irrespective of rank, role or experience with child sexual abuse, reported that child sexual abuse by clergy had personally affected them. Clergy reported feeling that they had become associated with child sexual abuse and felt they were treated with suspicion. They also felt that they had lost credibility and were no longer trusted by the public:

> "The word paedophile is associated with priest you see which is a terrible thing."

> ". . . with all the stuff that's been around there is no unearned status any more, you don't just come in as the priest."

> "In the past there was deference towards the priests. Now people look at you as the individual that you are, sizing you up because you could be one of these abusers."

> ". . . it has seriously damaged trust . . . at a priest level there has been a fairly serious undermining of their role."

The loss of trust and credibility was seen to have reduced morale among clergy:

> ". . . this is very disheartening . . . there is no two ways about it, it has been very demoralising. There is a lack of morale, there's no doubt about that."

> ". . . there is huge personal pain and you could almost say vocational pain among the members."

Interviewed clergy described feeling shock, anger, hurt and pain as a result of child sexual abuse by clergy and a sense that there was no respite from the issue. Some of the bishops interviewed described similar feelings but also described a sense of guilt and regret in relation to how they had managed cases of child sexual abuse:

> ". . . the whole problem has caused me more distress and more anxiety than anything else in my whole life . . . nothing has upset me and disturbed my peace of mind more than not having hindsight. It would be great if God could create us with hindsight . . ."

> "All I am is very sorry that in my ignorance and naivety that I would have contributed in any way to exposing young children to abuse and that I would have contributed to the suffering the Church is enduring now . . . It is a very painful way of learning your lesson."

> "I would have to say that one of the regrets I have is that I didn't consider the effects on the victims . . . I feel bad that I haven't been able to help . . ."

> "I never needed the Lord as much or friends as much as I did. Nothing has caused me anything like the agony of mind that this has caused me and still causes me . . . and the sense of guilt you feel and inadequacy and the regret that you couldn't have a chance to deal with it again. . . . People say, 'If I had my life all over again I'd do everything the same way.' I can't understand them at all — were they just lucky?"

The colleagues and priest advisor interviewed also described specific personal effects:

"I lost all confidence in my preaching . . . you stand up on a Sunday and you preach and you know this is going on and you say, 'Oh Jesus' . . ."

"It created huge fears around issues of human sexuality for me, I mean would I become like one of them?"

". . . how we treat children has gone to the opposite extreme, even how you treat your own nieces and nephews. One has become very conscious, I know this from talking with my colleagues as well, one becomes very conscious and the whole spontaneity and caring and gentleness goes out the window. It's as though many of the care elements in our profession have been driven by the legal profession, by the health boards and by fear. Fear is probably a good word. One becomes very conscious where one wouldn't have been before of how are people thinking of me."

". . . it did affect us . . . it was dreadful . . . it [being around children] was almost like going through a supermarket and clapping your hands for fear that you were going to be accused of stealing something because you were a known robber."

They also described incidences of harassment and verbal abuse they had personally experienced, or that other clergy they knew had experienced because they were clergy:

"One thing I had was there was a group of lads, about sixteen, sitting on the grass at the front of the Church. 'Here's the fucking priest, come over here Father and play with us. We won't tell the newspapers' . . . that kind of taunting."

The bishops who participated in the postal survey also reported similar personal effects. Twenty-nine per cent of bishops reported being shocked and saddened by the occurrence of clerical child sexual abuse:

"It has saddened me very much and made me feel very helpless in reaching any kind of healing."

Others (29 per cent) mentioned feeling demoralised as a result of revelations. One participant felt that it "has also killed joy and zest for daily living". These effects were similar to those mentioned by delegates.

Stress and Coping

The postal survey of delegates also showed a significant minority of delegates (23 per cent) reporting "lowered morale" and being depressed and drained as a result of the scandals. The loss of credibility and trust in the eyes of the public was another prominent effect. Some delegates reported not being able to "speak out on other matters because of the fear that this issue will be thrown back at me". They felt that the occurrence and the management of clerical child sexual abuse had "undermined what the Church is meant to be about". Another effect mentioned by delegates surveyed was a tremendous sadness for those abused. They felt saddened that many children had been sexually abused and felt a "deep sense of shame . . ." because of the betrayal of trust. The postal survey of delegates also showed that almost half (49 per cent) of the delegates described their role as "very stressful". Delegates who had dealt with cases (55 per cent of the sample) were much more likely to report that they found their role stressful (69 per cent) than those who had not yet had to deal with a case (11 per cent). Forty-six per cent of bishops found the experience of dealing with cases of clerical child sexual abuse "extremely stressful" with 40 per cent saying it was "very stressful". Fourteen per cent had not dealt with any cases. Thus, all bishops with practical experience have found the experience of managing cases of clerical child sexual abuse to be very or extremely stressful compared to 69 per cent of delegates who have had experience of dealing with cases.

Bishops were also asked about the resources they used to help them cope with the stress of dealing with allegations of child sexual abuse against clergy. Fifty-two per cent cited formal Church structures such as "advisory groups" and the appointment of delegates as being helpful. Thirty-eight per cent relied on "spiritual resources" such as prayer and faith in God. Professional consultation and advice was mentioned as a resource by 31 per cent of participants (e.g. counsellors, psychiatrists, health board officials and legal experts). Twenty-eight per cent received social support from friends and family. Twenty-one per cent listed personal attributes such as an "ability to listen" and an "attitude of responsibility and fairness" as important assets.

Fear

The clergy interviewed also described fear. This manifested in two ways. Firstly, there was the fear they experienced in the company of children, whether socially or in the context of their ministry. Secondly, there was the fear of a false allegation:

> "I'd be very conscious of, on the one hand, continuing to minister to young people and that I'm not going to be put into a box by what has happened . . . but also on the other hand that I need to take the precautions that are necessary to protect myself . . ."

> "The false allegation thing is a real fear."

> ". . . at one level anybody can say anything, that's a fear that's around for a lot of priests."

The majority of delegates (64 per cent) who participated in the postal survey said that they felt less comfortable in their interactions with children as a result of child sexual abuse by clergy and religious. Delegates were also asked if they found a change in the attitude of others towards them since the problem of clerical child sexual abuse had emerged. Over a third (35 per cent) of delegates agreed that they had noticed a change in attitudes (43 per cent of bishops also reported this change). These attitudes ranged from positive to negative, quite often a mix of the two; people had been either "extremely sympathetic and supportive" towards them or hostile. One-third of bishops reported an increased "embarrassment" and tension in relations with members of the public, and with family and friends. One bishop described how "people in general seem less inclined to make eye contact".

Effects on Self-image and Identity

Self-image and identity also seems to have been affected. Some reluctance was reported among the clergy interviewed concerning the wearing of clerical clothes or publicly displaying any sign that indicated that they were clergy:

> "On one occasion, I was in town. I rarely go into town because I'm so conscious of it now. Its almost like I'm wearing a paedophile uniform at this stage . . . a fellow ran after me and spat at me . . . he shouted, 'Child abuser, child molester'. More and more I'm anonymous. The only time I wear my clerical garb is when I'm walking around the parish."

> "It's an absolutely terrible situation to be in. It's almost as though I've become shamed of what I signify."

The need to conceal identity because of an unwillingness to be identified publicly as a member of the clergy had led some participants to question what they represent:

> ". . . I suppose the hardest thing for me to take was, 'Sure you are one of them anyway' and that identified me with the abusers and that brings in the personal element for me. At times . . . I wondered should I be a religious at all . . . it was the first time that I asked myself, 'Did I make the right choice?' I pitched my lot with a group of people who were not what I thought they were . . . is there something about the nature of religious life that drives people to abuse children? . . . three-quarters of my brain says no . . . the more damaging thing I have had to cope with myself is feeling less proud to declare that I'm a religious."

Impact on the Wider Church Community

The general public survey, which represented the views of the wider Church community, examined the extent to which child sexual abuse by clergy had affected religious practices, trust and perception of priests, perception of the Catholic Church, and trust in and relationship with God.

Impact on Religious Practices

When questioned about the effect of child sexual abuse by clergy on their own religious practices,[j] 59 per cent of the public surveyed said it had had no effect while 36 per cent reported a negative effect. Those who reported a negative effect said their attendance at mass and time spent praying was affected as was their attitude towards the Church and clergy.

Satisfaction with and Quality of Catholic Church and Clergy

Respondents were asked about satisfaction with Catholic clergy and the Catholic Church more generally. Over half (54 per cent) felt satisfied with Catholic clergy with one-third dissatisfied (32 per cent). Less satisfaction and more dissatisfaction was expressed with the Catholic Church with 44 per cent reporting satisfaction and 43 per cent reporting dissatisfaction (Figure 4.1).

Figure 4.1: Public Satisfaction Rates for Catholic Clergy and the Catholic Church as an Organisation

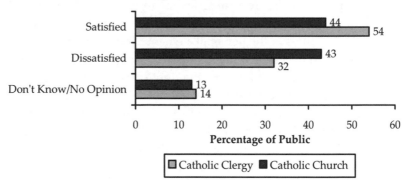

In a parallel question, respondents were asked if they thought the quality of Catholic clergy and the Catholic Church today was higher, lower or about the same as it was in the past (Figure 4.2). Most felt that the quality of clergy was higher (47 per cent) or

---

[j] Religious service attendance by Catholics appeared similar to that found in an equivalent survey in 1997 (with 63 per cent attending services at least weekly). These figures have consistently reduced from 91 per cent attendance in 1974.

about the same (26 per cent) while 12 per cent thought the quality was lower. For those who felt the quality of clergy was higher, three main reasons emerged: improved relationships with congregations, improved selection and training procedures, and greater "accountability" and "integrity". The most common explanation for a drop in quality was the occurrence and management of child sexual abuse by clergy. Regarding the quality of the Catholic Church, most respondents felt that the quality was about the same (38 per cent) or better (33 per cent). Those who thought the Catholic Church had improved referred to an increase in "openness" and "accountability" and improved relations with the wider Church community. Fifteen per cent of respondents thought the quality of the Church was worse today than in the past. Again, the management of child sexual abuse by clergy was cited for the decline in quality.

Figure 4.2: Public Ratings of Quality of Catholic Clergy and the Catholic Church Today Compared to the Past

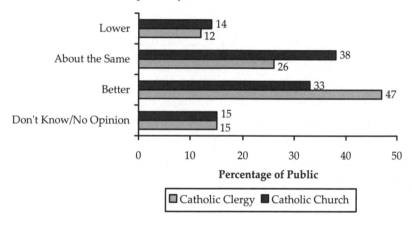

Impact on Trust and Perception of Priests

The extent to which child sexual abuse by clergy has affected the public's ability to trust clergy and whether the public idealised clergy and viewed them as spiritually and morally exceptional was examined (Figure 4.3). Respondents were equivocal on whether they were willing to trust a priest on first arrival in their neighbourhoods (41 per cent were not willing while 40 per cent were willing). The majority of respondents (76 per cent) did not regard choosing the priesthood as an indication of sexual problems and did not support the requirement that priests live a celibate life (74 per cent). Over half (52 per cent) did not believe that priests who sexually abused children were homosexual. There was less agreement on whether homosexual men should be ordained as priests (39 per cent agreeing that they should, 35 per cent disagreeing and 26 per cent unsure). The majority of respondents (76 per cent) felt that Catholics should not necessarily do what a priest tells them to do. Seventy-one per cent felt that priests were no closer to God than other people. However, 85 per cent believed that a priest's moral conduct should be better than other people's and 66 per cent said they looked to priests to provide moral leadership. The majority (72 per cent) of those surveyed felt that most clergy have been unfairly judged because of the emergence of child sexual abuse by clergy.

Confidence in the Catholic Church

Participants were asked if they thought that child sexual abuse by clergy had damaged the Catholic Church. An overwhelming majority of participants (94 per cent) believed that the Church has been damaged. Those who believed that the Church was damaged were asked whether they thought this damage was permanent and 52 per cent agreed.[k] Anecdotally, those who were unsure often qualified this by commenting that the permanence of damage was dependent on how the Church managed child sexual abuse in the future.

---

[k] Of the total sample, 49 per cent agreed, 36 per cent disagreed and 9 per cent were unsure.

Figure 4.3: Public Perceptions of and Trust in Clergy

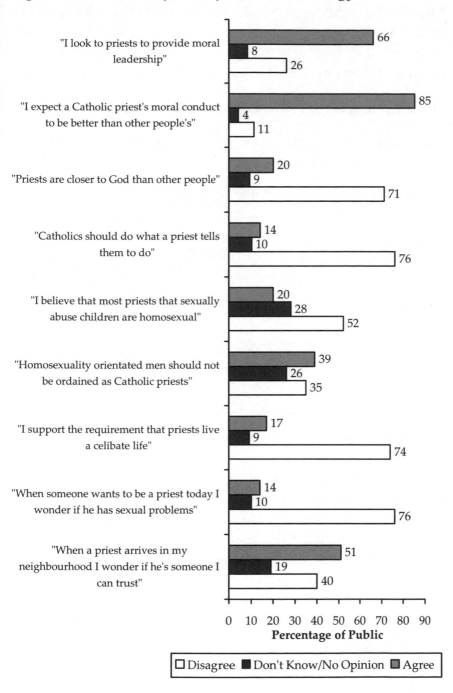

In relation to personal commitment to the Catholic Church, only a third of the public said that they looked to the Church to provide guidance on issues of human sexuality. Over two-thirds (65 per cent) said they would be pleased if their child became an altar server or if their son wanted to be a priest (56 per cent)[1] (Figure 4.4).

Figure 4.4: Aspects of Public Confidence in the Catholic Church

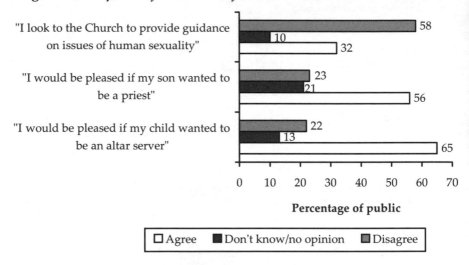

Impact on Trust and Relationship with God

Belief in God was high with 93 per cent of those surveyed reporting belief in a God. Those who indicated a belief in God were asked three questions about their personal relationship with, and faith in, God. The majority reported feeling close to (87 per cent) and loved by (88 per cent) God and 87 per cent were confident that prayers were heard and responded to by God.

Throughout this chapter attention has been drawn to the personal and public effects of the Church's management of child sexual abuse. Perspectives on the Church's initial response and ongoing management of child sexual abuse by clergy is discussed in the next chapter.

---

[1] Those without children answered the question hypothetically.

Chapter 5

CHURCH RESPONSE TO, AND MANAGEMENT OF, CHILD SEXUAL ABUSE BY CLERGY

SUMMARY

o Research indicates that responses to the disclosure of child sexual abuse have significant implications for recovery. Negative responses such as blame or disbelief can be damaging in both the short term and the long term.

o Before the Church had formal policies and procedures for dealing with child sexual abuse, a "moral fault" approach was taken. The act of abuse was considered a sin. A confessional approach tended to be adopted. This focused on the sinner rather than on the person abused. Clergy were generally removed from the "site of temptation".

o As the number of clerical abuse allegations grew and came to public attention in the late 1980s, attempts were made to develop Church procedures to manage child sexual abuse by clergy. Initial strategies consisted mainly of removing the accused person from ministry and sending the accused for treatment.

o Individual dioceses, notably St John's in Newfoundland, Canada and the Archdiocese of Chicago in the US, established inquiries in the 1990s. These inquiries recommended procedures and policies for dealing with allegations of child sexual abuse against clergy. They also began to consider the factors contributing to clerical child sexual abuse.

o The Catholic Church in Ireland issued a policy document on child sexual abuse by clergy (*Child Sexual Abuse: Framework for a Church Response*) in 1996. This document outlined a commitment to report all instances where it is known or suspected that a child has been, or is being sexually abused by a member of the clergy, to civil authorities.

o Preventative strategies became the focus of later Church policies as did the broadening of the focus on the behaviour of Church personnel to include lay Church workers and volunteers.

o According to canon law (the body of law that governs the Church), clerical offences such as child sexual abuse carry a maximum penalty of dismissal from the clerical state. Investigations into allegations against clergy are led by the bishop/superior and pursued in complete confidentiality. An administrative procedure such as suspension can be imposed or there can be a penal process whereby the case goes to trial under canon law.

o Specific Church policies on child sexual abuse do not include reporting procedures for accusations against bishops. Such accusations must be dealt with by canon law.

INTRODUCTION

This chapter provides a brief overview of formal Church responses to child sexual abuse by clergy in Irish and international settings. This is followed by the research findings from this study on the Irish Catholic Church's management of child sexual abuse. The main focus is on the experiences and attitudes of abused individuals and their families and also convicted clergy and their families. The experiences and attitudes of priests who were colleagues of convicted clergy, other clergy, Church delegates, bishops and the wider Church community are also discussed.

DISCLOSURE AND CHURCH RESPONSE

The response to disclosure is a crucial element in the recovery of children and adults who have been sexually abused. It has significant implications for the duration and extent of the effects of abuse.[146, 148] Disclosure can occur at different times and in different contexts. Individuals may, for example, speak of their childhood experiences in the context of a long-term relationship or details may emerge for the first time during psychotherapy.[163] The most damaging responses a person can encounter are blame and disbelief. Positive reactions to disclosure such as being believed and being allowed to talk about the experience are associated with less distress.[163, 164]

Research on disclosure has shown that few adults who experience sexual assault or rape, either as children or as adults, disclose their experience to professionals such as police, health professionals[1] or clergy.[165, 166] One study of women found that many who had disclosed rape or sexual assault (by non-clerical offenders) to clergy felt more injured by the response than by the assault itself.[167] The researchers attributed this to a general lack of understanding by clergy and to naïve views on sexual abuse and violence. In a separate study, attitudes of clergy to those who had been raped were examined. Clergy with sexist or religiously fundamentalist attitudes were found to react more negatively and attribute more blame to the abused person.[168]

Much of the literature on child sexual abuse by clergy has focused on the pastoral responses of the Church to those abused. Responses have generally been seen as inadequate and have often re-traumatised the abused individual.[138] Some of the more defensive reactions from the Catholic Church since the emergence of child sexual abuse by clergy have been categorised as follows:[169]

- Complete denial

- Acknowledgement of abuse with the caveat that it is rare and/or perpetrated by a small number of individuals

- Arguing that it is no more common in the Catholic Church than in other religious denominations

- Blaming the media for exaggerating the problem

- Arguing that there is no link between celibacy and child sexual abuse.

Moral Fault: Pre-policy Responses

Public outrage over clerical child sexual abuse in the Catholic Church has been due, in part, to the perceived mismanagement by the Church of the accused and those abused. Since the late 1980s, the Catholic Church has been producing specific guidelines and policies in many countries in an effort to formalise and standardise its responses.

Many commentators have considered the question of why the Church initially found it so difficult to deal with allegations of child sexual abuse and why so many cases were poorly managed. For example, it has been argued that the mistakes were due to ignorance and a general lack of awareness (also among the general population) about the pervasiveness of child sexual abuse at the time.[170] Furthermore, some superiors were willing to trust priests who had abused children and to allow them to continue in ministry in an attempt to salvage their priesthood.[171] In addition, efforts by Church personnel to avoid or limit legal liability resulted in an adversarial approach. This approach was guided more by legal advice rather than a pastoral response towards the abused person.[171]

It is speculated that some bishops viewed the issue in terms of the sixth commandment which prohibits adultery and that they relied on a traditional confessional approach to management.[172] In such a view, no distinction was made between breaches of chastity with a child and with an adult woman. The abused child was regarded as a "passive source of temptation" and the response of the Church was "sin-orientated" rather than "victim-orientated". If the priest was "truly sorry", the traditional response by the bishop was to remove temptation by moving the priest to another parish. Reporting the matter to the police would have jeopardised the priest's return to grace and would have created scandal. Clearly, in light of subsequent revelations, this so-called "geographical solution" was not an effective method for dealing with men who were sexually attracted to children.

DEVELOPMENT OF CHURCH POLICIES

First Generation Policies

The first comprehensive attempt to address the problem of child sexual abuse by clergy was produced in 1985 in the US. This report[a] was the result of the authors' direct experience of dealing with child sexual abuse by clergy. They felt it necessary to alert Church leaders about the growing problem and they advised the National Conference of Catholic Bishops (NCCB) in the US to establish a multidisciplinary national team to assist diocesan officials in responding to allegations of child sexual abuse at local level. The report did not have any great impact at the time in the US.

The Catholic bishops in the US issued several short statements in the late 1980s and early 1990s regarding clerical child sexual abuse. In summary, the following principles were recommended to guide those managing allegations:

- Investigate immediately

- Remove the priest where the evidence warrants it

- Follow the reporting obligations of civil law

- Extend pastoral care to the victim and the victim's family

- Seek appropriate treatment for the offender

- Deal as openly as possible about the incident with members of the community (within the confines of privacy).

---

[a] *The Problem of Sexual Molestation by Roman Catholic Priests: Meeting the Problem in a Comprehensive and Responsible Manner* (1985), by Rev. Thomas Doyle (canon lawyer), Ray Mouton (attorney) and Rev. M. Peterson (director of a psychiatric hospital). Available from www.thelinkup.com.

As the problem emerged in Canada, the Canadian Conference of Catholic Bishops (CCCB) issued general guidelines in 1987. They recommended a team approach to allegations.[b]

Church Inquiries: North America

Some dioceses commissioned their own inquiries to investigate child sexual abuse by clergy. The factors that contributed to the sexual abuse of children by clergy were examined and the findings were directed not only to clergy but to the whole Church.

The Archdiocese of Newfoundland, Canada established its own commission of inquiry in 1989. The report,[c] completed in 1990 and commonly referred to as the Winter Report,[d] included over 50 recommendations. It is considered highly significant because it examined past procedures and made recommendations for the future. It also identified factors and structures within the Archdiocese that contributed to the ongoing problem of abuse and to the failures to detect it.[e]

In 1992, the Canadian Conference of Catholic Bishops' *ad hoc* Committee on Child Sexual Abuse produced a report *From Pain to Hope*. This was addressed to the whole Canadian Catholic Church and included 50 recommendations covering a broad range of issues covering *inter alia* the pastoral care of those abused and their families, establishing advisory committees for dioceses, the management of accused priests and preventative strategies such as better formation of clergy and the promotion of research into human sexuality.

---

[b] These general guidelines were based on the 1985 report by Doyle, Mouton and Peterson.

[c] *The Report of the Archdiocesan Commission of Enquiry into the sexual abuse of children by members of the clergy*, vols. I, II, III, Newfoundland, Canada (1990).

[d] The inquiry was chaired by Gordon A. Winter.

[e] Shortly after the publication of the Winter Report, Archbishop Alphonsus Penney of St John's Diocese, Newfoundland, Canada (the person who had commissioned the inquiry) resigned.

The Archdiocese of Chicago issued a report in 1992 based on its investigations of known child sexual abuse cases in the diocese since 1963. The report examined risk factors for abuse and procedures for dealing with allegations from initial responses to the final disposition of cases. It referred only to priests and made no provision for lay persons working in the Church. The report is well known for its recommendation to establish an independent review board to "oversee the handling of allegations" and it has been used as a model for many other dioceses.[170]

Irish Church Policy: *Child Sexual Abuse: Framework for a Church Response* (1996)

In 1994, the Irish Catholic Bishops' Conference established a committee to advise on appropriate responses to an accusation, suspicion or knowledge of a priest or religious having sexually abused a child. The Committee, which included members of the clergy, legal representatives and members of the medical/psychology professions, was asked to formulate guidelines for Church policy and to suggest a set of procedures. In 1996, the Committee produced *Child Sexual Abuse: Framework for a Church Response*. This was endorsed by the Irish Catholic Bishops' Conference and the Conference of Religious in Ireland (CORI). The main guidelines were as follows (p. 18):

- The safety and welfare of children should be the first and paramount consideration following an allegation of child sexual abuse

- A prompt response should be given to all allegations of child sexual abuse

- In all instances where it is known or suspected that a priest or religious has sexually abused a child, the matter should be reported to civil authorities

- Care should be given to the emotional and spiritual well-being of those who have suffered abuse and their families

- There should be immediate consideration, following a complaint, of all child protection issues which arise, including whether the accused priest or religious should continue in ministry during the investigation

- The rights under natural justice, civil law and canon law of an accused priest or religious should be respected

- An appropriate pastoral response to the parish and wider community should be provided, with due regard to the right of privacy of those directly involved and to the administration of justice

- Adequate positive steps should be taken to restore the good name and reputation of a priest or religious who has been wrongly accused of child sexual abuse.

Each diocese and religious congregation was advised to adopt a protocol (reflecting the eight guidelines) for responding to complaints of child sexual abuse by clergy and to communicate the protocol to all clergy and the general public. The appointment of a delegate to oversee and implement the protocol in each diocese or religious congregation was also recommended. According to the *Framework Document*, the delegate should be "carefully chosen" and should undergo training. It was recommended that every complaint of child sexual abuse received by Church personnel should be communicated to the delegate for that diocese/religious congregation. It was also recommended that the bishop/religious superior appoint:

- A support person who should be available to each individual who experienced abuse and their family

- An advisor to be available to each accused priest or religious

- An advisory panel for each diocese, the members of which will be available to offer advice on a confidential basis, collectively and in their respective disciplines, when required. The panel should include lay people with qualities and expertise relevant to the issue of child sexual abuse.

- A media relations person.

The Committee also recommended that mechanisms for the exchange of information between religious congregations and dioceses be established, that methods for dealing with the concerns of the lay community be addressed and that assessment and treatment of priests and religious accused of child sexual abuse be considered. In relation to selection and formation of priests and religious, the Committee recommended that selection be based on signs of a real vocation and that psychological assessments should be used in screening potential candidates. It also highlighted the need for greater public awareness of child sexual abuse and recommended that priests, religious and teachers in Church-run schools should receive ongoing education and in-service training on the nature and effects of child sexual abuse. Arguably, in the absence of mandatory reporting in Ireland, the most significant aspect of this report was the recommendation that all known and suspected cases of child sexual abuse should be reported to civil authorities. However, the *Framework Document* was not directly binding on diocesan bishops or religious superiors.

The UK, Australia and New Zealand

Between 1994 and 1998 the Catholic Church in England and Wales,[f] Scotland,[g] Australia[h] and New Zealand[i] issued similar documents on child abuse. Some of the policies focused only on abuse by clergy but others included lay staff and Church volunteers. The reports had a number of common features:

---

[f] *Child Abuse: Pastoral and Procedural Guidelines* (1994) and *Healing the Wound of Child Sexual Abuse: A Church Response* (1996).

[g] *Child Sexual Abuse*, Report Commissioned by the Bishops' Conference of Scotland (1996).

[h] *Towards Healing, Principles and Procedures in Responding to Complaints of Sexual Abuse against Personnel of the Catholic Church in Australia* (1996).

[i] *A Path to Healing, Principles and Procedures in responding to complaints of sexual abuse by Clergy and Religious of the Catholic Church in New Zealand* (1998).

- A recognition of the dignity and rights of children

- An admission that child sexual abuse exists both in society and in the Church

- A willingness to respond appropriately and a commitment to prevent abuse

- A promise to develop structures and procedures in accordance with State policy, legislation and official documents

- An obligation to full and permanent co-operation with civil authorities

- A commitment to better selection and formation of priests, religious, lay staff and volunteers in the Church.

Second Generation Reports and Policies

As the response of the Church developed, the focus broadened to include preventative strategies aimed at creating a safer environment for children. In 1998, the Catholic Church of Scotland produced a report entitled *Keeping Children Safe*. This set out good practice for paid Church staff and volunteers to create a safe environment for children. It has been described as an "excellent example of informing people to the extent that they know exactly what to and what not to do to protect the welfare and safety of children".[173]

The document *Towards Healing*, produced by the Catholic Church in Australia, was revised in December 2000. The main changes were the proposals that the definition of abuse be extended to include physical and emotional abuse and that allegations against a Church employee, other than a member of the clergy, should be referred to the relevant employment body and investigated in accordance with employment laws.

In 2000, the Archbishop of Westminster established a body to examine and review arrangements for child protection and the prevention of abuse in the Catholic Church in England and

Wales.[j] The body produced an interim report in April 2001[k] and its final report *A Programme for Action* in September 2001. This recommended prioritising preventative policies and practices to minimise opportunities for abuse rather than focusing solely on responding to complaints of abuse. The recommendations covered a broad range of issues including the development of a code of conduct for those working with children, methods for record keeping, considerations regarding workers coming from abroad, false allegations and the problems associated with dealing with abusers in the congregation.

A document entitled *Charter for the Protection of Children and Young People* was produced in November 2002 by the US Conference of Catholic Bishops. It set out four principles on which policies would be adopted and implemented:

- To promote healing and reconciliation with victims/survivors of sexual abuse

- To guarantee an effective response to allegations of sexual abuse of minors

- To ensure the accountability of procedures

- To protect the faithful in the future.

The second principle underpinned the commitment to report all allegations of the sexual abuse of minors to public authorities. The most controversial aspect of the Charter stipulated that a priest who had sexually abused a minor (regardless of the time elapsed since the occurrence of the abuse) or who did so in the future would be permanently removed from ministry. The third principle authorised the establishment of a National Office for Child and Youth Protection to assist individual dioceses with the implementation of safe environment programmes. This office would

---

[j] Chaired by Lord Nolan.

[k] *Review on Child Protection in the Catholic Church in England and Wales* (2001) (The Nolan Interim Report).

assist dioceses to develop policies. It would also produce annual public reports on the progress made in implementing the standards set out in the Charter and list dioceses not in compliance with these standards.

Although the preamble to the Charter acknowledges that some bishops have sexually abused children (up to 12 bishops in the US have resigned because of allegations of sexual misconduct), there are no procedures in any Church policies, including the Charter, to deal with accusations against bishops. The procedures outlined in the Charter for priests accused and found guilty of child sexual abuse do not apply to bishops. According to canon law (canon 1401 and 1405), canonical trial of bishops is reserved to the Holy See (i.e. the Vatican).

Summary

First generation Church policies on child sexual abuse were limited in scope and focused mainly on the immediate context of the abuse and on the persons affected. The establishment of commissions to conduct independent inquiries in dioceses such as St. John's in Canada and the Archdiocese of Chicago have resulted in Church policies that are more comprehensive and much broader in scope. Many dioceses have borrowed from these policies in developing their own procedures and this has resulted in a common approach in many countries. Some policies focus only on clergy but others now include lay staff and volunteers. Second generation policies are continually being revised and developed and there is an increasing emphasis on prevention in these policies.

CANON LAW

Canon[1] law is the body of laws and regulations made by or adopted by ecclesiastical authority for the government of the Catholic

---

[1] The word canon is derived from the Greek word *kanon*, meaning a rule or practical direction and has acquired exclusive ecclesiastical significance (*Catholic Encyclopaedia*, 1999).

Church with the Pope as the supreme legislator. It is "intended to be an instrument to assist the People of God in living out their faith, as individuals and as members of the Church".[174] The ultimate purpose of canon law is "the salvation of souls . . ."[175] (canon 1752). Canon law was codified in 1917 and revised and updated in the wake of Vatican II, culminating in the promulgation of a Code of Canon Law in 1983. This second code has 1,752 canons, i.e. rules for the governance of the external life of the Church, which are concerned mainly with Church order and discipline.[176]

Canonical Issues in the Sexual Abuse of Children by Clergy: Provisions in the 1983 Code

Canon 1395 provides a penalty for clergy who violate their obligations of chastity by sinning against the sixth commandment.[177] Canon 1395 § 2 states:

> A cleric who has offended . . . against the sixth commandment of the Decalogue,[m] . . . with a minor under the age of sixteen years,[n] is to be punished with just penalties, not excluding dismissal from the clerical state if the case so warrants.

The person making an accusation has the right to be heard, the right to legal process and the right to the resolution of grievance according to canon 221.[178, 179] The accused member of the clergy has the right to defend himself, the right to due process of law, the right to an impartial investigation and the right to be penalised only in accordance with the law. In addition, canon 220 prohibits the unlawful damaging of a person's good reputation and the violation of privacy.[175] The accused person has the right to support, spiritual guidance and expert canonical help. The primary right of the accused is the right to an impartial investigation, a right shared by the person making the accusation.

---

[m] The Ten Commandments.

[n] This has been raised to 18 for abuse occurring after 1994 in the USA and after 1996 in Ireland (these derogations will be discussed later).

Investigation

Investigation is initiated by the "Ordinary"° and must proceed in a confidential manner. According to canon 1717 § 1:

> whenever the Ordinary receives information, which has at least the semblance of truth, about an offence, he is to enquire carefully, either personally or through some suitable person, about the facts and circumstances, and about the imputability of the offence, unless this enquiry would appear to be entirely superfluous.

Once sufficient information is gathered, the Ordinary must decide whether the process for inflicting or deciding a penalty can be set in motion on the basis of whether or not a crime has been committed. The Ordinary must consider whether the time for judicial action has not expired (prescription). In 1994, the US National Conference of Catholic Bishops was granted derogations by the Pope to change the statute of limitations for prosecuting clergy accused of sexually abusing a child and to allow such a prosecution until the minor's twenty-eighth birthday, for crimes committed after 1994.[180] The age at which the person sexually abused by a priest could be considered a minor was also raised from under 16 to under 18 years. In 1996, the Irish Bishops' Conference was granted similar derogations. For sexual abuse committed after 1996, criminal action was permitted until the abused individual has reached 28 years of age. For crimes prior to 1996, criminal action was permitted until the person has reached 23 years of age. Therefore, any allegation made after the person's twenty-third (pre-1996) or twenty-eighth (post-1996) birthday would not be subject to criminal action under canon law. Although the Ordinary would have to

---

° "In law the term Ordinary means, apart from the Roman Pontiff, diocesan Bishops and all who, even for a time only, are set over a particular Church or a community equivalent to it in accordance with can. 368, and those who in these have general ordinary executive power, that is, Vicars general and episcopal Vicars; likewise, for their own members, it means the major Superiors of clerical religious institutes of pontifical right and of clerical societies of apostolic life of pontifical right, who have at least ordinary executive power" (can. 134 §1).

look into the matter, he would not be able to institute a penal trial against the cleric, unless in a particular case the Holy See dispensed from the statute of limitations.

The investigation is concluded when the Ordinary decides that a crime has been committed and the penalty phase begins. However, if the Ordinary concludes that the accused is not canonically responsible for his actions (i.e. imputability cannot be proved), but is impaired due to psychological illness or other cause, he may declare the cleric impeded from exercising his orders, i.e. ministry (canon 1044). This is not a penal procedure but is disciplinary in the sense that it is similar to suspension. In some instances, once the preliminary inquiry is completed the Ordinary may decide to proceed by decree, rather than by a judicial trial. However, he cannot impose a perpetual penalty by means of a decree (canon 1342); a full trial is required so that the cleric may duly exercise his right of defence. An Ordinary may invoke the provisions of canon 1722, which are commonly identified as "administrative leave" as a protective measure pending the outcome of the process. Administrative leave is not a suspension — suspension is a canonical penalty.

A penal process is the "court of last resort", in canon law.[181] Canon 1341 states that the Ordinary should start a judicial or an administrative procedure only when methods of correction or pastoral means cannot sufficiently repair scandal, reform the accused and restore justice.[179] The various means of correction are listed in canons 1366 to 1340 and include deprivation of office, penal transfer, a prohibition against residing in a particular place or an order to reside in a particular place, a prohibition against the exercise of the power of order, canonical warnings and public or private penances. Other methods such as psychological treatment are not excluded.[181]

The Judicial Process

If the Ordinary decides to proceed judicially, he turns the entire matter over to the "promoter of justice"[p] who presents the case to a tribunal, if he judges that there is sufficient evidence. Judicial proceedings are held confidentially. If the accused has made no arrangements of his own it is the obligation of the tribunal to provide for the defence of the accused. Canon law requires that a tribunal of three judges adjudicate penal cases involving the penalty of dismissal from the clerical state (dismissal is not the only penalty in cases judged under canon 1395). If the judges find that the promoter of justice's case has not been established, the accused is absolved of the crime. Alternatively, if the offence of the accused is demonstrated and the person's imputability has been upheld, the tribunal must address the question of whether dismissal from the clerical state can be imposed both in law and on the basis of the facts.[181]

Canon law provides for the application of just penalties including dismissal from the clerical state for offences such as sexual misconduct with a minor. However, it does not require the application of dismissal. Thus, lesser penalties may be imposed. If proof exists that the accused has been reformed, or that scandal has been repaired, or if the accused is to be punished by the civil authorities, the tribunal can refrain from imposing dismissal even if the accused is found guilty. Once a decision is reached, the sentence is published and the accused has 15 days to appeal. If no appeal is lodged, the judge issues a decree stating that the sentence is to be executed.

Removal of the Accused from Ministry

The judicial process allows the bishop to prohibit the accused from exercising ministry once the accused has been cited. The bishop may remove the accused from ministry or from any ecclesiastical office or function, may impose or prohibit residence in a

---

[p] Priests usually serve in this office and also act as judges in penal actions.

given place or territory or prohibit public participation in Eucharist worship (canon 1722). These sanctions under canon 1722 are temporary measures.

Reassignment of Clergy who have Received Treatment Following Sexual Misconduct with Children

Clergy who suffer illness, incapacity or those in old age have the right to social assistance. Therefore, clergy removed from office can be provided with another assignment if they are suitable or they can be retired with a pension. It is only when clergy are dismissed from the clerical state that this "obligation-right" ceases and, even then, clergy must be supported if they are truly in need.[175] If a cleric has received treatment and is deemed suitable to return to ministry, restrictions can be canonically enforced. The Ordinary is not obliged to invent an office or ministry where no suitable position is available.

Clergy Not Suitable for Reassignment

In cases where clergy have been treated for sexual misconduct with minors and have been professionally judged unsuitable for ministry the options are voluntary retirement without faculties, voluntary laicisation, declaration that they are impeded from exercising orders or dismissal from the clerical state. Voluntary withdrawal from ministry due to illness or otherwise still entitles the person to social assistance and full or partial pension in accordance with diocesan norms.[175] Alternatively, the person may petition the Holy See for laicisation and, if granted, the Church has no further responsibility for assignment or support. Laicisation is only considered after long-term treatment if rehabilitation is unlikely. The Holy See is also willing, under certain conditions, to consider requests for imposed laicisation when the cleric has been sentenced to prison and refuses to petition personally for voluntary laicisation.

Dismissal from the clerical state can only be imposed judicially or by action of the Holy See. In 1999, an English Catholic priest serving a sentence for sex offences against children was dismissed by papal decree.[q] Normally, a penalty as serious as dismissal from the clerical state is imposed following a canonical trial but, in this instance, the Pope decided to bypass this process because of the seriousness of the convicted priest's crimes (*The Irish Times*, 6 October 1999). The problem, however, in terms of child protection, is that if all clergy who sexually abused children were laicised, they would not necessarily be under Church supervision. The concern is that they might then be more at risk of re-offending if they were adrift from any accounting mechanism. In a declaration of an impediment to the exercise of orders, an Ordinary may invoke canon 1044 and prohibit a person from the exercise of orders when that person is judged to be incapable of carrying out such ministry appropriately.[175] The person does not lose the right to support. He is bound by individual and penal precepts, which govern his ongoing treatment, monitoring and behaviour.

CONGREGATION FOR THE DOCTRINE OF FAITH

The Congregation for the Doctrine of Faith (CDF) is one of the main Vatican Congregations (departments) that handles a variety of matters for the Pope. In May 2001, the CDF issued a letter to bishops and other Ordinaries outlining several "norms" in relation to offences committed by clergy and clarifying who is competent to deal with such offences. This included the sexual abuse of minors. Cases involving child sexual abuse by clergy were to be referred to the CDF, which would review them and decide whether they should be handled locally or in the Vatican. The norms also stipulated that there should be a ten-year prescription period from the accuser's eighteenth birthday and that such cases must be handled in strict secrecy by courts staffed by priests.

---

[q] Three priests in the United States were dismissed from the clerical state for similar reasons in 1998 and in Ireland two diocesan priests were dismissed between 1992 and 1999.

Assigning jurisdiction over cases of child sexual abuse to the CDF represents an attempt to centralise the management of child sexual abuse cases in the Catholic Church. Prior to this, at least six different Vatican offices had some jurisdiction over such cases. The norms could allow the CDF to speed up canonical trial processes relating to the dismissal of clergy who have sexually abused children, particularly if dioceses lack the resources for a trial. In February 2003, some changes were made to the CDF document. In certain cases an Ordinary can now apply to the CDF to allow a lay person to serve as a judge, or for a priest to serve on the panel without a doctorate in canon law.

The following section outlines the views of the participants in the present study on the Church's management of child sexual abuse by clergy in Ireland in recent years.

CHURCH RESPONSE AND MANAGEMENT: FINDINGS FROM THE PRESENT STUDY

Summary

- Responses to those abused by Church personnel were characterised by lack of outreach, communication, sensitivity and compassion. The overall impression was that Church personnel were more concerned with legal issues, e.g. the fear of litigation against the Church, rather than concern for the person abused and their family. Some individuals who experienced child sexual abuse had to report their experience to more than one Church representative before it was addressed. Those who experienced abuse recommended the development of a system that would make it easier for people to report abuse. Suggestions included less intimidating venues for meeting complainants, the option of reporting to non-clerical personnel, a more timely and sensitive response and a willingness on the part of Church personnel to believe complainants.

- Colleagues of convicted clergy reported that the management of child sexual abuse by Church authorities reflected a concern to protect the Church as an institution. They were particularly critical of their own treatment during the investigation of the case. Most felt they were provided with little or no information or support.

- Clergy convicted of sexual offences against children felt that they were treated in a business-like manner by superiors who typically lacked understanding. All convicted clergy were sent for treatment. Financial support for legal and treatment services was not always provided by the Church. There were mixed feelings regarding support from superiors and peers during the legal process and during prison sentence.

- Convicted abusers and their families were concerned that future developments in the management of convicted clergy would be dictated by international developments and/or media pressure and might have negative consequences for them. For instance, they were concerned about permanent removal from ministry as recommended in recent US Church policy.

- Some family members of convicted clergy were critical of the Church's management of their relative. They described an administrative approach characterised by lack of concern for the individual. However, others felt that, given the nature of the crime their family member had committed, they welcomed any support from the Church.

- The Church management survey showed that delegates were more satisfied with their personal management of abuse cases than were bishops. Management strategies such as the over-emphasis on confidentiality and trusting the offender not to re-offend were described by senior clergy interviewed. Challenges to effective Church management of child sexual abuse such as poor procedures, and role confusion and conflict, were identified.

- The general public were highly critical of the Church's management of child sexual abuse. They felt they had not been kept informed and that Church authorities were not dealing adequately or directly with the issue. Over half felt that civil authorities should be mainly responsible for the management of allegations of child sexual abuse against clergy.

- There was little public awareness about any of the initiatives undertaken by the Church to address the problem of child sexual abuse by clergy. The majority were in favour of the provision of counselling for those who were abused but were unwilling to accept a clerical abuser back into Church ministry.

CHURCH RESPONSE AND MANAGEMENT: INDIVIDUALS WHO EXPERIENCED CHILD SEXUAL ABUSE AND THEIR FAMILIES

Of the seven participants interviewed who had experienced child sexual abuse, five reported their experience of abuse directly to Church personnel. The two other participants first reported their abuse to the Gardaí and have since met with Church delegates. The additional participant who experienced sexual abuse as an adult also reported the experience directly to Church personnel. Table 5.1 outlines the reporting pattern for the participants who reported their abuse directly to the Church (this is ordered from the earliest to the most recent case of reporting and includes the participant who experienced abuse as an adult).

Table 5.1: Reporting Profile of Those Who Reported Clerical (Child) Sexual Abuse Directly to Church Personnel

Participant	First Reported to:	Subsequent Management
1	(a) Local parish priest *(verbally, 1978)*	Promised to investigate but no further action taken.
	(b) Parish priest in the abuser's parish *(verbally, 1980s)*	Expressed concern. Sent a curate to talk to family but no further action taken.
	(c) Two local curates *(verbally, 1980s)*	One promised to report matter but no further action taken.
	(d) Priest known to participant *(verbally, 1983)*	Advised to report matter to bishop. Met bishop.
2	(a) Parish priest *(verbally, 1985)*	Advised that it was unlikely the priest was still abusing and refused to take any details. No action taken.
	(b) Bishop *(by letter, 1995)*	Received letter from senior Church representative approx. 2 weeks later — advised to make an appointment. Met this representative and subsequently met delegate.
3*	Bishop *(by letter, 1994)*	Prompt response (within one week). Matter passed on to priest. Met this priest but did not meet bishop.
4	Priest friend *(verbally, 1996)*	Encouraged to pursue the matter and arranged meeting with a priest of the same Order as the abuser.
	Provincial of the Order *(by letter, 1996)*	Prompt response from priest of the same Order. Also met with provincial of the Order.
5	Immediate religious superior *(verbally, 1996)*	Met superior and was instructed to contact Church representative. Received letter from Church representative (7 weeks later) referring the matter to Provincial of Order. Met provincial.
6*	Bishop *(by letter, 2002)*	Prompt reply from bishop by phone. Met bishop and delegate.

* These individuals were advised by Church personnel that their complaint had to be reported to the Gardaí.

What is evident from this chronological outline of cases is that some complaints were handled rapidly and by senior Church personnel. The first case and second case were both poorly managed.

Negative Experiences with Church Personnel

Although reporting patterns varied, the actual experience of reporting and the responses received were similar. Even though only a small number of people who experienced child sexual abuse by clergy participated in the study, the in-depth interviews revealed a number of important themes:

- Lack of outreach

- Lack of communication

- Listening versus action

- Necessity for personal determination and perseverance in reporting abuse

- Limited understanding of the impact and nature of child sexual abuse by Church personnel

- Lack of sensitivity and compassion

- Legal response taking precedence

- Self-protection by Church as an organisation.

Church Inaction

Many of the characteristics of Church responses to disclosure can be subsumed under the term "inaction". Participants described difficulties in making a complaint and in having the complaint heard. Complaints were not always responded to promptly and participants found that they had to follow up on progress themselves. Some had to arrange subsequent appointments themselves or put pressure on Church personnel in order to receive information. For example, one woman who had made an official complaint had not received any reply two months later. She then contacted the person to whom she had complained and waited another seven weeks for a reply. She described the experience as a struggle. Most of the participants had similar experiences of having to instigate contact and follow up on their own complaint:

> ". . . it took weeks to get a response from the Church and then it was a case of phone me and make an appointment. But this might have put people off pursuing it and that's the annoying part of it."

> ". . . it was a daunting thing to do but there was no question of them coming to me."

> ". . . they never get back to you and say 'Are you alright?' 'How are you after that experience?' . . . You feel abused again . . . I've always been the one to make the move towards them. They've never made the move towards me."

> "At the time, the damage that was done to my family could have been repaired but we were desperate for help . . . and that was never forthcoming . . . and desperate for a sense that it wasn't our fault . . ."

Most participants were not informed of the procedures that would be followed by the Church when they made their complaint. Two were told that their abuser had received treatment and was being monitored. However, they have since discovered that other complaints of child sexual abuse were made about the same abuser to Church authorities. Most were not given assurances about the protection of other children and were not given any advice or information about their complaint. One family member described a meeting with Church personnel:

> "The first meeting I had with [Church personnel] was horrendous. I came out of it and cried . . . he said, 'Where do they expect me to put [abuser], in a cage in the zoo?' . . . He said, 'We've done all we can and [the abused] has to get on with his life' . . . they were just listening. There was no advice, just listening and a pretence that they had never heard of this type of thing before."

Some participants had the sense that Church personnel were not interested in hearing their complaint, did not take the complaint seriously or were unwilling to deal with it:

> "I think [Church personnel] hoped it would go away or that I would go away . . . he was quite matter-of-fact and business-like. He was saying that it's a shame that these things happened in the Church but it wasn't sympathetic. It was more, 'it's a pity the Church has to deal with this'. I thought, typical Church. Run away from it, if we can give her some doubt maybe it will go away."

> ". . . our local parish priest said that he knew the [abuser] very well. 'There isn't a problem with him. You are being silly.'"

> ". . . [Church personnel] said, 'If you give me his name, I'll have to take some action and I doubt if [abuser] ever did it [abuse] again. And if he did, he is long left the priesthood so there is no point in me doing anything.'"

Two participants also sensed that they were viewed as making trouble for the Church:

> ". . . I was considered . . . an absolute nightmare for them, a troublemaker, a nasty individual because I stood up for what was right . . . they wanted me to go away and I know I was looked on as being troublesome . . ."

> ". . . when I meet [Church personnel] I feel his reaction is, 'Oh no. Here she is again.' . . ."

As a result of the inaction, some participants felt they had to persevere and were determined to see their complaint through in the interest of general child protection:

> "I think it was dealt with because I forced it to be dealt with."

> "If I hadn't been so determined, it [response] could easily have put me off . . ."

Some also pointed out that a person with fewer personal resources or determination may have been unable to pursue their complaint, given the number of obstacles they encountered along the way:

> "It was down to me and a less strong person may have let it go and not forced the issue."

> ". . . a lot of other people may not have the confidence to carry on because . . . if you relied on the Church there is no way a prosecution would be made. It makes it difficult for other people to come forward, I often wonder how many people start the process and then give up."

Such factors may mean that individuals with very difficult reporting experiences, which meant they did not persist to diocesan level, would not be represented in this study.

Overall, participants described the experience of initial reporting as a struggle with several barriers and obstacles:

> ". . . the whole process was unbelievable because instead of helping there was a fence at each step of the way and in many ways I think that was worse than the abuse itself because everything was a battle and every time you put your trust in someone you were let down."

> ". . . everything was done so I could give up at anytime and I always felt that I was being encouraged to give up . . . I really thought that every obstacle had been put in my way . . ."

> ". . . there are a lot of doors to get through and it's extremely hard to be heard . . ."

Inappropriate Actions by the Church: Lack of Sensitivity and Compassion

Some participants felt that Church personnel to whom they reported their abuse did not believe them. Similarly, most said they did not experience understanding, warmth or compassion from those to whom they reported. Some felt that this was because of a limited understanding of the nature and effects of child sexual abuse:

> "... I still feel the Church doesn't believe ... but I don't know if believe or understand is the right word ..."

> "They were very impersonal. To be honest [Church personnel] didn't seem to have any idea about the effect of abuse ... any understanding. And his attitude was, 'Sure it was only' ..."

> ". . . the experience would have been easier if I had been shown compassion and understanding."

> "... I didn't come away with the feeling of warmth and 'We want to thank you for coming and telling us about this', which was the reaction from [another authority]. . . . The Church don't seem to realise how something like that might affect your life."

One woman found it difficult to understand why she was not shown compassion:

> "... they're not what they're supposed to be about ... if Jesus came and stood in front of all the bishops, I'd say he'd let them have it because to me they're not what they are supposed to be because there's no compassion whatsoever."

Another woman reported her experience of abuse to a priest and the response she received showed a complete lack of understanding of the nature of child sexual abuse as well as lack of compassion and sensitivity:

> "... his reaction was I could stop worrying about it because I was forgiven ... he said it wasn't my fault that I had tempted this man [abuser] . . . and he wouldn't let me give him his [abuser's] name ... I felt he thought I was there to get some absolution ... he treated me like a leper ..."

This woman reported the abuse again a number of years later and her second experience was not much better. On her second attempt to report her abuse she described her first experience. Rather than being concerned with this response the second Church person to whom she spoke said that the first priest was probably "old-fashioned" and that men are generally "ignorant" of these things. Her second attempt at reporting was also unsuccessful:

> "He [Church personnel] said, 'You can't ruin a man's life for something he did thirty years ago' . . ."

Other participants also felt that the lack of understanding they were afforded by some Church personnel was because these clergy were "out of touch" or "far removed" from "real people and their lives" and the "normal world". One woman commented that the lack of compassion shown by clergy was because "it reminds them of their own fallibility". Others felt that, because they were men without children of their own, some clergy were unable to empathise with people who had experienced child sexual abuse.

The lack of sensitivity was also seen in the choice of location for the meetings which were often experienced as intimidating:

> ". . . the one thing I didn't like about that was the setting, there were so many of them at the table and I was like the child again."

Legal Responses Taking Precedence and Self-protection by Church as an Organisation

Most participants experienced a legal rather than pastoral or compassionate response:

> ". . . the whole morality went out the window. It was very much on legal terms. He even took down a book on canon law to quote to us, that type of thing . . . there was a sense of, 'I'm one step ahead of you and I'm going to stay ahead of you'."

> "I'd say he [Church personnel] has swallowed the canon law book. He just throws you the official line . . . not a very people-friendly person . . ."

> ". . . I found it very cold and authoritarian and detached . . . It seemed to say, 'If you are not telling the truth we are going to find out'. It was all very legalistic . . ."

Two participants described anger and frustration because the abusing priest remained working in a parish following their official complaints to Church personnel:

> ". . . they said their hands were tied unless he [abuser] admitted it and because he hadn't there was nothing they could do. They haven't dealt with it at all. I still think it's a disgrace that the Church authorities can't deal with an employee without it being heard in the High Court . . ."

> ". . . he's admitted to being an abuser but because he hasn't been found guilty in a court of law they are going to treat him as innocent . . ."

Most regarded this defensive and legal response as serving the Church's interest of organisational self-protection and of protecting the abuser:

> ". . . it was never about protecting children. It was about protecting themselves."

> ". . . they were trying to protect themselves rather than looking after you . . . they seemed less worried about future victims than court."

Positive Experiences of Disclosure to Church Personnel

Participants described some positive experiences with individuals they met through their dealings with the Church. Some showed them compassion and understanding. Being believed was very important to participants but it also caused frustration when no action was being taken on the basis of the complaint. Some participants, following previously unsatisfactory encounters with Church personnel, were relieved to find that other Church personnel were concerned about their experience of abuse and how the Church had treated them:

> "He spent three hours listening to the story and his reaction to everything was so compassionate and warm. Totally different to anyone high-up I had spoken to. He was horrified at the way I was treated and handled . . ."

"... he was a breath of fresh air. He listened ..."

"... he [bishop] was the loveliest man you could ever meet. He was what I expected, a thoroughly Christian man."

Expectations and Advice on a Constructive Church Response

Participants thought that the Church would want to know about their experience in order to prevent further sexual abuse of children:

"I started out with great faith in the Church. I believed that they wanted to find out about these priests and look after their laity and victims."

Most were dissatisfied with how the Church dealt with their complaints. Not all of their complaints were initially reported to the Gardaí. Some felt that they themselves had to go to the Gardaí because the Church was not dealing with their complaint. Four participants said that if they could change anything about their disclosure, they would now report their abuse directly to the Gardaí and not make any contact with the Church. There were two participants who had not reported their experience to civil authorities. One participant expressed regret about this while the other remained unwilling to pursue an investigation by the Gardaí.

There was some criticism of the Church's policy document (*Framework Document*), which outlines the procedures to be followed in the event of a complaint of child sexual abuse against clergy. Some felt that the procedures outlined were not being followed. Those who met with delegates were generally positive about them and found them helpful and supportive. However, one participant discovered that the delegate supported both the complainant and the accused. This was seen as a conflict of interests. Another was "devastated" to find that all discussions with the delegate were being reported to senior clergy. Participants felt that the handling of the complaint depended on who one spoke to in the Church. They described how they felt the Church should have responded to their complaint and how they should respond to others in the future. The following strategies were recommended by those who had been abused:

- Improved opportunities for making complaints, e.g.
    o More suitable, less intimidating venue for meetings
    o Public notices on how to go about making a complaint
    o Option of reporting to non-clerical Church personnel
    o Training for Church personnel
    o Selection of staff skilled in sensitive issues
- More compassionate and human response to people making complaints
- Honest approach to those reporting abuse
- Willingness to believe complaints
- More outreach and more contact with the person abused and their families
- More timely response
- Acknowledgement of the harm caused rather than efforts to minimise it
- More pastoral and less legal/defensive response
- Adherence to established Church guidelines
- Establishment of a fitness to practice board
- Ability to reflect and learn from mistakes
- Ombudsman or public inquiry to investigate how cases of child sexual abuse by clergy have been handled in the past.

Reflections on Church Management of Disclosure: A Caution

When considering the experiences of individuals reporting abuse to Church personnel, it is important to realise that they represent a minority of those originally invited to participate in the study (seven people sexually abused as children by clergy out of a possible 95). Such a low response rate illustrates the difficulties people have in discussing these issues. Furthermore, information from the individuals who participated in the SAVI study demonstrates that reporting clerical child sexual abuse to Church and/or civil authorities is rare. Of the 30 people who reported child sexual abuse by clergy in SAVI, only three reported the abuse to Church personnel at the time the abuse occurred. One of these individuals reported the abuse to the Gardaí 25 years later. Given this level of underreporting of abuse to Church and civil authorities and the understandable reluctance of those who have made such reports to speak about their experiences, this overview is necessarily incomplete.

CHURCH RESPONSE AND MANAGEMENT: CONVICTED CLERGY AND THEIR FAMILIES AND COLLEAGUES

This section considers Church responses to the complaint of abuse from the abuser's perspective (convicted clergy) and from that of their families and colleagues.

Convicted Clergy

Six priests and two religious brothers convicted of sexual offences against children were interviewed. Three of those interviewed were serving custodial sentences at the time of the study and were interviewed in prison. Three others had served their prison sentences and the remaining two participants received suspended sentences. Two of the priests interviewed had been laicised since their convictions. The remaining four priests had not been laicised but were not in any type of ministry.

Experience of Initial Detection and Management

None of the participants denied the allegations when confronted by their bishop or superior. One admitted that he had sexually abused children and went to his bishop for help. The procedure followed by the Church in each case was different. The one common feature was that all participants were initially sent for assessment and treatment. For most, the official meeting with their bishop/superior had a very significant effect and signalled the "beginning of the end":

> ". . . I felt that this was the end of my priesthood. It crystallised something that had been there for a couple of years . . . end of the world basically, total new territory for me. It was the end of everything I had built on and I knew there was no coming back from it once it went to the guards. And I knew at that stage I wasn't going to fight it . . ."

> ". . . I knew the sword was coming down on my head. I knew it was just a question of time . . . everything was falling . . ."

Some felt that their bishop/superior lacked understanding or compassion and treated them in a business-like manner:

> ". . . they are just officials carrying out their duties. I hoped that some of them would be human like Jesus, a human face under that mighty piety. I know they have to react and re-move priests but the man who dealt with me had no human qualities. When he looked at me he was looking at a God-forsaken sinner not a person . . . there was no attempt to talk about it or understand what happened . . . no allowance made for humanity of any kind."

One participant experienced anger from his superior and felt that he did not get a fair hearing:

> ". . . he [superior] said to me, 'If I ever felt like murdering any-one I do now' . . ."

Church authorities were seen to be clearer about financial support insofar as most were not completely supported financially. Some convicted participants paid their own legal fees, while others received a Church donation towards the cost. Some also paid part of the cost of their treatment. Financial assistance by the Church for clergy convicted of sexual offences has become a contentious issue. As a result, some of the convicted clergy reported feeling unable to approach the Church for financial help because they perceived there to be pressure on the Church not to help them:

> ". . . I don't think I'd go near them in the first place. I think I'd be begging. I get the sense that there is opposition saying, 'Don't give the bastard anything'."

Apart from the offer of treatment, participants felt that bishops and superiors did not know how to respond to them or what action to take:

> ". . . they were a bit bewildered . . . there was as much panic from them as from me . . ."

> ". . . didn't seem to be concerned about where I went. I don't think they had anything in place . . ."

Experience of Treatment

Before their court cases, all participants had attended a residential treatment facility.[r] One participant was dubious about the value of treatment but felt he had no option because of the climate in Ireland at the time regarding sex offenders and because his superior gave him no choice. Most participants were willing to attend for treatment. All participants found treatment difficult. The following terms were used to describe it: "challenging", "brutal", "savage", "psychological violence" and "surgery without anaesthetic". However, although participants described their treatment experience as tough, all but one said it was beneficial. For some, it was the first time they had spoken about their abusive behaviour. Overall, they felt that it opened up a new area in their lives and provided them with an opportunity to deal with personal issues in a way they had never done before:

> "It was the start of my life."

------

[r] Many, but not all, clerical sex offenders accept treatment or rehabilitation opportunities. Thus the views of those willing to participate in these interviews may not represent the full spectrum of clerical sex offenders.

"I was an emotional cripple. Therapy helped me to discover myself. It opened up a new life for me."

"It helped me to face a number of things that I wasn't aware of . . ."

Most found describing the specific details of their abusive behaviour the most difficult aspect of their treatment. A significant aspect of their treatment was "victim awareness" and dealing with their own sexuality:

"One thing I must say that I profited from was they emphasised victim awareness. I didn't know that [abused person] was my victim."

". . . therapy really helped me and showed me that abuse could be so damaging to people."

". . . [therapy] helped me face my sexuality in that I had made an inappropriate choice or way of life."

Some treatment programmes had a religious element and this was cited as important by three participants. One said that the religious/spiritual element in his treatment helped to restore his "spiritual life". Some attended relapse prevention groups following treatment and benefited from the ongoing support especially since they had left the security of prolonged residential treatment:

". . . one place I can go where I can talk about things that I couldn't talk to other people about. I mean I can talk to my priest friends about prison but sometimes they don't want to hear. I think it frightens them too."

One participant did not find treatment beneficial. He said he was not given any choice, that he found the environment intimidating, that he was unable to cope with group settings and, overall, treatment made him feel worse.

Experience of Legal Process and Prison Term

Once they became involved in the legal process, most felt a sense of inevitability about going to prison. All were advised to seek legal advice or were given the name of a solicitor. The first stage of the legal process, being interviewed by the Gardaí, was reported to be less traumatic than anticipated:

> "They were nice. They were good. They were doing their job but they were sensitive about it."

> "To be fair to them, they [Gardaí] treated me very well. I must say that, given the crime I had committed . . . but overall they treated me very well and the other thing was that they were very discreet. That story never broke at all until it went to trial because in the last while information does leak out and I'm certainly grateful for that . . ."

Not all participants experienced this level of discretion. One reported that the initial investigation did not remain confidential and "word got out". Another described being interviewed by the Gardaí as "psychological torture". Prior to sentencing, most felt as if they were in a type of "limbo". They were out of ministry and some were no longer living in their parish. Most kept in contact with the Church during this time. The most distressing time was awaiting the outcome of the investigation and their court case:

> ". . . my behaviour was getting totally erratic, drinking . . . so I overdosed and ended up in hospital . . ."

> "At the time I felt that a fatal heart attack would have been very welcome . . ."

The court case was also a distressing time. Most had the support of their families but they worried about the effect of publicity on their families. Having been through treatment, some felt prepared for their sentence:

> "I was taken down from the court, handcuffed, my tie and belt taken from me and all that sort of process. There were a lot of

other prisoners and of course I was the pariah among them and one of them was shouting at me. I declined to cover my head going out. They offered me a jacket. I just said I'd face it . . . I thought, 'I am what I am and I've done this'."

All found the initial experience of prison frightening. Some were quite isolated in prison while others had continuing support from family and friends. Two received visits and correspondence from former parishioners. One family member interviewed felt that his relative had coped remarkably well with prison:

> "Pretty well, much better than we expected, I wouldn't have lasted a week. He's done loads of courses . . . we're very proud of all he's done since he went in . . ."

While in prison, all of the convicted priests were visited by Church personnel. Many felt that the visits from their bishop were "duty visits". There were mixed feelings about support from peers while in prison:

> ". . . some of them found it very difficult and have been a bit more distant since and then there were others I didn't expect to see turned up . . ."

> ". . . I am left wondering . . . what the rank-and-file members think, my peers, because not many have come in to see me. . . . I think what a lot of them are doing for me is praying and I'm a bit cynical about that."

> ". . . the delegate came twice a year and was always available if I ever needed him. I felt that there was no problem if I wanted anything."

For those who completed custodial sentences, coming out of prison was associated with fear, uncertainty and shame. The Church made vocational and residential arrangements for some but others were laicised and had to make their own arrangements for life following prison:

"I was very ashamed and didn't go out. It was widely known
but not universally known. Some priests and friends fell away
and I wouldn't go to see my family as often as I used to . . ."

Following prison, participants reported that their lives were not as
difficult as they had anticipated. However, they described keeping a low profile and one now lives a very solitary existence. Some
received support from neighbours:

". . . the more I spoke to my family and friends the more I realised that I'd be much safer where I was known . . . the
neighbours were very good to me. When I came out first the
neighbour called within the first few days, welcomed me back
and offered me help if I needed it and that was very reassuring."

Disengagement from Priesthood/Religious Life

Most participants were advised that they could no longer remain
a priest or religious during the course of their treatment. Some
had accepted this loss while others were still trying to cope:

"I'm not doing what I want to do because priesthood is a way
of life. But having shed a lot of the darkness from my life, I
could be the sort of priest I always wanted to be. I will never
be a priest again but I still feel like a priest. I'm a red-carded
priest. I've been sent off."

One felt that he had made the wrong choice by entering religious
life:

"I don't think I should ever have joined [religious life] given
my background, coming from an unstable family background.
If I had been assessed I would have been sent for psychiatric
treatment . . . but I'm not blaming them for my behaviour."

Those interviewed who had been laicised felt that, if they could
no longer continue in ministry, laicisation was their only option.
They felt that they would eventually be forced to apply for laicisation or be dismissed so they wanted to take responsibility for the
decision themselves. Those who had not yet been laicised felt that

it is only a matter of time before they will be forced to apply. One felt that he had not been forced to apply because he did not rely on the Church for accommodation or financial support. If his situation changed and he required support from the Church, he suspected that laicisation would be forced upon him. Those who had not been laicised were not in any type of ministry, priests not yet laicised have had their faculties (e.g. saying mass, hearing confessions) removed and they are prohibited from wearing clerical dress and presenting themselves publicly as clergy. Preparation for life without priesthood/religious life was not a part of the Church's response to convicted clergy.

Family Members of Convicted Clergy

Five siblings of convicted clergy participated in the study. Two of the five family members of convicted clergy were positive about the way in which the Church had responded to and managed their brothers' cases. They felt that, considering the nature of the crime and how incongruent it was with priesthood/religious life, their relatives were fortunate to receive any support at all. Two relatives were in regular contact with a delegate and found this to be very helpful. The other three relatives interviewed were more critical of the Church's management. One sister said that, overall, there was no sense of "brotherhood". She recollected that, at her brother's ordination, the bishop described entrance into the priesthood as leaving one family and entering another. Adopting this perspective, she felt that the Church was a very "neglectful family". Some relatives felt that Church leadership was more interested in institutional protection than in responding to the abuser in a humane way. This lack of humanity was referred to by all of those critical of the Church's response:

> "... they were just obliged to look after him. They dealt with it administratively. He was treated as an abhorrent member of the tribe ... he was just a number. They were ruthless and not aware of him as a person ... he [convicted relative] assumed mutual care and responsibility ..."

> ". . . he has been shunned. They threw him in a corner and hoped he'd go away. They preach brotherhood but neglect people . . ."

One family member felt that support from the Church was particularly poor throughout the legal process and that this support further decreased when their relative was convicted and sent to prison:

> ". . . I felt that they had forgotten about him. He was out of the way and things had quietened down now."

This relative went to see the superior of the Order because of this but felt he had not achieved anything:

> "He didn't justify anything, didn't disagree, didn't argue with anything, he just listened to me. He [superior] is [the convicted abuser's] other family. He [superior] knows him better than I do . . ."

The relative was subsequently offered counselling via a telephone call from a priest he did not know. He was more concerned with the lack of support for his brother in prison. Some siblings did not feel confident about the ability of Church personnel to support their relatives on a continuous basis. They were worried about the future and felt that pressure from the media and/or decisions by the Catholic Church elsewhere might dictate the fate of their relative.

Colleagues of Convicted Clergy[s]

Three colleagues of convicted clergy and one priest advisor were interviewed. The colleagues of convicted clergy were extremely critical of how Church authorities had managed allegations of child sexual abuse. Priests working alongside alleged and subse-

---

[s] The experience of Church response and management for colleagues of convicted clergy are discussed separately from the experiences and perceptions of the other clergy interviewed face-to-face or surveyed (postal survey).

quently convicted abusers reported being given no information, support or resources unless they struggled to get these for themselves. They were not initially told of allegations and, as investigations progressed, they were often not kept informed:

"I was transferred without any explanation to his parish . . ."

"I was told that a guy was moving into the house and I was told that he had suffered a bit of a nervous breakdown. There was something going on and nobody would tell me what. I discovered the guy wasn't allowed leave the house and I was left in the house for a week not knowing why . . . nobody official rang me to tell me what was coming. Even in the week that the offence was reported. Nobody actually took up the phone to say this is what happened etc. So I was left in silence."

When colleagues discovered the nature of the problem from other sources some went to the Church authorities for advice. Some were not facilitated:

". . . about two years into his [abuser's] time there, we discovered some history from another curate, that this guy had abused children. So we felt that we should bring this to the attention of the authorities and we were immediately frowned on and pushed back. We were left there for a period of time in a sort of conspiracy of silence, not understanding, not knowing what was true . . ."

"I asked him [bishop] about saying something at mass and he said, 'Oh say nothing' and I said, 'Well you can't say nothing' and his advice was preach within the Gospel. He said that he was not empowering me to say anything. We [priests] get our information from the press."

One priest was given some background information about his accused colleague and was "horrified" to learn that some Church authorities were already aware of complaints of child sexual abuse against the accused but were willing to trust the alleged abuser on the basis of his promise not to re-offend. He felt that

Church authorities wanted to believe that the promise was genuine and naively thought their awareness of a previous offence would be enough to curb re-offending.

When parishioners became aware of complaints against a priest in their parish, colleagues reported both a sense of personal crisis and a crisis in the context of their ministry. Parishioners wanted to talk about the issue, needed reassurance, were worried about any contact they had had with the priest and were concerned about the sanctity of marriages and baptisms performed by the accused priest. Many wanted information but clerical colleagues reported not being given any information they could pass on:

> ". . . the parish knew about it and I was sort of in that situation where it was like, 'What am I in this? Am I a victim? Am I part of the problem? Am I here as someone to save the problem?' I was all over the place in that, obviously losing the sense of myself in it."

> ". . . everyone was phoning me and asking me what's going on . . . all these people wanted to come and talk. I'd go home and there would be 40 or 50 messages . . . the parish was divided. A girl assaulted me for not backing [abuser] up and people saying that we should pray for him . . . the whole parish was split according to those who thought he was guilty and those who thought he was innocent."

Church authorities were seen as impeding or preventing attempts by priests to resolve some of these problems at parish level. In some cases, they were actively prohibited from saying anything:

> ". . . at different stages I made representation to say, 'I'm not happy, this is not working', but I went to my authorities in good faith and found that you were fobbed off or made to believe that something was happening. Nowhere along the line was anything that I had to say taken seriously."

> "They left me to do whatever I could and they didn't empower me with information but it was difficult. I had appealed for a bishop to come out and address the parish but they

wouldn't hear of it. No one came but I felt that I couldn't cope and they were saying that they didn't have anyone to send. It took them six months to find someone who would share the responsibility."

One colleague wanted to make an appeal for any person in the parish who had experienced abuse to come forward but his authorities would not permit him to do so. Priests interviewed saw the Church as being unsure about how to handle the situation. This extended to the question of how to manage convicted clergy who had served their sentences or those who had received suspended sentences:

"The diocese was actually unsure of what they were supposed to do . . . what was he [abuser] to do. They [Church authorities] would have been afraid to give him [abuser] anything to do."

". . . there was no procedure for this sort of thing . . ."

Overall, the experience of priests who were colleagues of abusers was characterised by lack of communication and information from their superiors. The priests interviewed perceived this as a way of protecting the Church as an institution and of avoiding scandal.

CLERGY AND CHURCH PERSONNEL[t]

As part of the postal survey, delegates and bishops were asked about their level of experience with complaints of child sexual abuse. Fifty-seven per cent of delegates classified themselves as inexperienced, 33 per cent as quite experienced and 10 per cent as

---

[t] The research findings presented here includes data from the qualitative interview study phase whereby a number of clergy and Church personnel were interviewed face-to-face and also from the postal survey of delegates and bishops. Some of the bishops and delegates interviewed and surveyed had direct experience in the management of allegations of child sexual abuse by clergy while the opinions of others are based more on their observations and perceptions of how the Church, overall, managed child sexual abuse cases.

very experienced. Conversely, more bishops described themselves as quite experienced (62 per cent), with 29 per cent perceiving themselves as inexperienced in the area. Almost half of the delegates (45 per cent) said they had not yet dealt with a case. Thus a profile emerges of two groups of delegates; one very experienced group and a group with relatively little or no experience in the area. Eighteen per cent of bishops had not yet dealt with cases of clerical child sexual abuse. Delegates and bishops were asked to rate satisfaction with their management of these cases (Figure 5.1).

As Figure 5.1 shows, most delegates were satisfied or very satisfied (80 per cent) with their handling of child sexual abuse cases with only one delegate (2 per cent) dissatisfied. Forty-one per cent of bishops were satisfied while 14 per cent were dissatisfied with their own handling of cases. Thus, bishops expressed less satisfaction and more dissatisfaction with their management of cases than did delegates.

Figure 5.1: Personal Satisfaction Ratings with Management of Cases According to Delegates and Bishops

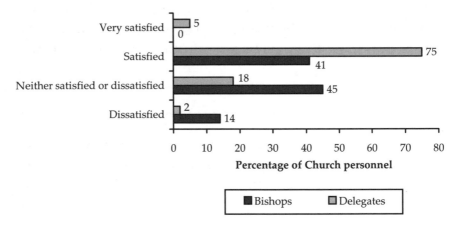

Preventing Scandal and Protecting the Church

The clergy and Church personnel interviewed described how the goals of preventing scandal and protecting the laity guided many decisions made in managing allegations of child sexual abuse. The approach was based on a "theology of scandal" and would have been seen as an important function of Church authorities:

> "It was protecting the Church. But Church was understood as the people because protecting the institution was no doubt also there. But I think it was broader than that . . . the original sense of scandal was to protect the people . . . now that seems a bit strange to us today. People are best to know things . . . but it reflects a different mentality."

> "There would be scandal about going to the secular authorities . . . there's a theology around scandal and different theories of scandal. It says that you avoid scandalising people, which implies making it public."

> ". . . it was a case of bad theology where the institution came first before the people. And the fact that most bishops and priests have . . . what the seminary does to them, tear away their personal identity and only gives them a role identity so they can't think outside the structure . . ."

Bishops interviewed also spoke about the emphasis on preventing scandal:

> ". . . the whole instinct on our part is that we must protect the Church so let's try and deal with this quietly . . . scandal was always regarded as one of the really serious sins. It was seen in some way as undermining the faith of people and the credibility of the Church . . . it was regarded as a very, very serious matter. If something came up like this, a priest sexually involved with somebody even whether it was adult or child . . . you must protect the people from being scandalised by this fact. Therefore, if you can in some way fix it by keeping everything quiet, . . . and I would say it was in some way regarded as legitimate, that it was better for everybody if this did not go into the public arena."

> "I suppose scandal theologically would be seen as possibly leading other people into sin. If my brother does something [bad] I'm not going to go and shout it from the roof tops . . . that sort of instinctive thing as well."

". . . I wished to avoid the great scandal of a priest being arrested for molesting a child . . . which again was wrong . . . at
the time one was protecting not so much the Church but the
priest and the priesthood and the people."

Challenges to Effective Management

The postal survey of bishops and delegates examined the challenges facing delegates and bishops in their respective roles. Their
role involves supporting not only abused individuals and their
families but also alleged abusers and their families and providing
pastoral care to the wider Church community. Delegates and
bishops were asked to rate the challenges of assisting each of
these five groups from 5 (most challenging) to 1 (least challenging). Experienced delegates rated dealing with the needs of the
abused individual as the most challenging while responding to
the needs of the parish or community where the allegation was
made was rated the least challenging. Inexperienced delegates
anticipated responding to the needs of the alleged perpetrator as
the most challenging and responding to the needs of the wider
parish or community as the least challenging. Experienced bishops also rated dealing with the needs of the abused individual as
the most challenging but rated dealing with the needs of the perpetrators' families as the least challenging. Bishops with no experience anticipated that dealing with the abused individual's
family would be the most challenging and dealing with the alleged perpetrator's family and the parish where the allegations
were made were anticipated as the least challenging. This shows a
difference between perceived and actual challenges in managing
cases of child sexual abuse. However, the most challenging aspect
according to both experienced bishops and delegates was responding to the needs of the abused individual.

The face-to-face interviews with members of the clergy also
drew attention to a number of challenges to the effective management of child sexual abuse by clergy. The main challenges described were unfamiliarity with the problem, lack of available

procedures, the nature of complaints, role confusion and responding to both the complainant and the alleged perpetrator.

Unfamiliarity with the Issue and Lack of Procedures

Lack of awareness and limited understanding of child sexual abuse was described as a challenge to effective management of allegations. Those interviewed who had received complaints described how, in the beginning, they did not know how to respond. There were no available policies or procedures to be followed. Procedures on misconduct in canon law were also unfamiliar and underutilised:

> ". . . the canon law process was totally unfamiliar . . . it was primarily a pastoral issue so it tended to be dealt with at that level and the whole thing about canon law and judicial processes was alien to the Church at that time . . ."

> " . . . there was a serious dearth . . . in people trained in canon law . . ."

Reliance on Legal and Other Professional Advice

In the absence of procedures or guidelines, and with limited understanding of child sexual abuse, those in positions of authority in the Catholic Church in Ireland generally sought legal and psychiatric advice. Much of the advice focused on protecting a person's good name, scandal and Church assets rather than on the crime that had been committed against the child and outreach to him or her.

Advice from psychiatrists and psychologists regarding the suitability of priests who had abused children to return to ministry was followed. Since this study did not examine individual cases in detail, it is not possible to comment on exactly what advice was given in the past by mental health professionals regarding the management of abusers. However, as discussed in Chapter 3, the first specific treatment programme in Ireland for sex offenders began in 1985. Structured treatment programmes for sex offenders and mental health professionals dedicated to the assessment and treatment of sex offenders have become available in Ireland since 1994. Therefore, the advice from mental health professionals prior to the 1990s is likely to have reflected their own particular professional orientation and probably, but not necessarily, an evaluation of the limited research literature of the time. The latter was evolving as international experience was obtained. Views on the most effective treatment for abusers and on the likelihood of re-offending changed significantly during that period. Furthermore, measurement instruments for risk assessment are a relatively new development in this area. In retrospect, the advice given to bishops on the management of abusers by mental health professionals may not have highlighted the risk of re-offending and thus, in some cases, led to further abuse. Some of the bishops interviewed in this study reflected on the type of advice they received from mental health professionals:

> "The local psychiatrist advised . . . that this man [abuser] now realised the wrongness of what he was doing and that he felt confident that he would never do it again. That was in the early '80s."

> "I don't want to be critical here because the psychiatrists I went to were very kind, very caring, very professional and very helpful but they got it wrong . . . I followed wrong advice in good faith. I shouldn't have been sending the priest offender to a psychiatrist but to . . . one who specialised in this particular problem . . . but that particular type of person didn't exist then but they were beginning to surface in the '90s . . ."

According to bishops and Church authorities interviewed, psychiatric advice was sought and followed in many cases during the 1970s and 1980s. Some bishops were advised that priests who had sexually abused children were unlikely to present further risk. There was very little professional expertise available at that time in Ireland. Even now, Marshall and Laws (2003) describe the field as in its "adolescence".[84] Irish bishops and other Church authorities no longer seek advice from just once source. Most dioceses have an "advisory panel", as recommended by the *Framework*

Document; a multidisciplinary group including health and child-care professionals and a civil and canon lawyer. Given that practice in this field is constantly being updated and revised, concerns have been expressed by bishops and other Church authorities that any advice followed today may also be judged as inadequate in years to come.

Nature of Complaint

The way in which complaints were made also presented challenges to Church authorities. In some cases, the person making the complaint insisted on complete confidentiality and indicated their unwillingness to have the matter investigated by civil authorities. The person receiving the complaint then typically could only preserve confidentiality by not reporting the matter to civil authorities:

> "Sometimes a complaint was brought to us by a parent who didn't want the guards involved and all they wanted was the priest to get help and an assurance that it wouldn't happen again. Now, perhaps we were too happy to take that line . . ."

> ". . . they wanted the priest put out of business but without anyone knowing why . . ."

One bishop described how a complaint was made to him and how it affected his response:

> "I think if it had come to me differently . . . if the parent had come roaring and shouting at me, it would have affected the response. It would have made me sit up more and be aware. The experience of having direct contact with a parent who was very angry and very upset would have alerted me more too. If someone had come thumping at the door outraged and making demands, which they are quite entitled to do, I would have learned a lot faster."

Confusion

The theme of confusion emerged as a factor that influenced responses. There was confusion about the issue in general and also confusion about the roles of those in authority. Many interviewees described a sense of confusion among Church authorities when they began receiving complaints:

> ". . . confusion, confusion surrounding the issue, confusion surrounding whether you could re-deploy a paedophile . . . treatment or whether you couldn't, whether there was a distinction to be made among paedophiles or whether there wasn't. My abiding memory of that time was a lot of confusion . . ."

> "Another one of the questions was, 'What in the name of God can you do if you have got paedophiles?' 'What do you do with them?' 'What is the just response?' Clarity begins to emerge as to what you should do in order to protect the victims but then what do you do and what do you do in justice to the person? Do you disown them entirely and then what happens? Is that another risk to society? What does the diocese or the religious order do? What are the real responsibilities in this situation?"

Attempts to increase their understanding of the problem led to more confusion rather than clarity for some of those interviewed:

> ". . . we had a gentleman from the USA coming and supposedly preparing us for the fallout that had already hit the American Church and saying that in certain situations that up to 90 per cent of paedophiles can be successfully treated. Eighteen months later another person came, another psychologist . . . saying the situation is that up to 90 per cent of them can't be treated. At that stage we wondered whom we could believe and you could see that there was confusion."

Role Confusion and Conflict

Church authorities receiving complaints of child sexual abuse against clergy had to acquire new roles and balance these with existing roles:

> "They are meant to be managers, they are pastoral and they are managers, they have two roles, which are quite difficult to hold together."

> ". . . the whole thing was so new that really at that stage I didn't know whose role it was. Now that there is a whole reporting scheme you see there are procedures and so on but then who did you go to? Whose role was it and whose responsibility was it? . . . I knew it was my responsibility in the sense that this man had done something very wrong."

Without procedures to follow and with a limited understanding of child sexual abuse, the person receiving complaints had multiple roles to consider:

> "We have a pastoral role and obviously we have to obey what the law says and we have to protect children. We have to have a pastoral role towards complainants because they have suffered a lot, we have to have a pastoral role towards the accused, the priests, who have their rights as well and towards the community. It is very difficult to combine everything because if you are seen helping one but you are neglecting others you're not neutral."

> "Usually one guy was trying to support victims and think about the priest and think what would the bishop say. It was just impossible and I would say that was the main structural flaw that the guidelines addressed and addressed fairly well . . . before '96 there was no separation of roles . . ."

> "The Church shouldn't have to be dealing with this, the guards should be dealing with this. It is not our arena, we are not policemen, pass it over to the civil authorities."

Responding to Both the Complainant and Alleged Perpetrator

Associated with this role confusion, there was a further challenge of responding to both the complainant and the alleged perpetrator. According to those interviewed, this posed significant challenges. Often the person making the complaint was not the main concern:

> "In retrospect now of course I would say that the Church didn't handle it as it should have done. It didn't take the victim's part as it should have done."

> ". . . the primary focus was on the perpetrator with very little reference to the effect on the person abused."

Some clergy and Church personnel also criticised the way in which the alleged perpetrator was treated. Once again this involved the issue of institutional protection:

> ". . . preserving the institution at all costs, what these people do to children is horrific and nobody can defend that but to demonise them [abuser] and discard them is not Christian at all."

> "The initial response was . . . get rid of him [abuser]. We have to preserve ourselves at all costs . . . it seemed to me the Church was more anxious to preserve itself as an institution than care for him, and the individual got lost along the way."

> ". . . the other side was absent, any degree of care for him [abuser], he suddenly was demonised and disposed of. It goes against all the Christian principles."

> ". . . priests who were convicted were subsequently obligatorily laicised by the bishop. That struck me as a further abuse of power in a sense and it was an attempt to say that there are a few rotten apples in the barrel but the barrel is sound . . . but the barrel is not sound. There are deeper systemic issues that need to be examined here and I felt that this was about institutional self-protection which got us in the mess we were in . . ."

> ". . . the other thing that I found very difficult to take, I had met guys in the '70s who had fallen in love . . . and wanted to leave and get married and weren't allowed as it were or were delayed. Then I find an abuser is laicised by the Pope . . . Holy Mother Church has cut your man off because there is money involved [risk of diocese being sued], that shocked me . . ."

Those in positions of authority with responsibility for managing cases of child sexual abuse described the difficulties they faced when responding to allegations before procedures were in place. One difficulty was responding to both the alleged perpetrator and the complainant:

> "I think initially I was trying to play a double role, trying to be on the side of the victim and at the same time trying to be just to the priest, I think in a way they are separate roles, there are several roles in it."

> "The most difficult thing is approaching the abuser. It's also very difficult to listen to people and hear their description of abuse. It is very sad, very difficult, it creates hurt, we have fought with abusers . . . we were in a very difficult situation, and sometimes we knew the abuser named in the complaint, it was very painful, we listened to them [abused] and believed them and then went to the abuser and he denied it. We didn't know where to go from there, we didn't know . . . it was very early days . . ."

The alleged perpetrator sometimes denied the allegation and this created additional challenges:

> "I often despaired getting anywhere. Meeting the alleged perpetrator was of course extremely difficult because you see you had this denial which meant it was difficult to make any progress . . ."

If the alleged perpetrator denied the allegation, this made the case and proceedings more ambiguous. The alleged abuser could be seen as a "victim" and the person in authority was not viewed as compassionate if he believed the complainant. According to those interviewed, the response from the Church has changed substantially in recent years; it has made "a complete U-turn", i.e. the focus was originally on the priest abuser, the Church and the person abused in that order. However, the order of priority has changed to the person abused, the Church and the abuser.

Focus on Confidentiality, Forgiveness and Reformation

The bishops/superiors interviewed described the nature of the priest–bishop/religious–superior relationship as somewhat parental with bishops/superiors often regarded as a confidant for clergy. When bishops/superiors became aware of allegations against clergy, the information was often treated with the utmost confidentiality in the context of these relationships:

> ". . . I did make mistakes and my biggest pastoral mistake was in confidentiality. I spent a lot of time ministering to priests as a bishop and that ministering was based on confidentiality. It was the only way which I could develop a trusting relationship . . . but my mistake was that I treated the priest abuser with the same confidentiality as I did a priest who had a different problem. Abuse thrives on secrecy so I would regard that as a major, on my part, pastoral mistake."

> ". . . I could see no point in a priest coming to his bishop or being sent for by his bishop if it was going to be everybody's business and I suppose that was some sort of extension of the confessional. I'm not justifying it now, because I can see in retrospect people would view it as secrecy."

In addition to preserving the confidentiality of the accused, there was also an attempt to reform him and salvage his priesthood/ religious life. In order to achieve this, the person was usually sent for treatment and moved from the site of the allegation, i.e. from temptation. The allegation was treated as a sin or moral failure rather than as a crime according to the bishops interviewed:

> ". . . our whole approach in the Church would have been restorative rather than punitive. You might say, 'Well wasn't that thinking simply of the offender' and I suppose it was in a

way without thinking about the harm to the abused person. But that wasn't clear to us."

"I never thought of it as a crime. I didn't see it as a crime at all. I saw it as wrongdoing."

". . . it never entered my head and even when I discussed the problem with a solicitor, he never said, 'You should go to the guards' or 'This is a crime'."

It was assumed that if the offending clergy member was sorry, promised not to offend again and agreed to get treatment, that this would be enough to deal with the problem. It was also presumed that a warning from a bishop or superior and the threat of being removed from the clergy would prevent further offending behaviour. As it was not considered a crime, civil authorities were not involved:

"I did believe that once I sent for him and warned him, 'You are getting a chance now to rehabilitate yourself or redeem yourself, a chance for survival as a priest' because I thought it was very important for me as a bishop to try and salvage the priesthood. I had no idea at all of the compulsive nature of the condition. I thought once he knew that I knew, once he knew the doctor knew and that his life in the sense of his professional life was on the line and he was getting counselling, that he would be all right."

"I remember saying to him [abuser] afterwards that 'If you don't go . . . for treatment I am going to call the guards' . . . I should have called them, but at that stage [1980s] it was beyond me that I would have one of my priests arrested. It was incomprehensible that I would betray him in that sense, because as bishop you are father to that family. I just have nightmares about that one now."

Bishops/superiors reported that they usually did not discuss the problem of allegations against clergy with their colleagues, as that would have been regarded as a breach of confidentiality:

". . . it wasn't a problem we even discussed among ourselves. That was a mistake . . . it is almost unbelievable, we got so used to working on our own . . . and I blame myself for that too. Not only did I not have insight, I didn't have foresight either."

Other Factors Contributing to Church Mismanagement of Child Sexual Abuse

Public debate about the Church's mismanagement of child sexual abuse by clergy has drawn attention to the structure and organisation of the Church. In the context of discussing the management of child sexual abuse in this study, clergy and Church personnel reflected on structural and organisational issues as factors contributing to the mismanagement of child sexual abuse.

Church Leadership and Structure

The priests interviewed criticised Church leadership and the way in which bishops are selected. The general consensus was that bishops were usually selected for being conservative and "safe":

". . . the appointment of bishops and way they're selected and the whole system of how likely candidates come up through the system . . . you won't find any radicals among the bishops. You won't find any creative thinkers or innovative people. You'll find the hierarchy full of safe pairs of hands."

Many of the priests interviewed felt that because the selection criteria were based on conservatism and orthodoxy, bishops were often not good managers or leaders:

". . . the criteria to be a bishop are a 'safe pair of hands', the criteria for selection I mean . . . these guys have played the game. Not all of them and I'm not saying that they are not good people but some of them are not leaders or good managers."

"The trouble with that is you end up with a team of goalies and no strikers."

The priests were also of the opinion that many bishops lacked pastoral experience and, as a result, were "detached from the real world" and "out of touch":

> "A lot of them come from academic backgrounds which is not sinful in itself. They are men who are out of the cut and thrust of pastoral life, no direct experience of what it's like on the ground. They tend to be somewhat detached from all that."

> "Stuff that cardinals and bishops are interested in is really not what your usual Sunday mass-goer is interested in. But the bishops would still see themselves with a duty to push this absolute line of orthodoxy. It happens because the amount of listening that goes on in the Church is negligible. Where is the forum for people to be heard? The bishops see themselves as the disseminators of truth, they stand up all the time and talk but they don't do too much listening."

> ". . . for these men [bishops], the Church isn't the people in the pews. The Church is the College of Bishops. They're the ones who draw up the rules. They live in a little world of clerical reality. Because most are men with little pastoral involvement, they almost live in fantasy world where the Church is 'Your Grace' and 'Your Lord'. The cardinal rule in the Church at the moment is conformity to Rome, the more people fall to Rome the happier they are . . ."

One of the bishops interviewed also described this level of detachment:

> ". . . the leadership needs to touch where the people are at. There is a kind of paralysis surrounding them [bishops] . . . they have a very narrow mindset. I think that one of the difficulties of the Church is that it is very difficult for someone to let go of office and one of the reasons for that is celibacy. All you have is your ministry . . . your whole identity is tied up with your ministry and therefore there is this tendency to stay on much too long. If you stay on too long then you are not in touch with your time."

Some priests also criticised how bishops had responded to child sexual abuse by clergy, particularly their inability to act and make any progress:

> "I feel angry about the inability of leadership to adapt and respond to it. They just react. Bishops are the leaders but I don't see any effective leadership, certainly not in this country. There are some exceptions but not much."

> "I'd say they are fatalistic. They are saying this problem is intractable, we will never solve it properly. Bishops think we are powerless, a persecuted Church in a hostile world. If I'm persecuted because I haven't done enough to prevent a child from being abused, that's different. That's being persecuted for having failed to do something you should have done."

In the postal survey, bishops were asked to rate their management and leadership skills, on a five-point scale ranging from excellent to poor. Half of the bishops gave themselves an "average" rating. Thirty-five per cent considered their management and leadership skills to be good and 15 per cent believed them to be fair. Twenty-nine per cent said they had received formal management and leadership training. However, most (89 per cent) bishops said they would now benefit, and/or would have benefited in the past, from management and leadership training.

In relation to the structure of the Church and how it operates, the overall views of those interviewed were that the Church was based on an outdated model, was slow to change and did not facilitate discussion or lay participation:

> "The structures of the Church are antiquated and they no longer serve the Church."

> "At the moment what we're doing is clinging desperately to a particular defunct model and in fact we are likely to be unfaithful to the mission that that model was once meant to serve. It's a maintenance model rather than a more creative or dynamic model that asks us where do we want to be."

"... it is not the kind of organisation that can respond rapidly to these kind of modern crises that break upon it and in trying to respond there is a long learning curve. It is not able to react quickly."

"We're in a Church where discussion of issues is forbidden. The Pope has forbidden the discussion on the issue of women priests. If I want to be removed from my parish I get up and give a homily in support of women priests. We have a lot of taboo subjects in the Church. It's a strange family where you can't sit down around the table and talk about issues ..."

"... they don't do enough listening, and there are no structures in the Church that facilitate a listening process. It's all from the top down with nothing going back."

In the postal survey bishops were asked to indicate aspects of the Catholic Church as an organisation that impeded the effective management of child sexual abuse cases. There were five main categories of responses:

- The structure of the episcopate and the dioceses
- The culture of secrecy
- The lack of knowledge and sound professional advice
- Canon law
- Precedence of organisation over the individual/preventing scandal.

Regarding the structure of the episcopate and dioceses, the "lack of any middle management structure" was viewed as problematic because it led to the concentration of authority in one person and to work overload. Some felt that the autonomy of individual dioceses led to a "lack of co-ordination between dioceses" and possibly to the "uneven application and implementation of the *Framework Document*". Bishops felt that, in the past, "excessive secrecy" was caused by a lack of knowledge and poor understanding of the nature of child sexual abuse coupled with a desire "not to give scandal". This level of secrecy was enabled by the autonomous nature of the dioceses. Bishops sought professional advice in relation to the treatment of perpetrators and some found this advice "wanting", i.e. inadequate. A number of bishops felt that processes within canon law impeded effective management.[u] Intentionally or unintentionally, the good of the organisation took precedence over the welfare of the individual in the management of complaints of child sexual abuse, according to 13 per cent of bishops surveyed.

Bishops were also asked to outline aspects of the Church's organisational structure that helped in managing cases. Responses were categorised as follows:

- Formal Church structures and procedures

- Relationships between bishops

- Personal attributes

- Relationship with the laity

- Expert advice from professionals.

Formal Church structures such as the *Framework Document*, the Child Protection Office and the Bishops' Committee on Child Protection were identified as helpful. Relations with other bishops were identified as helpful as they were a source of formal and informal support. Personal attributes such as listening skills were cited as important. Relationships with the laity were also a significant source of support. Good legal and psychological advice was identified as helpful in dealing with some cases. However, external professional advice was also viewed as unhelpful. For example, some of the bishops feel that given what they now know and the current status of knowledge on sexual offending they were ill-advised in relation to the management of abusers.

---

[u] Many did not elaborate beyond this.

Public Relations

The media were seen as instrumental both in highlighting the existence of child sexual abuse by clergy and in questioning the Church's management of allegations. Church personnel reflected on how the Church has been represented by the media and on the relationship between Church and media. Many felt that without the media, the problem of child sexual abuse by clergy would have remained hidden. This view was shared by the majority of the general population (as described in Chapter 3):

> "If it hadn't been for good journalists, a lot of this would not have come out."

> "I have to say in fairness to them that if they didn't do the job, much of it would still be hidden."

Most of those interviewed criticised the Church for inadequate public relations expertise and felt that the relationship between the Church and media was characterised by fear and distrust:

> "There is a lot of fear of the media in the Church . . . how much resources are the Church putting in media wise? It's nothing . . . we have a Communications Office . . . their work is more defensive than proactive."

> "We would get a minus mark for PR [public relations]. There is a fear of the media, there is a distrust of the media."

> ". . . it's all defensive and trying to rebut the charges . . . I think the Church is not communicating effectively. The communication problem is a very real problem . . ."

> ". . . they [bishops] are just frightened of the media and if you want to put the wind up the bishop, you tell him there's a reporter at the door."

The Church was criticised for its inability to handle public relations effectively. The media were also criticised for what was seen as unbalanced reporting of child sexual abuse by clergy:

"The media also have to face up to the truth and recognise that some of their reasons for being negative about the Church have nothing to do with child abuse."

"It is a society problem as well. The difficulty is, if you say that, they [media] say you are trying to get off the hook . . ."

"The reporting of these things can be unbalanced. I respect the responsibilities of the media but the manner in which they do it I don't always agree with. It may be well meaning but I think they are not sorry that this is a good story about the Church. I suppose it has something to do with a reaction to the position of the Church in Ireland."

"I put the press and the solicitors almost together in the way they have abused survivors throughout this whole thing. They have taken them up, made them into celebrities and then cast them aside."

"One of the allegations . . . was that this was a particularly Irish problem and an Irish religious problem and that we had brought it across the world . . . which was very, very hurtful and very worrying."

Child Sexual Abuse and the Church: General Effects of Mismanagement

General effects of child sexual abuse by clergy and mismanagement of the problem by the Church were discussed by clergy and church personnel. Participants identified two main effects: damage to the faith of the wider Church community and humbling of the Church. Most welcomed the idea of a more humble and transparent Church:

". . . it is no harm that the Church is down off its pedestal and that we are a more humble Church. We are a sinful Church and these people that have abused are our brothers whether we like it or not."

". . . our fundamental thing is to lead other people. I hope the Church rediscovers that and maybe starts off small and humbler . . ."

"There is good news in this but the good news comes at a huge price and the good news in this is that it may actually free the Church to return to its original way of being in the world . . . as a body of a Christ who subverted this way of power."

". . . most priests and religious are grieving because they have given their lives to this institution and have lost public respect and status . . . which we should never have had."

"Coming from 2,000 years in which they had their own power structures, their own ways of handling issues, and suddenly faced with being open and transparent, they are being accused of secrecy and they are not used to having to deal with things. Life has changed and the Church has had to go through the same opening-up process that the rest of society has."

Some went so far as to describe the process as one of purification while others cautioned that reflecting on the issue in terms of purification theologised the issue and focused on the individual offender rather than recognising structural elements that have contributed to the problem. The following section examines the organisational culture of the Catholic Church in Ireland.

Diagnosing Organisational Church Culture

It has been argued that the Catholic Church is resistant to any form of sociological or organisational analysis because the Church's view of itself is "endowed with a particular and essentially unchangeable structure of office". Four main types of organisational culture — the power, role, task/achievement and person/support cultures — are described in an assessment instrument Diagnosing Organisational Culture Questionnaire,[182] which is used to analyse organisational culture. This instrument was used in the survey of delegates and bishops to establish the current organisational culture within the Church and the culture that delegates and bishops would prefer in the Church. These four types of culture are described next.

Power-orientated Culture

The power-orientated culture is characterised by centralisation of power and unequal resource access with all authority, decision-making power and lines of communication flowing from the centre. It is found in organisations where power rests with a single individual or with a small nucleus of key individuals. As power-orientated organisations expand, they often run short of leadership talent because followers have been conditioned to be dependent. People in power-orientated organisations are motivated by rewards and punishments. Reward systems tend to be inequitable as they are based on the leaders' preferences rather than on objective systems. Power-orientated organisations tend to be highly politicised as decision-making rests with the individual rather than the group. Decisions tend to be made on the outcome of a balance of influence rather than on procedural or purely logical grounds. As the culture is essentially autocratic and resistant to challenge, low morale and feelings of powerless among the workforce are common. Rules and procedures are implicit rather than explicit. However, power-orientated organisations have the ability to respond quickly to changes and can provide satisfying work environments if leadership is based on strength, paternalistic benevolence and justice.

Role-orientated Culture

In the role-orientated culture, a system of roles and procedures are substituted for the centralisation of power. Authority and responsibility are located at the top of the hierarchy and delegated downwards. Role requirements, boundaries of authority and reporting arrangements are clearly defined. Thus, role cultures tend to be extremely status-conscious and often breed competition between departments and individuals. At its best, the role-orientated organisation provides stability, justice and efficient performance. It offers security and stability but can be impersonal. Innovative and risk-taking behaviour is often constrained as autonomy and discretion are not afforded to those at lower levels in the hierarchy.

Achievement/Task-orientated Culture

The achievement/task-orientated culture is based upon the assumption that organisational members have the potential to grow, to learn and to take responsibility for their own work and decisions. An achievement culture is a team culture that seeks to bring together the resources and people appropriate to the task. Individuals in an achievement culture tend to be internally motivated rather than externally motivated by rewards, punishments or systems. Work is organised according to the specific task requirements rather than by formal rules or regulations. Consequently, an achievement culture provides a highly flexible and autonomous environment for its members. This encourages creativity and increases job satisfaction. However, achievement-orientated organisations are frequently under-organised as they rely on members' motivation rather than on formal authority.

Support/Person-orientated Culture

The support-orientated culture is characterised by egalitarianism and mutual trust between the organisation and the individual. It offers members satisfaction from close relationships, a sense of belonging, connection and mutuality. In its purest form, it is more often found operating in communities and co-operatives such as a kibbutz. Control structures are minimal. Information, influence and decision-making are shared collectively. At its best, the support culture evokes high commitment and loyalty from its members. A certain amount of conflict and critical thinking is necessary in order to promote creativity and change and this may be lacking in a support culture. The support-orientated culture is the least common of the four types of cultures.

Existing and Preferred Organisational Church Culture

The Diagnosing Organisational Culture Questionnaire was used to identify aspects of the Catholic Church's culture from the perspective of delegates and bishops. The questionnaire contains 15 statements describing various aspects of organisational life such as work motivation, decision-making processes and relationships within and between groups as well as with the external environment.[v] The aim was to identify the most dominant organisational culture within the Church and the culture deemed to be most preferable, according to delegates and bishops. The findings also provided an opportunity to examine the possible gaps between how the organisational culture was perceived and what type of organisational culture participants would prefer.

Most Dominant Existing Organisational Culture

According to the delegates and bishops surveyed, the most dominant existing cultural orientation within the Catholic Church was a role culture. A role culture is like a bureaucracy. It involves a system of roles in which performance is organised by structures and procedures. The values of the role culture are order, dependability, rationality and consistency. The strengths of role cultures are seen to include stability, justice and efficient performance. A weakness of role organisations can be their impersonal nature. Authority and responsibility decrease as one moves down the organisational hierarchy thus restricting the autonomy and discretion of those at lower levels.

Least Dominant Existing and Preferred Organisational Culture

The least dominant existing culture was seen to be the power-orientated culture. The organisation of a power culture is based on inequality in access to resources. Leadership resides in one person or persons and is based on the leader's ability and willingness to administer rewards and punishments. People in power-orientated organisations are motivated by rewards and punishments and by the wish to be associated with a strong leader. The

---

[v] For each of the 15 statements, there were four responses (based on the power, role, achievement and support cultures). Each of the four options were ranked from 1–4 twice (i.e. 4 = the most preferred and most dominant existing culture while 1 = the least preferred and least dominant existing culture), for all 15 statements, to indicate (a) the type of culture that currently exists and (b) the preferred culture.

majority of participants felt that this set of values and assumptions was least representative of the Catholic Church's existing organisational culture. The power culture was also rated as the least preferred organisational culture.

Most Preferred Organisational Culture

The majority of delegates and bishops rated the support-orientated culture as their preferred organisational culture. The support culture is defined as an "organisational climate that is based on mutual trust between the individual and the organisation".[182] It is more people-orientated than results-orientated and is the least typical organisational climate seen in Western societies. It is characterised by the uninhibited flow of communication and resources throughout the organisation and by a warm and friendly climate. Support-orientated cultures offer members satisfactions that come from relationships rather than from achieving common goals or purposes. Managers and supervisors are supportive, responsive and concerned about the personal needs of those they supervised. In this type of organisational culture, decision-making processes are consensual.

The results from the Diagnosing Organisational Culture Questionnaire indicated that, although the Catholic Church was seen to contain elements of all four basic organisational cultures, the majority of bishops and delegates felt that a role-orientated culture, where roles and procedures are strictly delineated, was the most dominant organisational culture within the Church. However, the majority would prefer a support-orientated culture where structures and processes were more flexible. Further analysis showed a significant gap between their perceptions of the existing and their preferred organisational culture in the Catholic Church.

THE WIDER CHURCH COMMUNITY

The national survey examined public perceptions of the Church's management of child sexual abuse by clergy. Opinions and attitudes were sought about a number of aspects of the management:

the response of the Church, responsibility for the occurrence and management of child sexual abuse by clergy, initiatives taken by the Church to address the problem, tolerance of clergy who have abused children and preferred future responses by the Church in such situations.

Attitudes to the Church's Management

Most respondents were dissatisfied with the Church's handling of child sexual abuse (Figure 5.2).

Figure 5.2: Attitudes of the General Public towards the Management of Child Sexual Abuse by the Catholic Church

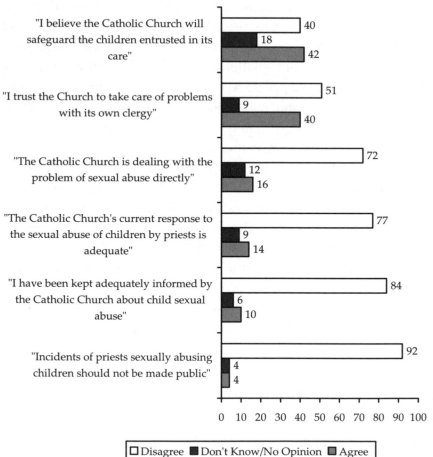

As Figure 5.2 shows, 84 per cent felt that they had not been kept adequately informed about child sexual abuse by clergy, 77 per cent felt that the Church's response has not been adequate and 72 per cent felt that the Church was not dealing with the problem directly. Only 40 per cent trusted the Church to take care of problems with its own clergy and 42 per cent believed that the Catholic Church would safeguard children entrusted to its care.

Responsibility for the Occurrence and Management of Child Sexual Abuse by Clergy

Only 16 per cent considered the Church hierarchy to be primarily responsible for the *occurrence of* sexual abuse of children with 70 per cent holding the individual abuser responsible. Thirty-nine per cent thought that the Church hierarchy was responsible for its *management*. The entire Church community (including lay people) was also seen as more responsible for management than for occurrence (14 per cent vs. 3 per cent).

Respondents could also nominate another group of their choice as responsible for the occurrence and/or management of clerical child sexual abuse. On further analysis of the "other" group the most commonly named source of responsibility for the occurrence of abuse was celibacy (one-third of this group; 3 per cent of the overall sample). The next common source responsible was the Catholic Church's policies (e.g. rigidity of rules and training and selection procedures).

Forty-one per cent of the sample identified non-Church groups as responsible for the management of clerical child sexual abuse. Most of these (56 per cent) believed that civil authorities (i.e. Gardaí, criminal justice system, State agencies) were responsible for its management, 15 per cent believed an independent body was responsible and 5 per cent believed that health and social services were responsible.[w]

---

[w] This question was asked in the same format as Rossetti's US study to facilitate comparisons. Our experience was that some participants may have used the word "responsible" to mean "culpable" (for the problem) while others used it to

Awareness of Initiatives Taken by the Catholic Church to Address Child Sexual Abuse by Clergy

Participants were asked if they were aware of any Catholic Church initiatives or actions taken to address the issue of child sexual abuse by clergy. Only one-third (33 per cent) reported being aware of any initiatives such as financial compensation, providing counselling and making apologies (30 per cent). Public statements, conferences and sermons made by the Church were noted by 23 per cent. Other initiatives identified included the Church's child sexual abuse guidelines (3 per cent), legal action against alleged perpetrators (3 per cent) and media-linked initiatives (9 per cent). Negative actions identified included the mishandling of clerical child sexual abuse cases by the Catholic Church authorities (11 per cent).

Respondents were asked if they were aware of the Irish Catholic Bishops' Advisory Committee guidelines/book called *Child Sexual Abuse: Framework for a Church Response*. Only one in ten (10 per cent) had ever heard of the book/guidelines.

Tolerance towards Convicted Clergy

The majority (92 per cent) of the public surveyed felt that a Catholic priest who had abused children should not be allowed to return to Church ministry (Figure 5.3).

When questioned about the rehabilitation of offenders, 63 per cent said they would not accept a priest who had abused children into their neighbourhood to work even if he had undergone psychological treatment and was being supervised by another priest. Only 24 per cent of those sampled found these safeguards acceptable (Figure 5.4a). Respondents who would not accept these safeguards (63 per cent of the overall sample) were asked if they would accept a priest who had abused children back into Church ministry in their neighbourhood if he had undergone treatment,

---

mean "mandated" (to find the solution). Thus, caution should be expressed in interpreting findings on this question.

Figure 5.3: Public Willingness to Accept a Priest Who had Sexually Abused Children Back into Church Ministry (unconditional acceptance)

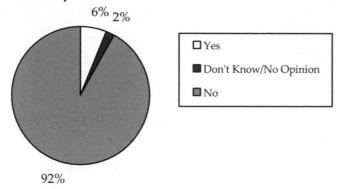

Figure 5.4a: Willingness to Accept a Priest Back into Ministry with Two Specific Safeguards (conditional acceptance)

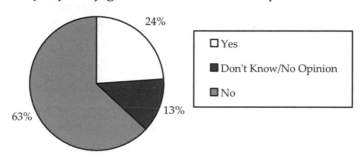

Figure 5.4b: Willingness to Accept a Priest Back into Ministry with Three Specific Safeguards (conditional acceptance)

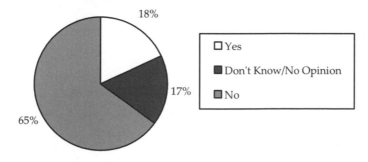

was supervised and his duties did not involve contact with children (Figure 5.4b). An additional 18 per cent of respondents were agreeable given these conditions (i.e. 12 per cent of overall sample). Overall, one in three people (36 per cent) would consider allowing former perpetrators to return to ministry if all three conditions (treatment, supervision and duties not allowing access to children) were met.

Actions Catholic Church Should Take to Help Those Who have been Abused by Clergy

Most (80 per cent) of the public believed that the Church should provide counselling for those abused, 65 per cent suggested financial support and 55 per cent felt that an acknowledgement by the Church was needed. An overwhelming majority of those in favour of counselling (90 per cent) felt that it should be provided by independent counsellors but funded by the Church. With regard to those recommending financial support, most (75 per cent) believed that the financial support should take the form of general compensation, while 22 per cent thought that the compensation should be used solely for counselling expenses. Most (94 per cent) who believed that a public acknowledgement was necessary, felt that the Church should make a public apology through the media. In summary, independent counselling, general financial compensation and public apologies were seen as the most useful actions to be taken by Church authorities to redress the damage caused to abused individuals.

Chapter 6

DISCUSSION AND CONCLUSIONS

Although research in the area of child sexual abuse is impeded because of the high number of unreported cases and the unknown proportion of sexually abused children who never become part of research studies, there are a number of areas of general consensus:

- Most child sexual abuse is perpetrated by someone known to the abused or the abused individual's family

- Child sexual abuse, like any other crime, occurs on a continuum, from inappropriate touching to rape and each type of child sexual abuse may be accompanied by force, violence or coercion

- Child sexual abuse is associated with adverse long-term effects

- Most child sexual abuse is not reported to civil authorities — only a fraction of those who commit sexual abuse are convicted for their crimes

- Although recidivism rates for sex offenders are difficult to establish and vary according to the definition of recidivism (e.g. defined as reconviction for same sex crime or arrests for similar sex crime), recent research studies reported recidivism rates of 12.7 per cent[183] and 14.4 per cent (treated) and 25.8 per cent (untreated)[184] for child abusers[a]

---

[a] A study of 400 male child abusers[198] found the highest recidivism rate (16.2 per cent) among men who had abused a child known to them but unrelated, followed by those in the abused child's extended family (10.8 per cent). Strangers had a recidivism rate of 9.7 per cent while stepfathers and biological fathers had the lowest recidivism rates (5.1 per cent and 4.8 per cent respectively).

- All sex offenders are not the same; they vary considerably in terms of remorse and openness to rehabilitation

- Although the vast majority of sex offenders are male, females also commit sexual crimes

- Most professionals agree that treating sex offenders is worthwhile.

Before this study commenced, and throughout the study process, child sexual abuse by clergy was the subject of numerous newspaper reports and television broadcasts. The public has been informed about this problem from many perspectives. However, this study was based on collective evidence from groups with direct experience, extending from the abused person through to families, colleagues and Church management as well as the Irish general public.

STUDY PHASES AND METHODOLOGY

The first phase of the study — the general public survey, was designed to assess the Irish public's knowledge of and attitudes to child sexual abuse by clergy. The high response rate, indicating that most of those contacted were willing to participate, and the spontaneous comments made by participants demonstrated a high level of interest in the subject.

There is no single explanation that best describes the experiences of those abused by clergy. Similarly, there is no one scenario that explains how the Church responded to, and managed, allegations of child sexual abuse against clergy. However, the second phase of the study, the personal experience study, demonstrated some patterns and commonalities across individual accounts.

The third phase, the Church management survey of delegates and bishops, was designed to represent the experiences of those involved in co-ordinating the Church's response to complaints of child sexual abuse. The high response rate gives confidence that the opinions and statements expressed are representative of delegates and bishops in Ireland today.

A small number of people who experienced child sexual abuse by clergy, and their family members, participated in the study. Every effort was made to increase the number of participants while respecting confidentiality limits. Given the nature of the study, it was disappointing but not surprising that the response rate was low. This pattern has been found in other similar studies. For example, using therapist face-to-face invitations or an official letter of explanation from services, only 34 per cent of over 1,000 clients of counselling services for those abused in institutional care in Ireland accepted an invitation to participate in a survey by this research group about their experiences of the service.[139] The low response rate means that the findings cannot be generalised to all those who experienced child sexual abuse by clergy. However, this does not mean that the contribution of those who participated is not valid. The in-depth nature of the qualitative interviews with those who were abused provided a compelling and often moving account of the experience of child sexual abuse.

Convicted clergy interviewed for this study may represent a specific category of offenders. All participants had admitted to the abuse when initially confronted, had expressed remorse and had received psychological treatment. By definition, they were also willing to participate in the study in an effort to make recompense. Thus, they may not be representative of the total population of convicted clergy or sex offenders in general.

AWARENESS OF CHILD SEXUAL ABUSE

Non-offending clergy and Church personnel described the development of their awareness of child sexual abuse. They mainly relied on the media in the 1980s and 1990s rather than on any formal introduction to the area from the Church. Bishops who received complaints initially felt ill-equipped to deal with them because of their own lack of awareness and because of a lack of organisational procedures. The procedures within canon law for sexual misconduct were under-utilised. Even those who used elements of canon law typically did not have expertise in this area. This was seen to partly explain the mismanagement of cases but a more significant aspect of the management approach was seen to be about protecting the Church and preventing scandal.

Public awareness concerning child sexual abuse by clergy was ascertained from the national survey. The public underestimated the number of priests and religious convicted of child sexual abuse in Ireland in the past ten years, despite the fact that the media are generally more likely to focus on the occupation of the offender where clergy are concerned than with any another occupational group. This tendency to underestimate the number of convicted abusers may reflect the fact that media coverage is of a small set of cases of abuse. These are widely reported, regularly revisited by the media and have become *causes célèbres*. It may be the case that only the more "famous" cases come to mind when someone is asked to estimate the number of convictions.

While the public underestimated the number of convictions, they overestimated the percentage of children who have been abused by clergy. The tendency to underestimate the number of convictions but to overestimate the prevalence of clergy among abusers may suggest that the public believe that cases of abuse by clergy go undetected. Conversely, it can be very difficult for the public to estimate prevalence in the absence of some wider perspective of the extent of the problem.

THE IMPACT OF CHILD SEXUAL ABUSE BY CLERGY

Based on interviews with those who were abused, specific risk factors for child sexual abuse by clergy can be identified. A strong familial Catholic faith could be a risk factor since it may engender an unquestioning trust in clergy and provide more opportunity for their interaction with children. Clergy were afforded access to families because of their position or, in some cases, because of circumstances within the family, such as illness. These factors also created barriers to disclosure because children felt that they would not be believed. Their developing faith also confused the issue because a real fear was that of being punished by God. Abusers manipulated this faith by affirming that, as clergy, their behaviour was not reprehensible but rather the child was responsible. In one case, confession of the abuse as a "sin" was used to convince the child of her guilt. The self-doubt created for children by such strategies delayed disclosure. Some needed the validation that it had also happened to someone else, while others needed therapy or the development of trust through an intimate relationship before they could disclose. The effects on those abused and their families have been persistent. Almost all of those interviewed have sought professional help as adults. Some have experienced a range of mental health problems and difficulties with relationships and intimacy. The experiences of those interviewed showed that disclosure was a process rather than a once-off occurrence. Thus, many people continue to live as adults at different stages of this process. This has implications for Church personnel receiving complaints as it indicates that an unknown and incalculable number of individuals in the general public may not have reached the disclosure stage yet but may possibly do so in the future.

There are few published personal accounts of convicted child sex abusers. This is in part because of a reluctance by the public to hear their stories and a reluctance on the part of abusers to allow them to be told: "it seems implausible that paedophiles have a story and inconceivable that they should be allowed to speak it".[185] The stories told by clerical abusers as part of this research conveyed struggle and loss. The struggle described by convicted priests and religious was mainly about leading a double life. Most of those interviewed described how they knew that the abuse they were perpetrating was wrong and was against what they stood for as clergy, yet they were unable to stop. Some described relief at being confronted about their abusive behaviour. They also experienced panic, suicidal ideation and a sense that the life they had led was over, i.e. that what had started with confrontation about allegations signalled prison and the end of their life as a priest or religious. Although the experience of treatment was difficult and emotionally demanding, most found it beneficial. For some, it created a personal awareness and taught them that their offending behaviour was indeed abuse. It also prepared them for prison while the spiritual element of treatment assisted some in their disengagement from priesthood/religious life.

This study provided a unique and anonymous forum where junior to very senior clergy could express their experiences of the issue of clerical child sexual abuse. While clergy in authority reported feeling guilt and regret over the issue of clerical child sexual abuse, individual priests and religious reported feeling disillusioned. The guilt and regret felt by bishops stemmed from mistakes they felt they had made in management, in particular their failure to extend care and concern to the abused. There was also guilt about the damage caused to the Church because of such mistakes. Non-offending clergy reported feeling stigmatised and a sense that they were being singled out unfairly for blame. Many of the findings from interviews with priests and religious are comparable to the findings from a contemporary survey of 323 Dublin diocesan priests on support, stress and future issues.[186] In this 1998 survey, priests reported that their greatest sources of stress were Church leadership followed by "clergy scandals". In the present study, the priests interviewed were highly critical of Church leadership and described how Church scandals had caused low morale among them. Similarly, the most important future initiative identified by priests in the 1998 survey was the development of an adequate lay ministry. Also in the top five most important future initiatives were the involvement of women at all levels of responsibility and developing a more collaborative ministry. Priests interviewed in this study also felt that these initiatives were important for the future of the Church. Despite the disillusionment and guilt expressed, there was also hope that if the Church could learn from the mistakes it had made, a changed and better Church would emerge.

Religious Faith and Practices and Belief and Faith in God

When confronted with a crisis, most people rely on their core beliefs, assumptions and values about the world. For religious people, these beliefs and values are often principles of faith. Therefore, it should not be surprising that some Catholics have experienced a crisis of faith in trying to come to terms with child sexual abuse by clergy. For individuals who experienced abuse and their families, confidence in the Catholic Church was significantly affected. For most, the institutional Church no longer had any significance or value in their lives. For most, this was because of the way in which their complaint of abuse was responded to and managed rather than as a direct result of the abuse *per se*. However, faith in God remained intact. Faith in God had also helped some of the convicted clergy to come to terms with their actions.

The religious practices of the general public were also somewhat affected by cases of child sexual abuse by clergy. More generally, attendance at religious services has fallen for Catholics in Ireland in the last decade. Child sexual abuse by clergy appears to have had no effect on public faith in God. The findings indicate that, for the public, institutional religion was not synonymous with a belief in or a personal relationship with a God. From a pastoral perspective this is reassuring — the spiritual well-being of the wider Church community does not appear to have been damaged by the emergence of Church personnel as perpetrators and "mis-managers" of child sexual abuse.

Impact on Perceptions of Church and Clergy

For those who experienced abuse, the Church's response to their disclosure and the subsequent management of their complaint, rather than the experience of abuse itself, was seen as responsible for their loss of confidence in the Catholic Church. The response from the Church was seen to lack compassion and concern for the individual. It also lacked a sense of urgency and was more legal than pastoral in its focus. Furthermore, there was a lack of concern for the future protection of other children. This was not what those disclosing their experience of abuse had expected from the Church. Coping with the revelation of child sexual abuse some decades ago, in a climate very different to the current one, meant that many families did not know where to go for help. Some thought that the Church would deal with it. There was even a reluctance to tell members of their extended family because they did not want to be accused of starting a "vendetta" against a priest. There was also the fear that they would not be believed or that they could be ostracised from their local community because people did not complain about priests at that time.

Some convicted clergy also reported a loss of confidence in the Catholic Church. They saw their future as uncertain and some found it more difficult than others to accept that they would never again be involved in any type of ministry in the Church. While in prison, many felt abandoned by the Church but also ashamed because of the abuse they had perpetrated and the damage they had caused to the reputation of the Church. However, some felt that Church authorities were unable or unwilling to understand that they were human and were too willing to dispose of them. Others were unwilling to criticise the Church because of their personal shame and guilt and the damage they felt they had caused to the Church.

The colleagues of convicted clergy described anger, hurt and disillusionment. They were angry with clergy who had sexually abused but were more angry about the overall management of child sexual abuse by Church authorities, in particular the response to complainants and the laity. They reported feeling hurt because they were not personally supported, kept informed by their authorities or empowered to reach out to the congregation where a priest had been suspected or convicted of child sexual abuse. They also reported that additional resources were not provided to assist them with their normal parish work and the crisis of having a priest in the parish under criminal investigation. The disillusionment reported was seen to stem from the fact that the Church was unable to use the principles of faith to respond to those who experienced abuse and because "front-line" clergy had to represent the Catholic Church publicly amid child sexual abuse scandals.

Members of the public surveyed were generally unhappy with the handling of these cases by the Church. They saw the Church as being damaged as a result of the abuse and its mismanagement. However, the overall quality of the Church was judged to be better than that of the past and satisfaction with priests today was generally high. A majority thought that the quality of priests was better today than in the past and that, in general, priests had been unfairly judged as a result of child sexual abuse by some clergy. Only half of the sample thought that damage to the Church's reputation would be permanent. When asked about the permanence of the damage caused to the Church by child sexual abuse by clergy, many felt that the damage would not be permanent or reserved their opinion until they could see how the Church would respond to complaints in the future.

The Irish public were generally positive and sympathetic towards individual priests. They expected priests to show moral leadership but did not accept them as authority figures. Priests were expected to show better moral conduct than others, but they were not seen as being closer to God, or deserving of total obedience from the laity. The public, particularly women, were less prepared to automatically trust a priest on first arrival in their community. While a less traditional view of priesthood appeared to prevail among the public, more than half the sample would be happy at the prospect of their son becoming a priest. That the public are no longer prepared to place unquestioned trust in clergy may be one of the major effects of clerical child sexual abuse. Clergy may have to work harder to earn the trust of parishioners. This could reflect a departure from the more traditional relationship of implicit trust between clergy and lay people. Overall, the study showed that confidence in the Catholic Church has been damaged while faith in God remains very high.

RESPONSE AND MANAGEMENT

The Church is meant to be a place of sanctuary and hospitality, particularly for vulnerable people. Instead, those who were abused often felt unwelcome. Many were disillusioned by the lack of pastoral care and concern offered. The business-like response from clergy receiving allegations of abuse may be an indication of disbelief or a strategy to preserve stability. If, historically, the response was poor because of ignorance, i.e. lack of awareness and information, then more recent and equally inadequate responses appear to have been influenced by legal anxieties and the fear of financial claims. One possible explanation for the poor treatment of complainants is that some Church personnel were suspicious of those making the complaint because they feared legal consequences. The clergy interviewed for this study reflected that, as pastors, bishops are usually available to meet with people in all types of crisis or trouble but in this case were unable to respond when the crisis involved their own Church. Many of those who reported abuse were clear that their motive was not financial compensation but to feel their story was listened to and acted on, and to prevent further abuse. They hoped the Church would feel the same way and that they would be treated compassionately.

The theme of protecting the Church and preventing scandal emerged many times throughout the research. This may partly explain how the Church handled complaints, as there was an attempt to keep the problem within the Church. This was done in an effort to protect the Church and to protect the laity. Ironically, while the Church's management of child sexual abuse often focused on preventing scandal, the actions of the Church have in fact created a far larger scandal than it tried to prevent.

The bishops interviewed attested to the approach of preventing scandal, as well as the restorative rather than punitive approach of the Church to the rehabilitation of the accused. Actions were aimed at salvaging priesthood/religious life. Many now regard this as a mistake on their part. Many also said they acted without the knowledge that child sexual abuse caused serious damage to the abused or that a sex offender was likely to re-offend. Alongside "preventing scandal" there was a focus on complete confidentiality. Some thought that a caution from senior clergy and the threat of removal from the priesthood was enough to prevent further abuse.

Some people making complaints to clergy requested complete confidentiality. In these cases the accused was often removed from the site of allegations and/or sent for treatment. However, an admission of guilt from the accused or co-operation with treatment was not always forthcoming. Once removed, formal monitoring structures were not put in place and this may have led to further abuse. Although procedures within canon law existed to remove priests from ministry for such offences, these were underutilised. It has been argued that a fundamental flaw in the teaching of moral theology within the Catholic Church was a somewhat narrow focus on "evil acts" rather than on the consequences of the acts.[162] Regarding Church management of child sexual abuse, the focus was on the "sinful" act rather than on the damage caused to the child and the criminal nature of the act. Administrative and structural elements of the Church were also seen to contribute to the mismanagement of child sexual abuse.

Challenges to the effective management of child sexual abuse by clergy were identified in the study. The most significant may have been the fact that the bishop was responding to both the complainant and the accused. With the introduction of the *Framework Document* in 1996, these roles were separated with the appointment of delegates. There are still problems, most notably that the same delegate deals with the complainant and the accused.

Many of the clergy interviewed for the study maintained that the Church's management approach had completely reversed from initially focusing on the accused to more recently focusing on the complainant to the neglect of the accused. There are two points on this issue. Firstly, it appears from this research that the institutional Church, rather than the accused, was the primary focus of protection in the management of cases of child sexual abuse (although this approach invariably works in favour of the accused). Secondly, while redirecting the focus of intervention from the Church to the complainant can be seen as a significant improvement, accused clergy also must be considered if the Church is serious about child protection in the future. Overall, from a management point of view, dealing with clerical child sexual abuse has been a bitter learning experience for the Church. It has moved the Church into a closer, if not comfortable, working relationship with civil authorities.

The vast majority of the Irish public surveyed felt they had not been kept adequately informed by the Church about child sexual abuse and that the Church was not dealing adequately or directly with the problem. There was little awareness of Church initiatives to address the problem of child sexual abuse by priests and religious. Few had heard of the *Framework Document*, which sets out the guidelines and procedures to be followed when responding to complaints. The public were more likely to be aware of actions such as homilies at Mass and media reports of a bishop's statement. The majority of respondents thought that counselling funded by the Church, but using independent counsellors, was most appropriate for those who have been abused. The Conference of Religious in Ireland (CORI) established *Faoiseamh* in 1997. This organises and funds counselling for those abused, yet the public were mostly unaware of its existence. These findings have implications for Church policy and for those responsible for publicising Church initiatives. The public's lack of awareness of actions the Church has taken to address clerical child sexual abuse may reflect a relative lack of media coverage. This may in part indicate the orientation of the media generally, i.e., to more individual case and sensationalist reporting (as is evident in media reporting of child sexual abuse more generally). However, it may also reflect the failure of the Church to effectively communicate its responses to the problem. Similarly, much of the media coverage of child sexual abuse by clergy has been highly critical of Church authorities. The coverage has focused largely on the mismanagement of cases, particularly the failure to report abusers to civil authorities and the transfer of abusers to other parishes. The often unsympathetic and sometimes hostile treatment of those reporting abuse was also widely reported. It is hardly surprising, therefore, that only 40 per cent of the sample trusted the Church to manage problems with its own clergy and most respondents felt that civil authorities should be responsible for the management of child sexual abuse by clergy.

Church authorities risk severing connections with their parishioners if they are not proactive in situations where clergy are accused or convicted of child sexual abuse. Absence of Church leadership in a time of crisis can create anger and alienation among the congregation. Too often the response of the Church has been seen to be about preventing scandal. As a result, the matter may not be responded to or discussed openly. It is this level of secrecy that appears to have most angered those abused and the congregation. Clear and direct information from the Church would mean that congregations do not have to rely solely on rumours or media coverage. This is, however, not a simple matter as due regard must be given to the rights of the accused person.

Many Church policies on child sexual abuse express a commitment to keep parishioners informed. However, if a priest is under criminal investigation (for certain types of sexual offences), both civil and canon law prevent information about the accused from being made public. This is an area of considerable tension between pastoral and civil requirements. Further examination and development is required to minimise these tensions and potential conflicts. Furthermore, because the policies produced by the Church in Ireland are not binding, implementation depends on individual bishops and priests rather than policy directives. Thus, the response may depend on the diocese rather than there being a consistent response across dioceses.

How should the Church respond? The Church hierarchy needs to publicly demonstrate its ongoing recognition of clerical child sexual abuse as a serious problem and continue to demonstrate its commitment to prevention, intervention and treatment for all concerned. A process of regular updating of policies should be established and made known to clergy and laity. Allegations should be dealt with in a compassionate and timely manner using trained support persons. Assistance should be provided in obtaining psychological and legal help and the complainant should be promptly informed about all decisions in relation to their complaint.

FUTURE MANAGEMENT ISSUES

This study has shown that, in relation to child sexual abuse by clergy, the Catholic Church in Ireland is in need of more effective leadership. The majority of delegates in the postal survey classified themselves as inexperienced in handling cases of child sexual abuse with just over half of them having dealt with a case. Bishops, on the other hand, tended to have long durations of tenure.

Many had dealt with between one and ten cases of child sexual abuse. Regardless of experience, the majority of bishops and delegates expressed a need for more training and education, more personnel to help with complaints of child sexual abuse, more supervision and consultation and better guidelines and procedures. A keenly expressed wish was for continuous training and development in all aspects of child protection and for support and consultation from experienced professionals in the area. Although clerical child sexual abuse has been an issue to the forefront of the Church's agenda since the early 1990s, there still remains a strongly felt need for training and education. The majority of bishops also expressed the need for specific management and leadership training. Only 29 per cent of bishops had received any formal management or leadership training. This, combined with the fact that "general Church leadership" was identified as the greatest source of stress in a recent survey of Dublin priests, points to the need for development in this area.

Delegates were evenly divided as to whether effective procedures were in place to deal with cases of child sexual abuse in the Catholic Church. Bishops tended to be more positive in their outlook on the future of the issue with the majority maintaining that while prevention and management would continue to be an issue, the procedures were now in place to deal with it. However, responding to a separate survey question, the majority of both bishops and delegates thought that existing guidelines required review.

Age (i.e. young age) is not the only criterion that renders individuals as vulnerable since many psychologically challenged and distressed individuals come into regular contact with clergy as do adults with learning difficulties. While not a specific focus of this study, it is clear that the sexual abuse and exploitation of adults within the Church also needs to be addressed. Overemphasis on sexual abuse of children rather than on abuse of all vulnerable individuals because of the extensive access and trust given to clergy neglects the wider issues involved and can also act as a barrier to disclosure if only "child" abuse is seen as noteworthy.

CHILD PROTECTION AND THE FUTURE
FOR CONVICTED CLERGY

The findings from the national survey show that most people would not accept a priest back into active ministry following treatment even with supervision and with restrictions on his ministry. Very few members of the public spontaneously suggested treatment for clergy who had sexually abused children as an action the Church should take in addressing the problem. Although this is not an unexpected finding, it presents a challenge to Church authorities. If convicted clergy were laicised but did not co-operate with the Church hierarchy, no further support or monitoring following release from prison could be provided by the Church. If they did co-operate, whether laicised or not, it is most unlikely that they would be accepted to engage in any type of ministry by the wider Church community. Internationally, there is evidence that the public are generally very intolerant of child sex offenders and that legal sanctions such as community notification of offenders are favoured more than "restorative justice" strategies to rehabilitate and heal all concerned in the context of child sexual abuse. Such responses may be time-dependent with groups moving from a purely "punitive" justice to a more restorative justice perspective and with distinctions being made between offences of varying severity. In Ireland, the situation may change over the coming years given an evolving understanding of the nature and extent of child sexual abuse.

Although a universal policy of automatic dismissal from the clerical state for clergy convicted of sexual offences may suit many dioceses and religious orders, in terms of offering a standard and uncomplicated approach to convicted clergy, such an approach has implications for child protection. Some dioceses currently run risk management and relapse prevention programmes for clergy who have been convicted. These mechanisms provide support and ongoing rehabilitation for these clergy while potentially reducing the risk of re-offending. A universal policy involving dismissal of convicted clergy could result in social isolation, financial difficulties and possible re-offending. In addition, a universal policy of dismissal does not fit well with the Christian doctrine of forgiveness. Dismissal should not be adopted as a public relations exercise or to limit legal liability. Instead, where convicted clergy are willing to co-operate with their diocese, ongoing support and rehabilitation should be facilitated in the interest of child protection. This may constitute a difficult "path" to negotiate with an already untrusting public. The challenge is to demonstrate that ongoing Church support of, and association with, convicted clergy is being undertaken in the spirit of forgiveness of the abuser and wider community protection rather than as a forum for condoning the actions of the abuser as a fellow Church colleague.

THE CHALLENGE OF FORGIVENESS

One of the most complicated issues for people who have experienced abuse is forgiveness and reconciliation. The clergy interviewed talked about forgiveness in relation to the abuser and the belief that no one is beyond redemption. This was seen as something unique that the Church could offer. The Church can still extend forgiveness and offer the chance for redemption to the abuser since forgiveness for past actions does not imply exemption from punishment or trust for the future. This must, however, be done in a way that protects children from abuse and also maximises co-operation from the abuser. The Church has been exposed as failing the complainants and is now endeavouring in many ways to undo this failure. However, this should not involve the demonisation of the abuser. There are many dimensions of forgiveness concerning this issue. For instance, can those who have experienced abuse and their families forgive the Church? How can the Church seek their forgiveness and counteract the doubt that surrounds leadership in the Catholic Church? Can the Catholic clergy and laity forgive the abuser? There may be few formal "rites of passage" out of a deviant identity. Is it really possible for abusers to renegotiate their social identity in the face of the current climate in relation to child sexual abuse in Ireland and in light of the continued media coverage?

A Changing Church

"An unexamined faith is not a faith. It is a superstition."[187]

One theory on the function of scandals in society is that they have significant consequences that bring about change.[188] A fear expressed by clergy interviewed was that Church authorities would regard the management of child sexual abuse within the Church as a purification process, i.e. ridding the Church of child sex abusers to sanitise it. This focus on the individual would ignore significant structural and administrative problems within the Church. In examining the issue of child sexual abuse within the Church, the institution must also be examined.

It has been suggested that the priest was understood to represent "the perfect body of Christ".[189] Both the faithful laity and the clergy were seen to want this image. Many priests were seen to have "bought into it, revelling in the unearned status that it brought". The status of clergy and willingness to trust clergy have suffered as a result of child sexual abuse by clergy. While some clergy described a "bereaved" response, others expressed relief at being considered nothing more than human. Most of the clergy interviewed felt that what had been lost — i.e. power — should never have been possessed. Furthermore, they looked forward to a "de-clericalist" approach to the administration of faith with more involvement from the wider Church community, particularly women.

Communication was also a major issue. It seems that within the Church itself, and from the Church to its laity, communication has been inadequate. Thus, when scandals about the Church were revealed, existing communication channels within the Church were unable to respond. By avoiding the media, Church authorities have (inadvertently) communicated to the wider Church community that they operate in silence and secrecy. Church authorities were seen to feel cornered by the media and to worry that they would do more damage by being available for questioning or discussion. They were seen to have opted for silence because they did not know what else to do. The Church needs to learn from the experience of dealing with cases of child sexual abuse in order to develop more effective means and methods for communication.

Both delegates and bishops perceived the existing culture of the Catholic Church in Ireland as most closely resembling a role-orientated organisational culture, i.e. bureaucratic with hierarchical relations between members and with formalisation and specialisation of roles. The majority of delegates and bishops said they would prefer a support-orientated culture. A support culture is characterised by egalitarianism and mutual trust between the organisation and the individual. Authority in a support-orientated culture is located within each individual rather than within the organisation. Support-orientated cultures offer members the satisfaction that comes from relationships rather than rewards for achieving common goals or purposes. The fact that both bishops and delegates would prefer a support culture is encouraging. However, it has been argued that structures within the Catholic Church are seen as "unchangeable" and therefore not subject to revision. Therefore, although delegates and bishops endorsed the same organisational changes, the existing organisational culture (role-orientated culture) identified by bishops and delegates means that there may not currently be mechanisms in place to put such aspirations into practice.

Individuals who have experienced abuse have done much to bring the issue of child sexual abuse by clergy to public attention. In Ireland, several courageous individuals have waived anonymity to keep the debate alive in the interest of child protection. Without these individuals, there would be no awareness. Their struggle for justice and accountability will hopefully improve child protection within the Church. In the US, many dioceses have Catholic lay groups who campaign for change. These groups have used the issue of child sexual abuse "scandals" to push more broadly for change in their Church. Catholics in the US have been coming to terms with the problem of child sexual abuse by clergy over a slightly longer timeframe than Irish Catholics. Whether lay members of the Catholic Church in Ireland will use "scandals" here as an opportunity to push for Church reform remains to be seen.

CONCLUSION

This study, in examining the impact of child sexual abuse by clergy, has drawn attention to the fact that the effects of abuse extend well beyond the individual abused. Although this is also true of abuse perpetrated by non-clerical abusers, it appears that the effects of abuse by clergy are more extensive because of the effects on colleagues and on the wider Church community. The study also shows that in some cases the Church failed to respond adequately and effectively to those who experienced abuse and their families, to the abusers and their families and to abusers' colleagues and general clergy. This has caused many to lose confidence in the Catholic Church as an organisation. Those in positions of authority interviewed for this study recognised the failures and mistakes made. It is clear that not enough was done to protect children from abuse. However, some of the mistakes and organisational failures identified through this research can be addressed.

This is the first study internationally to take a holistic perspective on the impact of child sexual abuse by clergy. In effect, the "ripples in the pond" from clerical abuse have been assessed. What it demonstrates is that clerical abuse represents loss at every level of Irish life — loss for those most closely involved as the "victims" of abuse but also loss for families and colleagues, for all Church personnel and for the wider Church community. This needs to be acknowledged in a system that has operated more on an "us" and "them" approach until now.

Church personnel are now better informed and have a better understanding of the nature and effects of child sexual abuse. They are in a better position to improve things for the future. The crisis created by child sexual abuse within the Church could be a catalyst for change at both local and national level. There has been, and continues to be, a period of anger. Child sexual abuse by clergy has generated a great deal of anger. People are angry that child sexual abuse should occur at all and particularly that those of whom high moral standards are expected should be the abusers. They are also angry at the mismanagement of child

sexual abuse by Church authorities. There is evidence that the issue has caused, and continues to cause, deep sadness among
Church personnel and among the wider Church community in
Ireland. This time can be seen as a period of seeking understanding as well as retribution. While this is a very dynamic period,
there is evidence from this survey that the public separate their
judgements of individual priests from those of the Church more
generally. They see today's Church as better than that of the past
and their own religious beliefs have not been damaged by the individual or collective actions of those representing the Church. It
is thus a time of opportunity for the Church to demonstrate its
commitment to clear and comprehensive management of the
problem of child sexual abuse by Church personnel. We are now
in an era where the public and professionals alike are being con-
tinuously educated about the nature and extent of child sexual
abuse in society. In this evolving context, the criterion for success
for the Church in managing child sexual abuse will not be a guarantee that abuse by Church personnel will never occur again.
Instead, it will be the development and enactment of a comprehensive strategy, for prevention, reporting and managing allegations. In a spirit of fairness and transparency, such a strategy can
serve to restore trust in the various institutions of the Church. It
can serve to repay some of the courage of those abused in bringing such painful and personal experiences to public attention for
the greater common good.

Chapter 7

RECOMMENDATIONS

The following recommendations aim to provide comprehensive coverage of the issues to be addressed in the future management of child sexual abuse by clergy. Some recommendations have already been stated in the 1996 *Framework Document* Guidelines and are being enacted. They are, however, restated here to ensure a single, updated and comprehensive set of recommendations is available.

A. PREVENTION OF CHILD SEXUAL ABUSE BY CHURCH PERSONNEL

The protection of children should be of paramount importance for the Church. Specific preventative strategies as developed by Church authorities should be genuinely proactive and developed in the interest of the protection and welfare of children rather than produced in response to particular cases or public pressure.

1. **The Church, as an organisation, should study the systems being put in place in other organisations to identify and manage various types of risk and to respond in a prompt and effective manner to crises.** Developments in the healthcare sector are particularly relevant. Notably, such developments have also been driven in the most part by crises, by evidence of poor management and by an increasing public demand for accountability and high standards. They have shown the necessity for systems-based thinking in identifying and manag-

ing risk and responding appropriately and proactively in dealing with crises.

2. **Child sexual abuse is a society-wide issue and the remit for child protection is broader than the Church. The Church should actively seek to work in co-operation with other agencies in this area in the interest of the best possible protection of children.** Contemporary government policies for the protection and welfare of children should form the framework for this co-operation (in 2003 this is *Children First*, 1999). The Church's own guidelines (*Framework Document*, 1996) should be reviewed in light of this report.

3. **Prevention strategies should be informed by relevant research as conducted by the Church or other agencies and should be communicated to all Church personnel, to the wider Church community and to the general public.**

4. **The Catholic Church in Ireland should seek to develop a model of best practice for child protection based on ongoing review of current guidelines.**

5. **Church procedures for prevention should be audited at appropriate intervals. This could be done by the Church or by an external agency using a quality assurance approach.**

B. MANAGEMENT OF COMPLAINTS OF SEXUAL ABUSE BY CLERGY

The findings from this study show that many allegations of child sexual abuse were not managed in an effective, considerate or consistent manner by the Catholic Church. At the outset, there were no procedures in place for receiving or managing complaints.[a] Complainants were rarely informed about how the complaint would be managed and, in many cases, it was up to the

---

[a] In this context, a complaint is defined as an official accusation by the person abused or a person acting on their behalf. Third-party reports, anonymous claims or hearsay do not constitute an official complaint.

complainant to check on progress. Church guidelines on the management of child sexual abuse were issued in Ireland in 1996. They provided a framework for responses and served to improve matters considerably. However, the guidelines are not binding on individuals, dioceses or religious congregations. Some subsequent complaints have not been managed in accordance with these guidelines. While Irish bishops work collectively on some issues, the current situation for dealing with individual complaints is that every bishop operates independently. The findings from this study show that most bishops are critical of the lack of co-ordination across dioceses. This may result in the uneven application of procedures relating to child sexual abuse.

6. **A clearly defined protocol for managing complaints, based on a standardised approach, should be put in place with due regard for the role of the bishop/superior in a diocese/congregation. This standardised approach could be facilitated by a national Child Protection Office (CPO) or similar national central body and should be widely communicated to the general public. Such a protocol would facilitate those who do not wish to approach clergy *per se* (including some whose first or main complaint is to civil authorities); would broaden the categories of Church personnel against whom complaints could be made; and would improve accountability for the management of complaints.**

7. **The protocol should provide, *inter alia*, clear and practical instructions for responding to disclosures of child sexual abuse for all Church personnel. The protocol should also provide information on onward referral of the complaint to the national central body/CPO. Training in complaints procedures should be mandatory for all Church personnel and should be audited at appropriate intervals to ensure adherence. Both training and audit might be best undertaken by an external agency.** There are many ways in which a person may make a complaint. They might report the matter directly to a bishop or contact their local clergy. Complaints might

emerge during the course of pastoral work by clergy, e.g. during marriage guidance/preparation.

8. As per the *Framework Document* (Church Guidelines on Child Sexual Abuse), complaints of child sexual abuse by clergy should be referred promptly to the Garda Síochána. This should be coordinated by the national central body/ CPO.

9. The national central body/CPO should notify the bishop, in the diocese where the abuse is alleged to have occurred, of complaints received. This notification should initiate a pastoral response from the local clergy/bishop in liaison with the national central body/CPO. A pastoral response by Church personnel should be initiated as soon as a complaint is received. It should accommodate the needs of all concerned — complainant, accused, families and associated Church colleagues. Active involvement of the bishop in this pastoral response is an important aspect of his leadership role. It signals commitment and openness to address the problem by Church authorities. The findings from this study show that local Church personnel can make a uniquely valuable contribution to the pastoral care and spiritual protection of a community when abuse is notified.

10. Complaints procedures should be widened in scope so that they facilitate complaints against all clergy and lay personnel who work for the Church.

11. Church policies regarding the prevention and management of child sexual abuse should be extended to include inappropriate sexual behaviour of clergy with those who have learning difficulties and mental health problems. In their work, clergy come in contact with many vulnerable groups. Overemphasis on the sexual abuse of children may signal that the Church is only interested in this type of complaint. This may inadvertently act as a barrier to those who wish to report abuse of other vulnerable individuals.

12. **All dioceses should have an advisory panel or board of management to deal with complaints of clerical child sexual abuse.** This study showed that disclosure is not a once-off event but, rather, a process. Individuals may be at different stages in this process at any given time. This has implications for Church response and policy. The protracted nature of disclosure means that instances of clerical child sexual abuse now exist where the abused individual is not yet ready to make the complaint but may reach that point at some future date. An assumption that all existing cases have already come to light, or will do so in the near future, is unwise.

13. **The *Framework Document* states that "adequate positive steps should be taken to restore the good name and reputation of a priest or religious who has been wrongly accused" (p. 19) but it does not describe the steps required. Policies for re-establishing the person's good name and the procedures to be followed should be developed.**

C. PROFESSIONAL DEVELOPMENT OF CLERGY

The roles and responsibilities of professionals across many disciplines have come under increasing scrutiny in recent times. Much of this has arisen from crises reflecting poor management and accountability. There is a growing public demand for high standards and accountability in public life. Healthcare professionals, those in the financial and banking professions and politicians are among the professional groups who have increasingly been called to demonstrate their commitment to high standards and accountability. Many of the lessons learned are relevant for the Church. An uncoordinated and poorly managed system with individuals claiming that they "didn't understand" or were "doing their best" is no longer acceptable as an explanation for incompetence when dealing with the public. Professionalisation is imperative. The development of a professional code of conduct for priests, ongoing training in personal and professional development and the provision of better support structures for priests are vital. Although only a minority of clergy are offenders, the provision of support and development programmes should assist all clergy.

14. **A code of professional conduct should be developed, in consultation with clergy, to clarify roles and boundaries in relationships, to assist clergy in managing these boundaries and to underpin the professionalism of the Church as an organisation.** Many of the participants in this study expressed the view that, as a professional body, they had no clear job descriptions and, apart from canon law, they had no professional code of practice. A code of professional conduct would provide support and guidance for clergy who are currently unsure about how to interact with children (and adults) in contemporary society. This would also serve to reassure the public that, like other professionals, clergy were operating with a specific code of conduct.

15. **The personal and professional development of clergy — both those in training and those already in ministry — should be advanced and should continue throughout their careers.** Most of the clergy who participated in this study reported that they had received little formation for celibacy. Neither did their formation prepare them for the changes that have taken place in Irish society. Current formation has improved and in some settings for example, candidates for the priesthood are now provided with opportunities for personal development by working with external human development counsellors. This should be maintained throughout life in ministry as ongoing personal development and reflective practice are essential for those whose work brings them into contact with the demands of the human condition.

16. **Support structures for clergy should be reviewed with a view to making support available on an ongoing basis. Personal development and spiritual support should be facilitated by these structures.** While procedures for selecting candidates for clerical life are important, it will never be possible to be completely assured that individuals with the potential to

sexually abuse others are not recruited into religious life. One strategy in preventing clerical sexual abuse is to provide opportunities for those who feel they are at risk of abusing to seek help.

17. **Those in leadership roles in the Church should receive professional training in management and leadership.** The overall response of the Church to complaints of child sexual abuse to date has lacked professionalism. As an organisation, the Church does not appear to have structures in place to support clergy throughout their ministry. Many of the clergy who participated in this study perceived the Church as lacking effective leadership. The surveys conducted as part of this study provided a unique opportunity for senior Church personnel to express their personal and managerial concerns in a confidential manner. If the Church, as an organisation, is to become more professional, skilled management and strong leadership are required.

18. **A programme of ongoing support and supervision for convicted clergy (including relapse prevention and preparation for life without ministry) should be developed. The programme should facilitate co-operation with clergy who have abused. Such a programme should be developed in conjunction with professionals working with sex offenders.** The treatment of child sex offenders is important for preventing child sexual abuse and for curbing potential re-offending. It is generally accepted that sex offenders benefit from psychological treatment and from relapse prevention programmes. This study found that almost all of the convicted clergy who had participated in such programmes benefited from their treatment. Some continue to be supported by their diocese by the provision of relapse prevention groups and individual counselling. However, in other dioceses, there are no such support systems. The overall management of convicted clergy after their release from prison and following treatment varies across dioceses. It is recognised that each case must be judged indi-

vidually and that diocesan provision may be influenced by factors such as age. However, in the interest of child protection, efforts should be made to support these men, as isolation and rejection could increase the risk of re-offending.

19. **Professional development procedures for clergy should be audited at appropriate intervals. This could be done by the Church or by an external agency using a quality assurance approach.**

REFERENCES

1. McGee, H., Garavan, R., de Barra, M., Byrne, J. and Conroy, R. (2002). *The SAVI Report: Sexual Abuse and Violence in Ireland*. Dublin: The Liffey Press.

2. Raftery, M. and O'Sullivan, E. (1999). *Suffer the Little Children*. Dublin: New Island.

3. Ferguson H. (2000). "States of fear, child abuse and Irish society". *Doctrine and Life*, 50 (1), 20–30.

4. Irish Catholic Bishops' Advisory Committee (1996). *Child Sexual Abuse: Framework for a Church Response*. Dublin: Veritas.

5. Muram, D. and Laufer, M.R. (1999). "Limitations of the medical evaluation for child sexual abuse". *The Journal of Reproductive Medicine*, 44 (12), 993–999.

6. Law Reform Commission, (1990). *Report on Child Sexual Abuse*. Dublin: Law Reform Commission.

7. Haugaard, J.J. and Emery, R.E. (1989). "Methodological issues in child sexual abuse research". *Child Abuse and Neglect*, 13, 89–100.

8. Finkelhor, D. (1979). *Sexually Victimized Children*. New York: Free Press.

9. Finkelhor D. (1994). "The international epidemiology of child sexual abuse". *Child Abuse and Neglect*, 18 (5), 409-417.

10. Haugaard, J.J. (2000). "The challenge of defining sexual abuse". *American Psychologist*, 55 (9), 1036–1039.

11. Department of Health and Children (1999). *Children First: National Guidelines for the Protection and Welfare of Children*. Dublin: Stationery Office.

12. MacIntyre, D. and Carr, A. (1999). "The epidemiology of child sexual abuse". *Journal of Child Centred Practice*, 6 (1), 57–85.

13. National Women's Council of Ireland, (1996). The Working Party on the Legal and Judicial Process for the Victims of Sexual and Other Crimes against Women and Children. Dublin: The National Women's Council.

14. Dublin Rape Crisis Centre (2000). *Jan '00 – Dec '00 Statistics and Financial Summary*. Dublin: Dublin Rape Crisis Centre.

15. Department of Health and Children (2002). *Provisional Childcare Statistics 2001*. Dublin: Department of Health and Children.

16. McKeown, K. and Gilligan, R. (1991). "Child sexual abuse in the EHB region of Ireland in 1988: An analysis of 512 confirmed cases". *The Economic and Social Review*, 22, 101–134.

17. Kennedy, M.T. and Manwell, M.K.C. (1992). "The pattern of child sexual abuse in Northern Ireland". *Child Abuse Review*, 1 (2), 89–101.

18. Market Research Bureau of Ireland (1987). *Child Sexual Abuse in Dublin, Pilot Survey Report*. Dublin: Market Research Bureau of Ireland.

19. Irish Marketing Surveys (1993). *Childhood Experiences and Attitudes*. Dublin: Irish Marketing Surveys Ltd.

20. Jones, L.M. and Finkelhor, D. (2003). "Putting together evidence on declining trends in sexual abuse: a complex puzzle". *Child Abuse and Neglect*, 27, 133–135.

21. Dunne, M.P., Purdie, D.M., Cook, M.D., Boyle, F.M. and Najman, J.M. (2003). "Is child sexual abuse declining? Evidence from a population-based survey of men and women in Australia". *Child Abuse and Neglect*, 27, 141–152.

22. Coldrey, B.M. (1996). "The sexual abuse of children". *Studies*, 85 (340), 370–380.

23. Schultz, L.G. (1982). "Child Sexual Abuse in Historical Perspective". *Journal of Social Work and Human Sexuality*, 1, 21–35.

24. Kenny, M.C. and McEachern, A.G. (2000). "Racial, ethnic and cultural factors of childhood sexual abuse: A selected review of the literature". *Clinical Psychology Review*, 20 (7), 905–922.

25. Gelles, R.J. (1975). "The social construction of child abuse". *American Journal of Orthopsychiatry*, 45, 363–371.

26. Lyons, J.B. (1997). "Sir William Wilde's Medico-Legal Observations". *Medical History*, 42, 437–454.

27. Bolen, R.M. (2001). *Child Sexual Abuse: Its Scope and Our Failure.* New York: Kluwer Academic/Plenum Publishers.

28. Krugman, R.D. (1995) "From battered children to family violence: What lessons should we learn?" *Academic Medicine*, 70 (11), 964–967.

29. Lynch, M.A. (1985). "Child Abuse before Kempe: A Historical Literature Review". *Child Abuse and Neglect*, 9, 7–15.

30. Gleaves, D.H. and Hernandez, E. (1999). "Recent reformulations of Freud's development and abandonment of his seduction theory: Historical/scientific clarification or a continued assault on truth?" *History of Psychology*, 2 (4), 304–354.

31. Smart, C. (2000). "Reconsidering the recent history of child sexual abuse, 1910–1960". *Journal of Social Policy*, 29, 55–73.

32. Bender, L. and Blau, A. (1937). "The reaction of children to sexual relations with adults". *American Journal of Orthopsychiatry*, 7, 500–518.

33. Bender, L. and Grugett, A.E. (1952). "A follow-up report on children who had atypical sexual experiences". *American Journal of Orthopsychiatry*, 12, 825–837.

34. De Young, M. (1982). "Innocent seducer or innocently seduced? The role of the child incest victim". *Journal of Clinical Child Psychology*, 11, 56–60.

35. Caffey, J. (1946). "Multiple fractures in the long bones of infants suffering from chronic subdural haematoma". *Journal of Roentgenology*, 56 (2), 163–173.

36. Kempe, C.H., Silverman, F.N., Steele, B.F., Droegemuller, W. and Silver, H.K. (1962). "The battered-child syndrome". *Journal of the American Medical Association*, 181, 17–24.

37. Leventhal, J.M. (1999). "The Challenges of Recognising Child Abuse: Seeing is Believing". *Journal of the American Medical Association*, 281 (7), 657–659.

38. Goddard, C. (1996). "Read all about it! The news about child abuse". *Child Abuse Review*, 5, 301–309.

39. Green, A.H. (1993). "Child sexual abuse: Immediate and long-term effects and intervention". *Journal of the American Academy of Child and Adolescent Psychiatry*, 32 (5), 809–902.

40. Taylor, L. and Newberger, E.H. (1979). "Child Abuse in the International Year of the Child". *New England Journal of Medicine*, 301 (22), 1205–1212.

41. Department of Health (1983). *Guidelines on Procedures for the Identification, Investigation and Management of Non-accidental Injury to Children*. Dublin: Department of Health.

42. Department of Health (1987). *Child Abuse Guidelines: Guidelines on Procedures for the Identification and Management of Child Abuse*. Dublin: Department of Health.

43. Bays, J. and Chadwick, D. (1993). "Medical diagnosis of the sexually abused child". *Child Abuse and Neglect*, 17, 91–110.

44. Finkelhor, D. (1984). *Child Sexual Abuse: New Theory and Research*. New York: Free Press.

45. Olafson, E., Corwin, D.L. and Summit, R.C. (1993). "Modern history of child sexual abuse awareness: Cycles of discovery and suppression". *Child Abuse and Neglect*, 17, 7–24.

46. Silverman, F.N. (1972). "Unrecognized Trauma in Infants, the Battered Child Syndrome, and the Syndrome of Ambroise Tardieu". *Radiology*, 104, 337–353.

47. Summit, R. (1981). "Beyond belief: The reluctant discovery of incest". In Kilpatrick, M. (ed.). *Women in Context*. New York: Plenum.

48. Finkelhor, D. (1992). "What do we know about child sexual abuse?" Childhood Adversity Conference, Trinity College, Dublin, July 1992.

49. Gelles, R.J. and Cornell, C.P. (1983). "International perspectives on child abuse". *Child Abuse and Neglect*, 7, 375–386.

50. Kemp, A. (1998). *Abuse in the Family: An Introduction*. USA: Brooks/ Cole Publishing Company.

51. Naylor, B. (1989) "Dealing with child sexual assault: Recent developments". *British Journal of Criminology*, 29 (4), 395–407.

52. Hiner, N.R. (1979). "Children's rights, corporal punishment, and child abuse: Changing American attitudes, 1870–1920". *Bulletin of the Menninger Clinic*, 43 (3), 233–248.

53. O'Mahony, P. (1993). *Crime and Punishment in Ireland*. Dublin: Round Hall.

54. Thearle, M.J. and Gregory, H. (1988). "Child Abuse in Nineteenth Century Queensland". *Child Abuse and Neglect*, 12, 91–101.

55. McGee, C. and Westcott, H.L. (1996). "System abuse: Towards a greater understanding from the perspective of children and parents". *Child and Family Social Work*, 1, 169–180.

56. Pfohl, S. (1977). "The 'discovery' of child abuse". *Social Problems*, 24, 310–323.

57. McGuinness, C. (1993). *Report of the Kilkenny Incest Investigation*. Dublin: Government Stationery Office.

58. Sgroi, S.M. (1999). "The McColgan case: Increasing public awareness of professional responsibility for protecting children from physical and sexual abuse in the Republic of Ireland". *Journal of Child Sexual Abuse*, 8 (1), 113–127.

59. Dhooper, S.S., Royse, D.D. and Wolfe, L.C. (1991). "A statewide study of the public attitudes toward child abuse". *Child Abuse & Neglect*, 15 (1–2), 37–44.

60. Calvert J.F. and Munsie-Benson, M. (1999). "Public opinion and knowledge about childhood sexual abuse in a rural community". *Child Abuse & Neglect*, 23 (7), 671–682.

61. Finkelhor, D. (1994). "Current information on the scope and nature of child sexual abuse". *The Future of Children*, 4 (2), 31–53.

62. Waterman, C.K. and Foss-Goodman, D. (1984). "Child molesting: variables relating to attribution of fault to victims, offenders and non-participating parents". *Journal of Sex Research*, 20, 329–349.

63. Broussard, S.D. and Wagner, W.G. (1988). "Child sexual abuse: Who is to blame?" *Child Abuse and Neglect*, 12, 563–569.

64. Back, S. and Lips, H.M. (1998). "Victim age, victim gender and observer gender as factors contributing to attributions of responsibility". *Child Abuse and Neglect*, 22 (12), 1239–1252.

65. Daro, D.A. (1994). "Prevention of child abuse". *The Future of Children*, 4, 198-223.

66. National Commission of Inquiry into the Prevention of Child Abuse (1996). *Childhood Matters, Vol. 1, The Report*. London: Stationery Office.

67. West, D. (2000). "Paedophilia: Plague or panic?". *Journal of Forensic Psychiatry*, 11 (3), 511–531.

68. Blumer, H. (1971). "Social problems as collective behaviours". *Social Problems*, 18, 298–306.

69. Goddard, C. and Saunders, B.J. (2001). "Child abuse and the media". *Issues in Child Prevention*, No. 14. Australia: National Child Protection Clearing House. Available from: URL: http://www.aifs.org.au.

70. Nelson, B. (1984). *Making an Issue of Child Abuse*. Chicago: University of Chicago Press.

71. Franklin, B. (1989). "Wimps and bullies: Press reporting of child abuse", in Carter, P., Jeffs, T. and Smith, M. (eds.), *Social Work and Social Welfare Yearbook, Vol. 1*. Milton Keynes: Open University Press.

72. Horsfield, P. (1997). "Moral panic or moral action? The approximation of moral panics in the exercise of social control". *Media International Australia*, No. 85.

73. Kitzinger, J. (1996). "Media representations of sexual abuse risks". *Child Abuse Review*, 5, 318–333.

74. Kitzinger, J. (1988). "Defending innocence: Ideologies of childhood". *Feminist Review*, No. 28, 77–87.

75. Goddard, C. and Saunders, B.J. (2000). "The gender neglect and textual abuse of children in the print media". *Child Abuse Review*, 9, 37–48.

76. Wilczynski, A. and Sinclair, K. (1999). "A moral panic? Representations of child abuse in the quality and tabloid media". *Australian and New Zealand Journal of Criminology*, 32 (3), 262–284.

77. Katz, J. (1987). "What makes crime 'news'?". *Media Culture and Society*, 9, 47–75.

78. Cameron, P. and Cameron, K. (1998). "What proportion of newspaper stories about child molestation involves homosexuality"? *Psychological Reports*, 82 (3), 863–871.

79. Breen, M. (2000). "The good, the bad and the ugly: The media and the scandals". *Studies*, 89 (356), 332–338.

80. Ferguson, H. (1995). "The paedophile priest: A deconstruction". *Studies*, 84 (335), 247–256.

81. Gillespie, A. (2000). "UK Perspective". *Jurist*, July 24.

82. Costin, L.B., Karger, H.J. and Stoesz, D. (1996). *The Politics of Child Abuse in America*. New York: Oxford University Press.

83. McDevitt, S. (1998). "Media trends in child abuse reporting: The United States and the Republic of Ireland". *Journal of Child Centred Practice*, 5 (2), 11–28.

84. Marshall, W.L. and Laws, D.R. (2003). "A Brief History of Behavioral and Cognitive Behavioral Approaches to Sexual Offender Treatment: Part 2. The Modern Era". *Sexual Abuse: A Journal of Research and Treatment*, 15 (2), 93–120.

85. Fagan, P.J., Wise, T.N., Schmidt, C.W. and Berlin, F. (2002). "Pedophilia". *Journal of the American Medical Association*, 288 (19), 2458–65.

86. Finkelhor, D. and Araji, S. (1986). "Explanations of pedophilia: A four factor model". *The Journal of Sex Research*, 22 (2), 145–161.

87. Bagley, C. and King, K. (1990). *Child Sexual Abuse: The Search for Healing*. London: Routledge.

88. Clark, T.O. (1992). "Recidivist paedophiles: Treating the untreatable". *Australian Journal of Forensic Sciences*, 24 (1–2), 31–34.

89. Cole, S.A. (2000). "From the sexual psychopath statute to 'Megan's law': Psychiatric knowledge in the diagnosis, treatment, and adjudication of sex criminals in New Jersey, 1949–1999". *Journal of Historical Medicine and Allied Science*, 55 (3), 292–314.

90. Hanson, R.K. and Thornton, D. (1999). *Static '99: Improving actuarial risk assessments for sex offenders, User Report 99-02*. Ottawa: Department of the Solicitor General of Canada.

91. Laws, D.R. and Marshall, W.L (2003). "A Brief History of Behavioral and Cognitive Behavioral Approaches to Sexual Offenders: Part 1. Early Developments". *Sexual Abuse: A Journal of Research and Treatment*, 15 (2), 75–92.

92. Grossman, L.S., Martis, B. and Fichtner, C.G. (1999). "Are sex offenders treatable? A research overview". *Psychiatric Services*, 50 (3), 349–361.

93. Rosen, R.C. and Hall, K.S.K. (1992). "Behavioural Treatment Approaches for Offenders and Victims", in O'Donohue, W. and Geer, J.H. (ed.), *The Sexual Abuse of Children: Theory and Research*. New Jersey: Lawrence Erlbaum.

94. Department of Health (1966). *Commission of Inquiry on Mental Illness*. Dublin: Government Stationery Office.

95. Gilligan, R. (1989). "Policy in the Republic of Ireland: Historical and current issues in child care". In Carter, P., Jeffs, T. and Smith, M. (ed.), *Social Work and Social Welfare Yearbook, Vol. 1*. Milton Keynes: Open University Press.

96. O'Connor, P. (1992). "Child care policy: A provocative analysis and research agenda". *Administration*, 40 (3), 200–219.

97. Ferguson, H. (1993). "Child abuse inquiries and the Report of the Kilkenny Incest Case: A critical analysis". *Administration*, 41 (4), 385–410.

98. Peillon, M. (1987). "State and society in the Republic of Ireland: A comparative study". *Administration — Journal of the Institute of Public Administration of Ireland*, 35 (2), 190–212.

99. Pratt, J. (2000). "Sex crimes and the new punitiveness". *Behavioural Sciences and the Law*, 18 (2–3), 135–151.

100. Presser, L. and Gunnison, E. (1999). "Strange bedfellows: Is sex offender notification a form of community justice?" *Crime and Delinquency*, 45 (3), 299–315.

101. Zevitz, R.G. and Farkas, M.A. (2000). "Sex offender community notification: Managing high-risk criminals or exacting further vengeance". *Behavioural Sciences and the Law*, 18 (2–3), 375–391.

102. Philips, D.M. (1998). *Community notification as viewed by Washington's citizens*. Washington: Washington State Institute for Public Policy.

103. Plante, T.G. (ed.) (1999). *Bless Me Father for I have Sinned: Perspectives on Sexual Abuse Committed by Roman Catholic Priests*. Connecticut: Praeger.

104. Edgardh, K. and Ormstad, K. (2000). "Prevalence and characteristics of sexual abuse in a national sample of Swedish seventeen-year-old boys and girls". *Acta Paediatrica*, 89, 310–319.

105. MacIntyre, D. and Carr, A. (1999). "The effects of child sexual abuse". *Journal of Child Centred Practice*, 6 (1), 87–126.

106. Bartoi, M.G. and Kinder, B.N. (1998). "Effects of child and adult sexual abuse on adult sexuality". *Journal of Sex and Marital Therapy*, 24 (2), 103–122.

107. Fleming, J. (1998). "Childhood sexual abuse: An update". *Current Opinion in Obstetrics and Gynaecology*, 10, 383–386.

108. Lipovsky, J.A. and Kilpatrick, D.G. (1992). "The child sexual abuse victim as an adult". In O'Donohue, W. and Geer, J.H. (ed.), *The Sexual Abuse of Children: Theory and Research*. New Jersey: Lawrence Erlbaum.

109. Saywitz, K.J., Mannarino, A.P., Berliner, L. and Cohen, J.A. (2000). "Treatment for sexually abused children and adolescents". *American Psychologist*, 55 (9), 1040–1049.

110. Cuffe, S.P. and Shugart, M. (2001). "Child abuse and psychic trauma in children", in Vance, H. Booney, and Pumariega, A.J. (eds.), *Clinical Assessment of Child and Adolescent Behaviour*. New York: John Wiley & Sons, Inc.

111. Litrowinik, A.J. and Castillo-Cañez, I. (2000). "Childhood maltreatment: Treatment of abuse and incest survivors" in Snyder, C.R. and Ingram, R.E. (ed.) *Handbook of Psychological Change: Psychotherapy Processes and Practices for the 21st Century*. New York: John Wiley & Sons.

112. Brandon, S., Boakes, J., Glaser, D. and Green, R. (1998). "Recovered memories of childhood sexual abuse". *British Journal of Psychiatry*, 172, 296–307.

113. Kendall-Tackett, K., Myer Williams, L. and Finkelhor, D. (1993). "Impact of sexual abuse on children: A review and synthesis of recent empirical studies". *Psychological Bulletin*, 113 (1), 164–180.

114. Beitchman, J.H., Zucker, K.J., HoodGranville, J.E., daCosta, A. and Akman, D. (1991). "A review of the short term effects of child sexual abuse". *Child Abuse and Neglect*, 15 (4), 537–556.

115. Beitchman, J.H., Zucker, K.J., HoodGranville, J.E., daCosta, A., Akman, D., and Cassavia, E. (1992). "A review of the long-term effects of child sexual abuse". *Child Abuse and Neglect*, 16, 101–118.

116. Paolucci, O.E., Genius, M.L. and Violato, C. (2001). "A meta-analysis of the published research on the effects of child sexual abuse". *Journal of Psychology*, 135 (1), 17–36.

117. Finkelhor, D. (1990). "Early and Long-Term Effects of Child Sexual Abuse: An Update". *Professional Psychology: Research and Practice*, 21 (5), 325–330.

118. Browne, A. and Finkelhor, D. (1986). "Impact of child sexual abuse: A review of the research". *Psychological Bulletin*, 99, 66–77.

119. Hill, J., Davis, R., Byatt, M., Burnside, E., Rollinson, L. and Fear, S. (2000). "Childhood sexual abuse and affective symptoms in women: A general population study". *Psychological Medicine*, 30 (6), 1283–1291.

120. Lange, A., De Beurs, E., Dolan, C., Lachnit, T., Sjollema, S. and Hanewald, G. (1999). "Long-term effects of childhood sexual abuse". *Journal of Nervous and Mental Disease*, 187 (3), 150–158.

121. Mullen, P.E., Martin, J.L., Anderson, J.C., Romans, S.E. and Herbison, G.P. (1993). "Childhood sexual abuse and mental health in adult life". *British Journal of Psychiatry*, 163, 721–732.

122. Murphy, S.M., Kilpatrick, D.G., Amick-McMullan, A., Veronen, L.J., Paduhovich, J., Best, C.L., Villeponteau, L.A. and Saunders, B.E. (1988). "Current psychological functioning of child sexual assault survivors". *Journal of Interpersonal Violence*, 3, 55–79.

123. Sykes Wylie, M. (1993). "The shadow of a doubt". *Family Therapy Networker*, 17 (5), 18–29.

124. Pilkington, B. and Kremer, J. (1995). "A review of the epidemiological research on child sexual abuse". *Child Abuse Review*, 4, 191–205.

125. Glaser, D. (1991). "Treatment Issues in Child Sexual Abuse". *British Journal of Psychiatry*, 159, 769–782.

126. Koenig, H. and Larson, D. (2001). "Religion and mental health: Evidence for an association", *International Review of Psychiatry*, 13 (2), 67–78.

127. Myers, D.G. (2000). "The funds, friends and faith of happy people". *American Psychologist*, 55 (1), 56–67.

128. Walsh, K., King, M., Jones, L., Tookman, A. and Blizard, R. (2002). "Spiritual beliefs may affect outcome of bereavement: Prospective study". *British Medical Journal*, 324: 1551.

129. Kennedy, M. (2000). "Christianity and child sexual abuse — the survivors leading to change". *Child Abuse Review*. 9 (2), 124–141.

130. Reinert, D.F. and Smith, C.E. (1997). "Childhood sexual abuse and female spiritual development". *Counseling and Values*, 41, 235–245.

131. Finkelhor, D., Hotaling, T., Lewis, I.A. and Smith, C. (1989). "Sexual abuse and its relationship to later sexual satisfaction, marital status, religion and attitudes". *Journal of Interpersonal Violence*, 4, 379–399.

132. Kane, D., Cheston, S.E. and Greer, J. (1993). "Perceptions of God by survivors of child sexual abuse: An exploratory study in an under-researched area". *Journal of Psychology and Theology*, 21, 228–237.

133. Lawson, R., Drebing, C., Berg, G., Vincellette, A. and Penk, W. (1998). "The long-term impact of child abuse on religious behaviour and spirituality in men". *Child Abuse and Neglect*, 22 (5), 369–380.

134. Lebacqz, K. and Barton, R.G. (1991). *Sex in the Parish*. Louisville, Kentucky: John Knox Press (cited from McLaughlin, 1994, reference 136 below).

135. Fuentes, N. (1999). "Hear our cries: Victim-survivors of clergy sexual misconduct", in Plante, T.G. (ed) *Bless Me Father for I have Sinned: Perspectives on Sexual Abuse Committed by Roman Catholic Priests*. Connecticut: Praeger.

136. McLaughlin, B.R. (1994). "Devastated spirituality: The impact of clergy sexual abuse on the survivors' relationship with God and the Church". *Sexual Addiction and Compulsivity*, 1 (2), 145–158.

137. Rossetti, S. (1995). "The Impact of Child Sexual Abuse on Attitudes Toward God and the Catholic Church". *Child Abuse and Neglect*, 19 (12), 1469–1481.

138. Farrell, D.P. and Taylor, M. (2000). "Silenced by God — an examination of unique characteristics within sexual abuse by clergy". *Counselling Psychology Review*, 15 (1), 22–31.

139. Leigh, C., Rundle, K., McGee, H.M. and Garavan, R. (2003). *SENCS: Survivors' Experiences of the National Counselling Service for Adults who Experienced Childhood Abuse*. Dublin: National Counselling Service.

140. Durham, A. (2003). "Young men living through and with child sexual abuse: A practitioner research study", *British Journal of Social Work*, 33, 309–323.

141. Rossetti, S. (1997). "The effects of priest-perpetration of child sexual abuse on the trust of Catholics in priesthood, Church and God. *Journal of Psychology and Christianity*, 16 (3), 197–209.

142. Castelli, J. (1993). "Abuse of Faith: How to understand the crime of priest paedophilia". *US Catholic*. September, 6–15.

143. Cradock, C and Gardner, J.R. (1990). "Psychological intervention for parishes following accusations of child sexual abuse". In Rossetti, S. (eds.) (1990). *Slayer of the Soul: Child Sexual Abuse and the Catholic Church*. Connecticut: Twenty Third Publications.

144. Bacik, I., Maunsell, C. and Gogan, S. (1998). *The Legal Process and Victims of Rape: A comparative analysis of the laws and legal procedures relating to rape, and their impact upon victims of rape, in fifteen member states of the European Union*. Dublin: Dublin Rape Crisis Centre.

145. Hill, A. (2001). "'No-one else could understand': Women's experiences of a support group run by and for mothers of sexually abused children". *British Journal of Social Work*, 31, 385–397.

146. Grosz, C.A., Kempe, R.S. and Kelly, M. (2000). "Extrafamilial Sexual Abuse: Treatment for Child Victims and their Families". *Child Abuse and Neglect*, 24 (1), 9–23.

147. Allison, J. and Wrightsman, L. (1993). *Rape: The Misunderstood Crime*. California: Sage.

148. Esquilin, S. (1987). "Family responses to the identification of extra-familial child sexual abuse". *Psychotherapy in Private Practice*, 5, 105–113.

149. Foley, T.S. (1985). "Family response to rape and sexual assault". In Burgess, A.W. (ed.) *Rape and Sexual Assault*. New York: Garland.

150. Manion, I., Firestone, P., Cloutier, P., Ligezinska, M., McIntyre, J. and Ensom, R. (1998). "Child Extrafamilial Sexual Abuse: Predicting Parent and Child Functioning. *Child Abuse and Neglect*, 22 (12), 1285–1304.

151. Legg, A. and Legg, D. (1995) "The offender's family" in Myer Hopkins, N. and Laaser, M. (eds.), *Restoring the Soul of a Church: Healing Congregations Wounded by Clergy Sexual Misconduct*. Collegeville, MN: The Liturgical Press.

152. May, H. (2000). "Murders' relatives: Managing stigma and negotiating stigma". *Journal of Contemporary Ethnography*, 29(2), 198–221.

153. Lefley, H.P. (1987). "Family burden and family stigma in major mental illnesses". *American Psychologist*, 44(3), 556–560. (cited from May, 2000, reference 152 above)

154. Haskin, D.K. (1995) "Afterpastors in troubled congregations", in Myer Hopkins, N. and Laaser, M. (eds.) *Restoring the Soul of a Church: Healing Congregations Wounded by Clergy Sexual Misconduct*. Collegeville, MN: The Liturgical Press.

155. McDonough, K. (1995). "The effects of the misconduct crisis on non-offending clergy", in Myer Hopkins, N. and Laaser, M. (eds.) *Restoring the Soul of a Church: Healing Congregations Wounded by Clergy Sexual Misconduct*. Collegeville, MN: The Liturgical Press.

156. Hopkins, N.M. (1991). "Congregational intervention when the pastor has committed sexual misconduct". *Pastoral Psychology*, 39 (4), 247–55.

157. Hopkins, N.M. (1998). *Congregational response to clergy betrayals of trust*. Collegeville, MN: The Liturgical Press.

158. Vogelsang, J.D. (1993). "From denial to hope: A systematic response to clergy sexual abuse". *Journal of Religion and Health*, 32 (3), 197–208.

159. Conway, E., Duffy, E. and Shields, A. (1999). *The Church and Child Sexual Abuse: Towards a Pastoral Response*. Dublin: Columba Press.

160. Dardis, J. (2000). "Speaking of Scandal". *Studies*, 89 (356), 309–323.

161. Rossetti, S.J. (1993). "Parishes as victims of abuse". *Human Development*, 14 (4), 15–20.

162. Irish Marketing Surveys (1997). *Religious Confidence Survey*. Dublin: Irish Marketing Surveys.

163. McNulty, C. and Wardle, J. (1995). "Adult disclosure of sexual abuse: A primary cause of psychological distress?" *Child Abuse and Neglect*, 18 (7), 549–555.

164. Campbell, C., Ahrens, C. E., Sefl, T., Wasco, S.M. and Barnes, H.E. (2001). "Social reactions to rape victims: Healing and hurtful effects on psychological and physical health outcomes". *Violence and Victims*, 16 (3), 287–302.

165. Ullman, S.E. (1996). "Do social reactions to sexual assault victims vary by support provider". *Journal of Interpersonal Violence*, 11, 143–157.

166. Golding, J.M., Siegel, J.M., Sorenson, S.B., Burnam, M.A. and Stein, J.A. (1989). "Social support following sexual assault". *Journal of Community Psychology*, 17, 92–107.

167. Walters, C. and Spring, B. (1992). "How your Church can help victims of sexual assault find healing and hope". *Christianity Today*, 36, 330–333.

168. Sheldon, J. and Parent, S. (2002). "Clergy's attitudes and attributions of blame toward female rape victims". *Violence Against Women*, 8 (2), 233–256.

169. Sipe, R. (1999). "The problem of prevention in clergy sexual abuse". In Plante, T.G. (ed.) *Bless Me Father for I have Sinned: Perspectives on Sexual Abuse Committed by Roman Catholic Priests*. Westport, CT: Praeger.

170. Rossetti, S. (1996). *A Tragic Grace: The Catholic Church and Child Sexual Abuse*. Collegeville, MN: The Liturgical Press.

171. Parkinson, P. (1997). *Child Sexual Abuse and the Churches*. London: Hodder and Stoughton.

172. Longley, C. (2000). "Wrong mindset on sex abuse". *The Tablet*, 26 August.

173. De Fleurquin, L. (2001). *Paedophilia and Episkopen*. Paper presented at the Annual Conference of The Canon Law Society of Great Britain and Ireland, 17 May 2001, England.

174. McGrath, A. (2000). "Is Canon 1395 a cause of disrepute for the Church". *Irish Theological Quarterly*, 65, 51–60.

175. Griffin, B.F. (1991). "The Reassignment of a Cleric Who Has Been Professionally Evaluated and Treated for Sexual Misconduct with Minors: Canonical Considerations". *The Jurist*, 51 (2), 326–339.

176. Coriden, J.A. (1991). *Introduction to Canon Law*. Mahwah, NJ: Paulist Press.

177. Provost, J.H. (1995). "Offences against the Sixth Commandment: Toward a canonical analysis of canon 1395". *The Jurist*, 55, 632–663.

178. Paulson, J.E. (1988). "The Clinical and Canonical Considerations in Cases of Paedophilia: The Bishops' Role". *Studia Canonica*, 22, 77–124.

179. Proctor, J.G. (1987). "Clerical Misconduct: Canonical and Practical Consequences". *Canon Law of America Proceeding*, 49th Annual Meeting, pp. 227–224.

180. Beal, J.P. (2000). "At the Crossroads of Two Laws: Some Reflections on the Influence of Secular Law on the Church's Response to Clergy Sexual Abuse in the United States". *Louvain Studies*, 25, 99–121.

181. Ingels, G. (1999). "Dismissal from the Clerical State: An Examination of the Penal Process". *Studia Canonica*, 33, 169–212.

182. Harrison, R. and Stokes, H. (1992). *Diagnosing Organisational Culture*. Amsterdam: Pfeiffer & Co.

183. Hanson, R.K. and Bussière, M.T. (1998). "Predicting relapse: A meta-analysis of sexual offender recidivism studies". *Journal of Consulting and Clinical Psychology*, 66, 348–362.

184. Alexander, M.A. (1999). "Sexual offender treatment efficacy revisited". *Sexual Abuse: A Journal of Research and Treatment*, 11 (2), 101–114.

185. Plummer, K. (1995). *Telling Sexual Stories: Power, Change and Social Worlds*, London: Routledge.

186. Lane, D.A. (1998). *Reading the Signs of the Times: A Survey of Priests in Dublin*. Dublin: Veritas.

187. Wills, G. (2002). *Why I Am A Catholic*. Boston: Houghton Mifflin Company.

188. Dorr, D. (2000). "Sexual Abuse and Spiritual Abuse". *The Furrow*, 51 (10), 523–531.

189. Conway, E. (2002). "Touching our Wounds". *The Furrow*, 53 (5), 263–270.

190. Finkelhor, D. and Dziuba-Leatherman, J. (1992). "Children as victims of violence". *Paediatrics*, 94 (4), 413–420.

191. Behl, L.E., Conyngham, H.A. and May, P.F. (2003). "Trends in child maltreatment literature". *Child Abuse and Neglect*, 27, 215–229.

192. McKay, S. (1998). *Sophia's Story*. Dublin: Gill and Macmillan.

193. Gil, D. and Noble, J.H. (1969). "Public knowledge, attitudes and opinions about physical child abuse". *Child Welfare*, 49, 395–401.

194. Larsson, I. and Svedin, C.G. (2002). "Teachers' and parents' reports on 3- to 6-year-old children's sexual behaviour — a comparison". *Child Abuse and Neglect*, 26: 247–266.

195. Rind, B., Bauserman, R. and Tromovitch, P. (1998). "A meta-analytical Examination of Assumed Properties of Child Sexual Abuse using College Samples". *Psychological Bulletin*, 124 (1), 22–53.

196. Goode, E. and Ben-Yehuda, N. (1994). "Moral panics: Culture, politics, and social construction. *Annual Review of Sociology*, 20, 149–171.

197. Mendes, P. (2000). "Social Conservatism versus Social Justice: The portrayal of child abuse in the press in Victoria, Australia". *Child Abuse Review*, 9, 49–61.

198. Greenberg, D., Bradford, J., Firestone, P. and Curry, S. (2000). "Recidivism of child molesters: A study of victim relationship with the perpetrator". *Child Abuse and Neglect*, 24 (11), 1485–1494.

Appendix I

THE STRUCTURE OF THE CATHOLIC CHURCH IN IRELAND

The Second Vatican Council teaches that the one Church of Christ "constituted and organised as a society in the present world, subsists in the Catholic Church, which is governed by the successor of Peter and by the bishops in communion with him" (p. 357).[a] This Church exists in and consists of particular Churches; most of these in the Latin Church are called dioceses. A diocese is defined first and foremost in terms of its being a "portion of the people of God" entrusted to the care of a bishop (canon 369). There are 26 dioceses in Ireland whose boundaries were defined many centuries ago. These are gathered into four provinces which are presided over by one of the bishops, known as a Metropolitan, with the title of Archbishop. Some bishops also have an auxiliary bishop to help with the pastoral care of God's people. That pastoral care is effected through parishes which are defined in accordance with canon 515. Each parish has its own parish priest and sometimes one or more curates, or other priests in residence. Alongside the hierarchical structure of the Church, there exist many religious institutes of men and women each with its own internal government, autonomous from the government of diocesan bishops. In matters of public worship or apostolic activity of any kind, religious may be subject to the supervision of diocesan bishops. These institutes are dedicated to prayer and other work.

---

[a] Flannery, A. (ed) (1966). *Lumen Gentium 8*, Vatican Council II. Dublin: Dominican Publications.

Several Commissions and groups have been set up to advise and assist the Irish Bishops' Conference (based in St Patrick's College, Maynooth, County Kildare) in areas such as:

- Catechetics and Education
- Child Protection
- Communications
- Doctrine and Theology
- Ecumenism
- Emigrants
- European Affairs
- Finance
- Justice and Peace
- Laity
- Liturgy
- Missions
- Pastoral Commission (such as *ACCORD* and *CURA)*
- Pastoral Renewal
- Religious
- Research and Development
- Social Welfare
- Trócaire.

These Commissions and groups do not have an independent authority. For a more extensive list see www.catholicireland.net.

Tables A1 and A2 show the number of parishes, churches and the Catholic population in each diocese and the number of priests and religious in each diocese.

Table A1: Number of Parishes and Churches and the Catholic Population for each Diocese in Ireland (2002)

Diocese	Parishes	Churches	Catholic Population
Armagh	61	147	210,342
Dublin	200	238	1,041,100
Cashel & Emly	46	84	78,536
Tuam	56	131	121,536
Achonry	23	47	34,826
Ardagh	41	80	71,806
Clogher	37	86	86,047
Clonfert	24	47	32,600
Cloyne	46	107	129,823
Cork & Ross	68	124	220,000
Derry	53	104	228,508
Down & Connor	88	151	315,381
Dromore	23	48	63,200
Elphin	38	90	68,500
Ferns	49	101	100,446
Galway	40	72	98,157
Kerry	54	105	127,850
Kildare & Leighlin	56	117	183,105
Killala	22	48	38,115
Killaloe	58	133	110,170
Kilmore	36	95	53,995
Limerick	60	94	169,500
Meath	69	149	212,858
Ossory	42	89	76,049
Raphoe	33	71	80,500
Waterford & Lismore	45	85	135,879
Totals:	*1,368*	*2,643*	*4,088,829*

Source: Irish Catholic Directory, 2003 (Veritas)

Table A2: Number of Priests and Religious in each Diocese in Ireland (2002)

Diocese	Diocesan Priests		Religious Orders		
	Active in Diocese	Others*	Clerical	Brothers	Sisters
Armagh	129	24	58	41	362
Dublin	473	92	975	505	2,736
Cashel	107	14	20	8	185
Tuam	147	23	28	48	393
Achonry	43	13	0	0	95
Ardagh	74	12	5	9	272
Clogher	88	7	6	4	156
Clonfert	51	15	39	0	176
Cloyne	127	34	0	12	258
Cork & Ross	117	23	141	40	680
Derry	118	18	5	4	119
Down & Connor	190	37	71	40	305
Dromore	50	20	26	11	156
Elphin	57	13	6	3	130
Ferns	104	35	9	10	190
Galway	65	22	53	12	221
Kerry	98	30	10	18	306
Kildare & Leighlin	106	17	93	54	380
Killala	42	15	4	3	70
Killaloe	120	20	29	20	235
Kilmore	86	10	16	2	71
Limerick	130	20	70	25	348
Meath	113	21	119	30	267
Ossory	76	16	19	58	239
Raphoe	68	25	12	3	57
Waterford & Lismore	97	17	147	65	438
Totals:	*2,876*	*593*	*1,961*	*1,025*	*8,845*

* Refers to Priests of the Diocese retired, sick, on study leave, or working in other dioceses in Ireland and abroad.

Source: Irish Catholic Directory, 2003 (Veritas)

Appendix II

STUDY METHODOLOGIES

The research protocol was given ethical approval by the Research Ethics Committee of the Royal College of Surgeons in Ireland.

PHASE 1: NATIONAL SURVEY OF THE GENERAL PUBLIC

A general population survey was thought to be the best way to represent the views of the wider Church community on child sexual abuse by clergy. Such a survey could reflect all levels of faith and commitment to the Catholic Church; from those describing themselves as Catholics or as "lapsed" Catholics to those of other religions or those without a belief or faith.

Telephone Surveys

There are many potential methods available for a general population attitude survey. One option is the telephone survey. The telephone methodology is seen to provide many of the benefits of the face-to-face interviews (e.g. the ability to establish rapport and monitor for distress), yet has fewer "costs" associated with it. Both participant and interviewer well-being and safety can be more easily managed, as neither party need travel or put themselves in an unfamiliar (and possibly unsafe) situation. In addition, the telephone interview is seen as more "anonymous" than a face-to-face interview. Thus, the participant may be more assured about confidentiality and anonymity and more likely to report difficult experiences or diverse views about the subject matter under review. The response rate is generally higher than that of postal surveys, which often achieve response rates of approximately 30 per cent.

Although not a widely used option in Ireland, the use of telephones to conduct surveys is increasing. The Economic and Social Research Unit (ESRI) conducts monthly surveys of 1,400 randomly selected households as part of a European Union-wide research system assessing social, health and economic indicators. Participation rates of 62–64 per cent are reported as typical in these studies (James Williams, ESRI; personal communication). Some market research companies in Ireland also use telephone survey strategies. For prevalence studies of sexual violence, the telephone survey has evolved as the method of choice internationally over the past decade. It has recently been successfully used in a prevalence study of lifetime experiences of abuse: *Sexual Abuse and Violence in Ireland* (SAVI).[a] In that study of over 3,000 adults, the response rate was 71 per cent.

In summary, the relative benefits of the telephone survey methodology and its apparent acceptability in discussing sexual abuse with Irish people resulted in its selection as the methodology to be tested in a feasibility study.

Methods Used to Encourage Participation Prior to the Population Survey

Response rates are critical to the validity of a study. A low response rate severely limits the researcher's ability to generalise study results to a larger population. A variety of methods have been used in previous research to encourage participation even before a study commences. These include an introductory letter before a telephone call to set up an interview, or media advertisement via TV, radio, or newspapers. It was felt that advance media attention to this study might be counterproductive given the topic under consideration. The telephone calls made to the

---

[a] McGee, H., Garavan, R, de Barra, M., Byrne, J. and Conroy, R. (2002). *The SAVI Report: Sexual Abuse and Violence in Ireland*, Dublin: The Liffey Press.

general public were consequently "cold calls", i.e. the participant had no advance notice to expect a call or to know the topic of the study.

Methods Used to Encourage Agreement to Participate in the Survey

Several strategies for increasing the likelihood that potential participants would take part in a telephone survey and feel comfortable about their participation were adopted for this study. Those to be contacted needed assurance that the study was legitimate, was conducted by a reputable agency and that guarantees such as those about anonymity or confidentiality were genuine. To achieve this, introductory scripts were carefully developed for the interviewers to help them explain the purpose of the study, its importance, and how their telephone number was obtained. Several levels of explanation were developed so that the study could be authenticated for participants. A free-phone number to the research team was offered so participants could ring to authenticate the study before participation or recontact the team if they had any further questions or concerns (following study participation). Alternatively, they could telephone the main switchboard of the Royal College of Surgeons in Ireland. Where potential participants were anxious or unconvinced by interviewer reassurances about the study itself, the interviewer could offer to fax a letter confirming the study to the person's local Garda station. Interviewers also offered to call back those participants who indicated that the interviewer had reached them at an inconvenient or inappropriate time. Finally, participants who initially refused were followed-up with a "conversion call" to allow a second chance at participation. These calls are a standard part of telephone survey work and are explained in more detail in the section on study procedures.

Methods Used to Ensure Data Quality

The survey instrument was initially piloted by the research team. Measures were taken to maintain anonymity of the data collected. In order to ensure the quality of the data collected and to verify that calls were conducted in an ethical and professional manner, calls were monitored in two ways. First, tape recordings (of the interviewer's side only) of randomly selected telephone conversations were made and reviewed by the survey co-ordinator. The aim of this was to provide feedback on research techniques. Secondly, for a random selection of approximately 4 per cent of completed interviews, the co-ordinator conducted follow-up calls to verify that the original call had taken place and to ask the participant for an evaluation of the quality of the initial call.

Management of Participant Distress

The interview did not ask individuals about experiences of abuse but since the topic of the study had the potential to raise this issue for individuals, it was felt necessary to anticipate possible disclosures of abuse and to have procedures in place. All of those disclosing abuse (even if they did not appear distressed) were asked if they wished to avail of counselling services. Where participants said "yes", they were asked for their general geographic location (county of residence or elsewhere if preferred) and they were given the name of a contact person in the nearest sexual abuse service. The Dublin Rape Crisis Centre and the National Network of Rape Crisis Centres facilitated the study by agreeing to provide a priority appointment to any person contacting them saying that they were part of the "Church Abuse Study" (this procedure had been used successfully in the SAVI study). In addition, if the abuse disclosed involved clergy, participants were asked if they wished to report this abuse to the Child Protection Office of the Irish Bishops' Conference. Those who disclosed abuse were called approximately two days later to ensure that participation in the survey had not caused undue distress and to reiterate the availability of counselling. In this and other unpredictable and serious circumstances, it was arranged that the research team be consulted regarding the management of the situation. In each case, a detailed record of the management of the case was made.

Interviewer Selection, Training and Support

Researchers (N=3) worked a maximum five hours daily making telephone calls during the survey period. All telephone calls were made from the work setting (in a dedicated telephone survey room). This meant researchers had constant access to fellow interviewers and co-ordinators to allow immediate support and management of difficult problems if necessary. Regular supervision meetings were also held to allow time for debriefing.

Feasibility Study

The aim of the feasibility study was to assess the suitability of the interview schedule developed for evaluating the attitudes of the general public to child sexual abuse by clergy. The feasibility study was also necessary to find out if the planned approach would yield an acceptable response rate, i.e. would people participate in a study of this nature. The feasibility study was conducted during December 2001. A total of 51 participants (65 per cent response rate) participated in the feasibility study within the time period allocated. This response rate was deemed acceptable to proceed to a full telephone survey.

Conducting the Telephone Survey

Sample Considerations

The survey methodology was developed in consultation with the Survey Unit at the Economic and Social Research Institute (ESRI). Based on the feasibility study, a target sample size of approximately 1,100 members of the general public aged 18 years or older was estimated to be necessary to achieve the aims of the main study. In order to ensure that the sample would be representative of the general population, quota estimates by gender and age (young, middle, older age) were drawn up.

Number Generation

Telephone numbers were generated using a system called random digit dialling (RDD). This allows the widest coverage of telephone numbers by enabling contact with ex-directory numbers and with new numbers not currently listed in telephone directories. Only landline telephone numbers at private households were used.[b] Recent UK evaluations suggested this to be an appropriate strategy since the vast majority of households with mobile coverage have this in addition to landline telephones. Using both sets of numbers (landlines and mobiles) is problematic since it would give many households a double or greater chance of being included in sampling. Landline telephone coverage in private households in Ireland is very high at 95.6 per cent.[c]

Lists of telephone numbers were generated as follows using the RANSAM system of the ESRI. The area code was randomly selected from among possible Irish codes and possible "stems" were then identified. The "hundreds bank" method was used where a local telephone number was generated and the last two digits were used to create a full set of 100 numbers ranging from "XXXXX00" to "XXXXX99". A total of 200 sample points (i.e. unique numbers) were generated across the country and the 17 numbers generated within each of these produced clusters of numbers for contact.

Call Methodology

A strict telephone calling and outcome coding system was developed to standardise the methods. Each number dialled was allowed to ring ten times before cutting off. If there was no reply,

---

[b] Private household contact and telephone contact *per se* excludes the views of many more marginalised or institutional groups, e.g. homeless people or those in prison. This is a limitation of the study. However, it conforms to international standard practice.

[c] *Living in Ireland Survey* (2001). Dublin: Economic and Social Research Institute.

numbers were recalled later on the same day or in a different time-block (morning, afternoon or evening) on the next day. Engaged numbers were re-called after ten minutes. All numbers were called a maximum of ten times. After six unsuccessful calls, the call sheet was passed to a supervisor for review to formally consider the most likely strategy to achieve an answer. Where there were answer machines, messages were not left because this may have caused undue concern. Numbers with no replies after ten attempts were checked with Eircom Directory Enquiries to clarify whether they were disconnected, not yet assigned or were public telephones. Where a reply was received, the researcher first clarified whether she was in contact with a private household (only private households were included to maximise privacy for participants).

Conversion Calls

A methodology unique to telephone surveys is the "conversion call" for those people who have declined participation in an initial unsolicited call ("cold call"). The rationale is to provide an otherwise unavailable opportunity for the potential participant to reconsider participation. The aim is to do this in a way that is facilitating rather than coercing. Conversion calls were made by a different interviewer one to two days after the first call. The reasons for re-contact ("it provides you with the possibility to reconsider your decision to participate"), and an assurance that this was the only re-contact, were explained.

Survey Content and Measures

Table A2.1 provides an overview of the questionnaire items according to the main topics covered. There were 59 items in the interview schedule.

Table A2.1: National Survey Questionnaire Items and Topic Sections

Items	Topics
	Interview introduction and agreement to participate
1–21	Attitudes towards/trust in the Catholic Church
	Attitudes towards/trust in Catholic priests
	Assessment of/trust in Church's response to child sexual abuse
22–23	Effect of child sexual abuse by clergy on religious practices
24–31	Willingness for children to participate in Church activities/ associate with clergy and choose religious life
32–35	Belief in God
	Relationship/trust in God
36–37	Estimates of the prevalence of child sexual abuse by clergy
38–39	Quality of clergy (past and present)
	Quality of Catholic Church (past and present)
40–42	Origin of knowledge about child sexual abuse
	Origin of knowledge about child sexual abuse by clergy
	Assessment of media coverage of child sexual abuse
	Assessment of media coverage of child sexual abuse by clergy
43–44	Effect of child sexual abuse by clergy on how clergy are judged
	Effect of child sexual abuse by clergy on the Catholic Church
	Estimation of the number of clergy convicted of sexual offences against children
45–49	Awareness of actions taken by the Catholic Church to address the problem of child sexual abuse by clergy
	Awareness of Church guidelines on child sexual abuse
	Opinions on who is responsible for the occurrence and management of child sexual abuse by clergy
	Suggestions for ways the Catholic Church could help those who have been abused
50–57	General demographic characteristics of participant
58–59	Religious denomination of participant
	Attendance at religious services by participant

Items 1–10, 12–22, 28–31, 33–39 and item 41 were adapted with permission from a US survey with a similar focus (Rossetti, 1995[d]; 1997[e]). Rossetti organised these items into several themes based on factor analysis. These themes are:

- Assessment of/trust in the Church's response
- Commitment to Church leadership
- Idealisation of priests
- Trust in priests
- Trust in/relationship with God
- Evaluation of the Church
- Tolerance of priest perpetrators.

Items 42 (d), 43 & 44 and item 59 were adapted, with permission, from the Irish Marketing Survey's 1997 Religious Confidence Survey. These allow comparison with previous studies.

Interview Structure

Introduction. The first section was a standardised survey introduction. Key characteristics, such as who was conducting the study, its purpose and its confidential and voluntary nature were outlined. Following agreement to participate, the participant's present availability and privacy (i.e. not being overheard) were checked and the participant's age (i.e. must be over 18 years) were confirmed.

Items 1–21. This was the largest section of the interview. The statements in this section asked about attitudes towards the Catholic Church generally, towards clerical perpetrators of child

---

[d] Rossetti, S. (1995). "The Impact of Child Sexual Abuse on Attitudes Toward God and the Catholic Church". *Child Abuse and Neglect*, 19 (12): 1469–1481.

[e] Rossetti, S.J. (1997). "The Effects of Priest-Perpetration of Child Sexual Abuse on the Trust of Catholics in Priesthood, Church and God". *Journal of Psychology and Christianity*, 16(3): 197–209.

sexual abuse and towards the management of child sexual abuse by the Catholic Church. All of these items (except item 11) were adapted, with permission, from Rossetti (1995; 1997). Some statements were modified slightly for use with an Irish population (e.g. "Catholic" was placed before the word "priest" and "Church", and "neighbourhood" was used instead of "parish") since the questions would also be asked of non-Catholics. The Rossetti study dealt only with Catholic respondents.

Items 22–23. Item 22 (taken from Rossetti) asked if cases of child sexual abuse by clergy had affected the respondent's religious practices. If yes, participants were asked how they had been affected (e.g. time spent praying, attendance at religious services).

Items 24–31. Willingness to allow one's children to participate in Church activities was evaluated by these items. Items 24–27 asked if the participant had children, if they were of school-going age, the age range and the number of boys and girls. Items 28–31 asked the participant if they would be pleased if their child became an altar-server, if they would permit their child to go to a Catholic summer camp or holiday with a priest and if they would be pleased if their child wanted to be a priest. For participants who did not have children questions were put hypothetically (i.e. "If you had a child").

Items 32–35. Participants were asked if they believed in "a God" and if so, what was the nature of their relationship with God.

Items 36–37. Two items evaluated respondent estimates of the prevalence of child sexual abuse by clergy. They were asked to estimate the percentage of clergy involved in the sexual abuse of children and to estimate the percentage of children sexually abused by clergy. They were also asked to compare clergy to other men in society and to estimate whether they abused children more, less or the same as other men.

Items 38–39. Participants were asked to judge the quality of Catholic clergy and the quality of the Catholic Church today, compared to the past.

Items 40–42. This section focused on the source of the public's knowledge about child sexual abuse in general and child sexual abuse by clergy. Participants were also asked to judge whether media coverage of child sexual abuse by clergy was damaging or beneficial (and for whom) and if it was fair.

Items 43–44. Participants were asked if they thought that clergy, as a result of child sexual abuse by clergy, had been unfairly judged and if the Church had been damaged. If they answered yes, they were asked if they thought this damage was permanent. They were also asked to estimate the number of clergy convicted of sex offences against children in Ireland in the last ten years.

Items 45–49. These items examined awareness of actions taken by the Church to address the problem of child sexual abuse by clergy, evaluated perceived responsibility for the occurrence and management of child sexual abuse by clergy and sought opinions on what the Church should be doing to help those who have been abused.

Items 50–57. Participant gender, age, occupation and marital status were obtained.

Items 58–59. The last survey items asked participants about their own religious denomination (if any) and if they had always been a member of this identified religion or if they had changed. They were also asked about frequency of attendance at religious services.

Conclusion. The concluding section of the survey was also standardised. Participants were thanked for their participation, were given the opportunity to make further comments and were told they could contact the research team via the freephone number.

Survey Procedures

Data collection began on 22 January 2002 and was completed by 31 May 2002. The average duration of telephone interviews was 15 minutes.

Response Rate

Over 3,700 unique telephone numbers were contacted for the study. Call outcomes were categorised and the response rate calculated using international standards. Figure A2.1 outlines the broad categories of call outcomes and the number of each type obtained.

Figure A2.1: Profile of Unique Telephone Numbers Called and Interviews Conducted for the General Population Survey

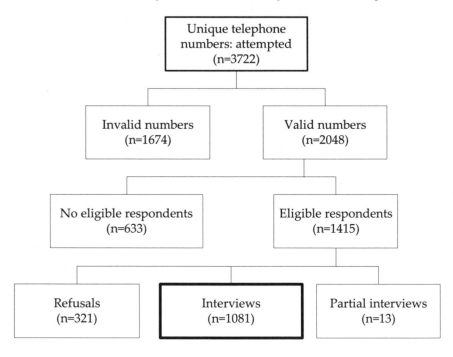

Of the 3,722 unique telephone numbers called, 2,048 were valid. Invalid numbers included disconnected numbers, commercial numbers, faxes and numbers where there was no reply after ten attempts. The valid numbers were categorised into eligible (n =1415) and ineligible respondents (n= 633). Ineligible respondents were private households where the person contacted was unable to take part in the interview. Reasons for this included language barriers, respondent impairments (e.g. deafness), major life events (e.g. recent bereavement) or temporary absences for the duration of the study. Of the 1,415 eligible respondents, 1,081 completed interviews, 321 refused and there were 13 partially completed interviews. The overall response rate for the study was 76 per cent. This is notably high for a public survey in Ireland. Overall, the high response rate suggests that the results can be considered to represent the views of the general population.

PHASE 2: PERSONAL EXPERIENCE STUDY

A qualitative research method employing in-depth interviews was deemed the most appropriate method to examine the experiences of those abused and their families, convicted clergy and their families and clergy and Church personnel in general. Qualitative interviewing uses a biographical or narrative approach rather than a formal question-and-answer format and aims to bring the researcher closer to the individual's perspective on issues.[f]

Sampling and Access

A total of 48 individuals were interviewed; the study sample included:

- Individuals who had experienced child sexual abuse by clergy (7)[g]

- Members of their families (3)

---

[f] Chamberlain, K., Stephens, C. and Lyons, A.C. (1997). "Encompassing Experience: Meanings and Methods in Health Psychology". *Psychology and Health*, 12, 691–709.

[g] Another individual who experienced sexual abuse as an adult was also interviewed.

- Clergy convicted of sexual offences against children (8) and their family members (5) and colleagues (4)

- Clergy and lay people who work for the Church (20).

Sampling becomes more difficult the more sensitive the topic under investigation. A purposive sampling technique known as networking or "snowballing" was initially used to recruit individuals to participate in the study. This sampling technique begins with an initial set of contacts, "gatekeepers", who pass on information (a study information sheet) about the study to the target population. It is recognised as having considerable potential for the sampling of rare and vulnerable populations.[h] The study information sheet outlined the purpose of the study; the groups who were being interviewed for the study; what participation in the study necessitated; that participation was confidential; and how the research team could be contacted. A freephone number was also provided to facilitate contact with the researcher.

Initial contacts for individuals who had experienced abuse by clergy were:

- Church delegates[i]

- *Faoiseamh* counsellors[j]

- Non-delegate clergy

- Media personnel.

A total of 95 information sheets were sent out to these initial contacts; 72 to delegates, 10 to *Faoiseamh* counsellors, 12 to individual clergy and one to a member of the media. Eight people responded

---

[h] Lee, R. M. (1993). *Doing Research on Sensitive Topics*. London: Sage.

[i] Church delegates are individuals (usually a priest or religious) nominated by each diocese or Religious Order to respond and manage allegations of child sexual abuse against a priest or religious

[j] Faoiseamh was set up by CORI (Conference of Religious of Ireland) in February 1997 to listen to and, if required, arrange face-to-face counselling with independent counsellors, for those abused by members of Religious Orders.

and were interviewed. By definition all had reported their abuse to Church authorities. Two have not reported the abuse to the civil authorities, four have investigations ongoing and two have had civil investigations and the abusers have been convicted.

Those individuals who experienced abuse and participated in interviews were asked if they were willing to invite a family member/significant other to participate in the study to discuss the family member's perspective. Where they agreed, they were given an information sheet to pass on to the designated person. Three people interviewed declined this offer. A total of six information sheets were distributed. Three family members responded and participated in the study.

Delegates and other clergy were used as initial contacts for clergy convicted of sexual offences against children. A total of 26 information sheets were sent to clergy: those currently serving prison sentences (n=10) and those who had either received a suspended sentence or who had served their sentence (n=16). Permission to interview clergy in prison was granted by the Director General of Irish Prisons following review of the study protocol by their Research Ethics Committee. Eight convicted clergy were interviewed for the study.

Clergy convicted of sexual offences against children who were interviewed were also asked if they were willing to invite a family member/significant other to participate in the study to give their perspective. If agreeable they were given an information sheet to pass on to the designated person. Four declined to ask any of their family members. Information sheets (n=10) were also forwarded to a support group for family members of convicted sex offenders and to Church delegates (n=9). A total of 23 information sheets were provided for relatives of convicted clergy. Five family members of convicted clergy were interviewed.

Clergy and lay people who work for the Church were contacted directly and asked to participate in the study. The clergy in this group consisted of priests, religious (male and female), bishops, retired bishops, and religious superiors/provincials. Some of the clergy were delegates or were priests who had worked in the

same parish as convicted priests. The twenty-four clergy interviewed were selected because of their varied roles and experience
in dealing with cases of child sexual abuse by clergy.

National Random Sample of Those Abused as Children by Clergy

Random sampling is generally not an option for research on sensitive topics since individuals concerned are often difficult to identify. However, this study was able to obtain a random sample of
individuals from the general population who had been sexually
abused by clergy in Ireland. This sample had already taken part in
a national prevalence study on sexual abuse and violence (SAVI).
The SAVI study involved 3,120 anonymous telephone interviews
with adult members of the general public in Ireland. Of those
3,120 adults, thirty-nine reported experiences of sexual abuse by
clergy. Thirty of these individuals reported they were abused as
children (less than 17 years).

Experiences of abuse ranged from episodes in the 1940s to the
1980s. Most (22 of 30) of the cases reported involved boys and in
almost half of the cases (12 of 30) the abuse began before the person was 10 years old. Half of the cases (14 of 29 where duration
was known) involved more than one episode of abuse. Physical
contact was involved in most cases with 2 cases involving ongoing penetrative abuse. Most cases of abuse of boys (16 of 22) occurred in schools while no girls were abused in school settings.

At the end of the original SAVI interviews, participants were
asked if they were willing to be contacted for future studies.
Twenty-five of the 30 people abused by clergy as children agreed.
With notification to the original sponsors of the SAVI study and
following Research Ethics Committee approval, these individuals
were re-contacted by the director of the SAVI Project (Hannah
McGee) and invited to participate in the present study.

As in the original study, potential SAVI participants were contacted by phone. It was explained that this was a separate study
from SAVI; that its aims were to better understand child sexual
abuse by clergy and to inform recommendations for improved

management in the future; and that the Catholic Church had funded the study. Those contacted were invited to consider whether they wished to be involved in this separate study and were invited to take the time needed to make their decision about participation. Individuals were preferentially interviewed by telephone at a time suitable to them (to preserve anonymity as in the original study). Where those willing to take part preferred a different form of interview, this was facilitated. A total of 14 individuals (who originally participated in the SAVI study) were interviewed by telephone for this study. One individual also requested a face-to-face interview and this was facilitated.

Management of Participant Distress and Disclosure of Ongoing Abuse

Research on sensitive topics raises ethical concerns such as the extent to which participation in the research may encroach on people's lives. The invitation to participate in research may be regarded intrusive because it involves dealing with areas that are private, stressful or emotionally charged.[k]

To facilitate participants taking part in the face-to-face interview study, they were offered a choice of venue for interview. Participants were also advised that they could withdraw from the interview at any stage. Interviews were taped with participant permission. The interviewer monitored and managed distress as necessary during the interview (e.g. asking the participant if they would like to change the subject, return to it later or reschedule the interview). Interviews concluded with a period of discussion on less sensitive issues as a way of disengaging from the serious topics being addressed to facilitate participant well-being. Participants could contact the interviewer following the interview if necessary. They were telephoned two to three days following the interview, with permission, to check on their well-being.

A contact number/address for sexual abuse services (in their own geographic area or elsewhere if preferred) was available if

---

[k] Lee, R. M. (1993). *Doing Research on Sensitive Topics*. London: Sage.

participants asked for counselling. This ranged from freephone telephone services through *Faoiseamh* (the CORI[1]-funded independent counselling service) to priority appointments with sexual abuse services in their geographical area.

Confidentiality and Anonymity

The study information sheet, provided in advance for participants, explained the confidential and anonymous nature of participation. Potential participants were advised that interviews would be tape-recorded (with agreement) and that these tapes would be destroyed once transcribed. Names would not be recorded on transcripts of interviews. No names or any other identifying information would be used in the final report.

Procedure

Intending participants contacted the interviewer directly by telephone having received the study information sheet. Interviews were arranged at a time and place to suit the participant. This was usually the person's home. Some chose to be interviewed at the Royal College of Surgeons in Ireland. Clergy currently serving custodial sentences were interviewed in prison. Participants were required to sign a consent form prior to interview.

All face-to-face interviews were conducted with the same interviewer. Interviews lasted from one to four hours depending on the participant's desire to talk about their experiences. Almost all interviews (n=44) were tape-recorded. When transcribed, the tapes were destroyed. Interviews were conducted between February 2002 and March 2003.

Data analysis

The interview schedule was designed to focus on the following study objectives:

---

[1] Conference of Religious in Ireland.

- To examine the psychological and social impact, and the impact on faith, of child sexual abuse by clergy

- To examine the experience of disclosure and response in relation to child sexual abuse by clergy.

Qualitative analysis involves data reduction and this is achieved through a process of selecting, condensing and transforming the data. Transcribed interviews and field notes were initially examined using the three main interview schedule headings:

- The experience of disclosure and the response received

- Experiences with Church personnel and overall management by the Church

- The personal impact of experiences.

All the text from transcribed interviews was coded on paper using an open-coding method. Coding is a way of transforming raw data (i.e. text) into data for analysis, organising data into manageable sections and putting similar sections of data together. This open-coding involved assigning sections of text from each interview to one of the three main interview schedule headings. This was done systematically, by reading through each interview and labelling large sections of text (i.e. D + R for the experience of disclosure and response received, CP + CM for experiences with Church personnel and management by the Church and PI for personal impact) until all of the text in each interview was labelled according to these descriptive codes. This first phase of coding organised the data into three large portions of text. These portions were then coded separately into new subcodes. Coding at this stage was exhaustive (i.e. all text assigned to at least one code) and generated a number of codes. New subcodes were created when text for existing codes could no longer be found. Subcodes that occurred across interviews were deemed central and were pulled together to form themes. In the interest of reliability, a second person coded a sample of interviews and codes were compared. In relation to validity, one study participant, who had experienced child sexual abuse, was asked to review the report in draft form.

PHASE 3: POSTAL SURVEY OF CHURCH PERSONNEL WITH RESPONSIBILITY FOR MANAGING CASES OF CLERICAL ABUSE

Both bishops and delegates play an important role in the management of complaints of child sexual abuse against clergy. Time constraints meant that it was not possible to interview all Church delegates and bishops (current and retired). In order to have as many representative perspectives as possible, a postal survey of all delegates, all members of the Irish Bishops' Conference and all retired bishops in Ireland was conducted. The survey was completed over a six-month period (July to December 2002).

Sample and Access

All current religious and diocesan delegates, members of the Irish Bishops' Conference and retired bishops were surveyed. At the time of the study there were 50 diocesan and 103 religious delegates in Ireland. There were 33 members of the Irish Bishops' Conference (25 bishops and 8 auxiliary bishops) and there were 11 retired bishops in Ireland. Names and addresses for delegate and bishops were provided by Church sources.

Survey Procedure

Diocesan delegates were receiving training at the time of the survey so questionnaires and an explanatory letter were distributed at these training sessions. Questionnaires were posted to religious delegates. Questionnaires were also posted directly to all bishops. Many delegates and bishops had already been introduced to the study and the researchers at a briefing meeting in May 2001.

Survey Content and Measures

Delegate Questionnaire

The delegate questionnaire consisted of two main sections. The first section pertained exclusively to the delegate role while the second section examined perceptions of the Catholic Church's organisational culture. The first section contained a mix of 14 open-ended and closed items (fixed-choice responses, e.g. agree, disagree etc.) designed by the research team. The first three questions examined delegates' experience of clerical child sexual abuse cases and their satisfaction with their management of them. The next set of questions consisted of a list of statements about attitudes on the role of delegate. Respondents had to choose their answer from a five-point Likert-scale ranging from strongly agree to strongly disagree. Questions 5 and 6 were open-ended and examined the strengths and weaknesses of the *Framework Document*. Delegates were asked to rate the challenges pertaining to their role and to choose the most salient support options. The questionnaire also contained a series of questions on the personal and spiritual effects of child sexual abuse on the respondent. The last question in this section examined delegates' perceptions of the future of the clerical child sexual abuse issue for the Catholic Church in Ireland.

The second main section of the delegate questionnaire was *Diagnosing Organisational Culture*.[m] This instrument contains 15 items that examine different aspects of organisational culture ranging from decision-making processes to assignment of tasks and motivation. Overall, this questionnaire establishes the most dominant and least dominant existing organisational culture within an organisation and the organisational culture most and least preferred by respondents. Respondents were required to rank four possible response outcomes from 1-4 (4 represented the most dominant existing and the most preferred organisational culture and 1

---

[m] Harrison, R. and Stokes, H. (1992). *Diagnosing Organisational Culture*. Amsterdam: Pfeiffer & Co.

represented the least dominant existing and least preferred organisational culture). Two rankings were required: one to reflect the organisational culture that currently exists and the second time to reflect the preferred organisational culture.

Bishop Questionnaire

As with the delegate questionnaire, the questionnaire sent to bishops was divided into two sections. The first section had of a mix of 22 open-ended and closed items designed by the research team. The first five questions covered demographic information relating to age, length of tenure, type of experience with cases of clerical child sexual abuse and satisfaction with their management of them. Bishops were then asked to rate the challenges pertaining to their role and to choose the most salient support options as in the delegate questionnaire. Bishops were asked to describe the personal and spiritual effects of child sexual abuse. They were also asked about organisational aspects that may have created problems in dealing with abuse cases and about their management and leadership training and experience. Perceptions on the future of the issue of child sexual abuse by clergy were assessed. Section 2 of the survey consisted of Harrison and Stokes's (1992) *Diagnosing Organisational Culture* instrument.

Response Rate

Following invitations and one postal reminder, completed questionnaires were received from 32 of 50 diocesan delegates (a response rate of 64 per cent) and 70 of 103 religious delegates (a response rate of 68 per cent). Thus, from a total sample of 153 delegates, 102 took part (a response rate of 67 per cent). Thirty-five of 44 bishops replied (response rate of 80 per cent). Across the two groups the response rate was 70 per cent. Postal surveys of the general public, even with follow-up reminders, typically achieve much lower response rates. The high response rate for this survey suggests that the results can be considered as broadly representative of the views of delegates and bishops.

Appendix III

CHILDCARE POLICY AND LEGISLATION IN IRELAND

This Appendix is a brief chronological outline of childcare policy and legislation pertaining to sexual offences in Ireland.

CHILDCARE LEGISLATION

National Society for the Prevention of Cruelty to Children and The Cruelty to Children Act 1889

Procedures and policies on child neglect, orphaned children and the removal of children from their homes were practically non-existent in late nineteenth- and early twentieth-century Ireland.[a] In 1889, the Irish branch of the NSPCC was founded (now the ISPCC). The Cruelty to Children Act criminalised child cruelty and gave inspectors of the ISPCC new powers to remove children who were being neglected or mistreated by parents or guardians. By the 1930s, there were 26 inspectors covering Ireland's 32 counties.[b] The main objective was not removing children from parents but enforcing parents' responsibilities towards their children. Only about 2 per cent of all children came into contact with the ISPCC and few

---

[a] Skehill, C., O'Sullivan, E. and Buckley, H. (1999). "The nature of child protection practices: an Irish case study". *Child and Family Social Work*, 4, 145-152.

[b] Ferguson, H. (1996). "Protecting Irish Children in Time: Child Abuse as a Social Problem and the Development of the Child Protection System in the Republic of Ireland". *Administration*, 44 (2): 5–36.

children were actually removed from parents. Children who were taken into care were usually placed in industrial or reformatory schools or in homes and family services established by Catholic religious orders with State funding. Children could be placed in an institution by voluntary agencies or by concerned individuals such as the local parish priest with notification to the State.

Children from institutions could be "boarded out", i.e. fostered by families. Private arrangements for fostering (called "at nurse") could be organised by families themselves. From 1902, an Inspector of Boarded Out Children was appointed to regulate the fostering of children and to visit children in institutions. Assessment of potential foster parents largely consisted of one visit and a letter of recommendation from the local parish priest. Up to the 1940s, assistance officers monitored foster homes and from the 1940s on, public health nurses, in addition to their other duties, visited these boarded-out children. The first report of the ISPCC, published in 1957, recorded a few cases of assault, some incest and many cases of neglect.[c]

Children Act, 1908

Offences against children and offences by children were covered by the Children Act 1908. A child was defined as a person under 15 years of age. It was an offence under this Act for a person over the age of 17 who had custody, charge or care of a child to assault, abandon or expose the child to suffering, injury or mental derangement. The Act made provisions for a child to be taken to a place of safety, by a constable, if there was reason to believe that an offence was committed against the child. At the time the Act was passed, a place of safety was any workhouse, police station, hospital or other "suitable place".[d] Industrial and Reformatory

---

[c] Ferguson, H. (1996). "Protecting Irish Children in Time: Child Abuse as a Social Problem and the Development of the Child Protection System in the Republic of Ireland". *Administration*, 44 (2): 5–36.

[d] Greene, D. (1979). "Legal aspects of non-accidental injury to children". *Administration*, 27(4): 460–474.

schools provided most childcare for orphaned, homeless and "delinquent" children.[e] Removal of the child was temporary until the child was committed to the care of a relative or other fit person by the court. The organisation named in a Fit Person Order retained legal custody of the child until they were 16. Up until 1970, the ISPCC investigated and processed most childcare cases coming before the courts. The Act was amended by the Children Act 1934, 1941, and 1989 and the Children (Amendment) Acts 1949 and 1957.[f] Parts of the Children Act 1908, as amended, formed the principal legislation for the protection and welfare of children until the Child Care Act 1991.

The Health Act 1970

The Health Act in 1970 established eight health boards (now ten) and recruited social workers and community care teams.[g] The State took the responsibility for childcare and protection from the ISPCC and the foundations of the present care system were established. This eventually developed into a more sophisticated, multidisciplinary childcare protection system.

The Children Act 1989

Although the health boards were established in 1970, they had no power under the 1908 Children Act to act as a "fit person". The 1989 Children Act was enacted to enable health boards to act as "fit persons".

---

[e] Richardson, V. (1999). "Children and Social Policy", in Quinn, S., Kennedy, P., O'Donnell, A. and Kiely, G. *Contemporary Irish Social Policy*. Dublin: University College Dublin Press.

[f] Shatter, A.J. (1997). *Family Law in the Republic of Ireland* (4th ed). Dublin: Butterworths.

[g] Ferguson, H. (1996). "Protecting Irish Children in Time: Child Abuse as a Social Problem and the Development of the Child Protection System in the Republic of Ireland". *Administration*, 44 (2): 5–36.

The Child Care Act 1991

The Child Care Act 1991 was the first comprehensive piece of child welfare legislation enacted since the foundation of the State.[h] Its central concern was the protection of children rather than offences committed against or by the child as in the Children Act 1908. It addressed three main areas: child protection, alternative care for children who cannot remain at home and family support. The underlying principle of the Act is that each health board should be actively "promoting the welfare of children who are not receiving adequate care and protection". Health boards were now required to regularly review their support services for children and families. The Act was fully implemented between 1991 and 1995.

The Act recognised that the child should be cared for within the context of the family. Historically and constitutionally, the family has been considered the fundamental unit of society and has received considerable protection and support in Irish society and law. The provisions of the Act were based on the premise that it is in the best interest of a child to be raised by their own family. The emphasis was on "family support services" and only when all efforts to accommodate the child within the family failed should powers to remove the child be applied. However, for the first time the child was recognised as having individual rights. The rights of the child included the right to protection from abuse or other adversities threatening to development or welfare and the right, subject to age, to have due consideration given to their wishes and the right to accommodation when homeless.

Each health board was required to establish childcare committees to advise the board on the performance of its functions, consult with non-governmental bodies, review the needs of children and report to its health board on service provision. However, the health board was not obliged to accept the recommendations of the committee. A child was defined as a person under 18 unless they were then or had been married. The Act raised the age limit

---

[h] Gilligan, R. (1993). "The Child Care Act 1991: An Examination of its Scope and Resource Implications". *Administration*, 40 (4), 345–370.

for children to remain in care from 16 (the Children Act 1908) to 18 years of age. It improved intervention measures by introducing emergency care orders and supervision orders. Emergency care orders made provision for a health board to apply to the District Court to place a child under its care. However, the Gardaí may also enter a house, without a warrant, where there is an immediate risk to health or well-being of the child when there is insufficient time for the health board to apply to the courts for an Emergency Care Order. Once the child is removed to safety, the health board must then apply for an Emergency Care Order. Supervision Orders are where the District Court can authorise the health boards to visit a child's home regularly and may also require the parents of the child to take the child for medical or psychiatric examination, assessment or treatment. It also provides for the appointment of a non-legal guardian, *ad litem*, to represent the child in care proceedings.

State Guidelines on the Identification, Reporting and Management of Child (Sexual) Abuse

Six sets of guidelines on the identification, reporting and management of child abuse have been issued by the State. An Irish Committee on Non-Accidental Injury (NAI) to Children was established in 1975. The establishment of the Committee was influenced by the "Battered Child Syndrome" paper by Kempe et al., (1962). The *Report of the Committee on Non-Accidental Injury to Children*, which was published in 1976, recommended the need for the early identification of "battered children" through increased distribution of knowledge and training for professionals working with children. In response to these recommendations, the Department of Health issued the first set of formal guidelines to professionals on child protection in 1977 entitled *Memorandum on Non-Accidental Injury to Children*.

In 1980 the second set of guidelines, entitled *Guidelines on the Identification and Management of Non-Accidental Injury to Children* were issued. In these guidelines, the monitoring and management co-ordination of non-accidental injury to children was the responsibility of the health boards while the relevant Director of Community Care or Medical Officer of a Health Board was given overall responsibility for cases within their health boards. A checklist was provided for professionals to aid the identification of cases and the case conference method was espoused as a valuable and effective method for dealing with child abuse.

The third set of guidelines, *Guidelines on Procedures for the Identification, Investigation and Management of Non-Accidental Injury to Children*, were issued in 1983. Identification and management of NAI remained unchanged from the 1980 guidelines but there were new sections clarifying the investigating role of the general practitioner and hospitals and the emphasis on inter-agency and inter-professional co-ordination was increased. In addition, it was recommended that parents be kept informed of decisions being made in relation to their children. The most significant aspect of the 1983 guidelines was that for the first time in official guidelines, reference was made to "injury resulting from sexual abuse". However, because it was mentioned within the context of physical abuse there were no specific guidelines on the identification and management of child sexual abuse.

In 1987, *Guidelines on Procedures for the Identification, Investigation and Management of Child Abuse* were issued by the Department of Health. These guidelines used the term "child abuse" rather than "non-accidental injury". The term child abuse included physical, sexual and emotional abuse and neglect. The 1987 guidelines made it clear that, although the procedures to be followed when dealing with child sexual abuse do not differ from those of the 1983 general guidelines, the identification and validation of child sexual abuse is different. This signified a development in official guidelines as the 1983 guidelines made no provision for the distinction between sexual abuse and other forms of abuse. The 1987 guidelines defined not only the roles of the caring professions but also provided guidance on the roles of teachers, Gardaí and others in contact with children. Under the guidelines, a health board was expected to notify the Gardaí of any alleged case of child abuse.

In 1995, agreement was reached between health boards and the Gardaí whereby social workers and Gardaí would be required to notify each other of suspected cases of child abuse. The report, *Notification and Reporting of Suspected Cases of Child Abuse*, was issued in 1995. These guidelines were particularly prescriptive about the handling of suspected cases of child abuse. The emphasis was on accountability. Employees of a health board who suspected that a child had been abused or neglected were now required to notify the Gardaí even before confirmation of the abuse was available. This 1995 document on procedures amended the original 1987 Department of Health guidelines.

In 1998, the Minister of State at the Department of Health and Children established a working group to review the guidelines on procedures for the identification, investigation and management of child abuse and the notification of suspected cases of child abuse between health boards and Gardaí. In 1999, the Department of Health and Children issued new guidelines (the sixth and current set of guidelines), *Children First: National Guidelines for the Protection and Welfare of Children*. The aims of the guidelines are ". . . to assist people in identifying and reporting child abuse and to improve professional practice in both statutory and voluntary agencies and organisations that provide services for children and families". Reporting procedures for child services and the general public are outlined. If a person suspects that a child is being abused they are advised to contact their local health board. However, in an emergency, the report should be made to the Gardaí. Guidelines on the responses of the health board and Gardaí in terms of assessment, management and investigation are also outlined. There are additional guidelines for vulnerable children including children with disabilities, homeless children and children in foster and residential care. Procedures for dealing with allegations of abuse against employees and volunteers are outlined. These include the employer's responsibility to report allegations of abuse to statutory authorities. The guidelines also address training, supervision and support issues for child protection workers.

INQUIRIES

State inquiries concerning abuse are included in this outline as, in most instances, findings from inquiries resulted in legislative change or development.

Cussen Report, 1936

The first post-Independence inquiry into how industrial and reformatory schools were run in Ireland was commissioned by the Minister for Education in 1936. Although the report did express some concern regarding training, education, lack of local authority support and the stigma attached, it concluded that the reformatory and industrial schools provided the "most suitable method of dealing with these children . . .".[i]

Tuairim Report, 1966

The report issued by Tuairim, an independent organisation, was more critical of the industrial and reformatory schools. This report was not State-sponsored. In their report *Some of Our Children*, the lack of social policy and legislation passed in Ireland since Independence was highlighted. It reported that corporal punishment in industrial and reformatory schools was either unsuitable or excessive; it called for new legislation to replace the 1908 Children Act and for childcare services to be co-ordinated by the Department of Health.

Commission of Inquiry on Mental Illness, 1966

The Commission of Inquiry on Mental Illness published a report in 1966 reviewing the health services available for the "mentally ill". Chapter 6 of the report examined the provision for "special classes" which included children and adolescents. Industrial and

---

[i] c.f. Richardson, V. (1999). "Children and Social Policy" in Quinn, S., Kennedy, P., O'Donnell, A. and Kiely, G. *Contemporary Irish Social Policy*. Dublin: University College Dublin Press.

reformatory schools were not included in the Commission's terms of reference but it did express concern "with the provisions made in such schools for psychiatric and psychological services and with the possible effect of the schools on the emotional development of children sent to them" (p. 73). Industrial schools were criticised for inadequate provision of psychological services and for not segregating children according to their educational, social and psychological needs. The Commission recommended that the "problem" of industrial schools be examined (p. 74).

Committee on Reformatory and Industrial Schools, 1966–1970

In response to the Tuairim Report and the Inquiry on Mental Illness, the Minister for Education established a Committee in 1966 under Justice Eileen Kennedy to examine the industrial and reformatory school system.

The Kennedy Committee investigated the industrial and reformatory schools culminating in a report, published in 1970. This report was "one of the most damning indictments of the operation of any State system ever produced in this country".[j] The Committee visited all the industrial and reformatory schools. They described the system as being "far from satisfactory" and reported a lack of awareness of the needs of children in care. The Committee also found that statutory obligations had not been fulfilled since inspection of the schools had been ineffective. It called for two of the institutions to be immediately shut down and for an end to the institutional model of childcare. It proposed that:

- The present institutional system of residential care be abolished and replaced by group homes which would approximate as closely as possible the normal family unit

- Administrative responsibility for all aspects of child care be transferred to the Department of Health

---

[j] Raftery, M. and O'Sullivan, E. (1999). *Suffer the Little Children*. Dublin: New Island.

- The criminal age of responsibility be raised from 7 to 12 years

- A new Child Care Act be enacted to update laws relating to childcare

- An advisory body with statutory powers be set up to ensure that the highest standards of care are attained and maintained.

Industrial schools were closed during the 1970s.

Kilkenny Incest Case and Investigation, 1993

The Kilkenny Incest Case involved a father who had sexually abused his daughter from 1976 to 1992. There was widespread concern at the failure of the health services to take action during that time. The case resulted in the first major child abuse inquiry of its kind in Ireland. The Minister for Health established the inquiry within a week of the case gaining public attention. The terms of reference were as follows:

- To carry out an investigation, insofar as the health services are concerned, of the circumstances surrounding the abuse and in particular to establish why action to halt the abuse was not taken earlier

- To make recommendations for the future investigation and management, by the health services, of cases of suspected child abuse.

Poor communication and lack of co-ordination between agents of the health services were identified as reasons for failure to detect the abuse. Furthermore, despite widespread circulation of the 1987 Department of Health Guidelines, the inquiry found that these were not being implemented and many professionals were not even aware that they existed.[k] The inquiry did not blame individual professionals but concluded that the system of child protection

---

[k] McGuinness, C. (1993). *Report of the Kilkenny Incest Investigation*. Dublin: Government Stationery Office.

needed reform to prevent similar situations. Had the report singled out individuals, there may not have been pressure on the Government to examine the child welfare and protection system. Following publication of the report the Government granted £35 million to fully implement the 1991 Child Care Act and the Child Care Policy Unit was established in the Department of Health.

Madonna House Case and Inquiry, 1996

In 1993, a maintenance man who worked at Madonna House, a residential child care facility run by the Sisters of Charity, was sentenced to four years imprisonment for sexually abusing children residing there during the 1980s and 1990s. The Sisters of Charity and the Department of Health jointly appointed a Committee in 1994 to investigate child sexual abuse in Madonna House. In 1996, the Department of Health published the report of the inquiry into the operation of Madonna House.

The West of Ireland Farmer Case and Report of the Review Group, 1995–1998

In 1995, a man was convicted of raping and abusing four of his children over a 20-year period. He was sentenced to 283 years in prison, the largest cumulative total sentence in Irish legal history. However, the sentences were to run concurrently which meant he would actually serve 12 years. Two years later, his daughter Sophie McColgan sued the North Western Health Board and a general practitioner for failing to intervene during the time she and her siblings were abused. The case was the first of its kind in Ireland. The statute of limitations for civil liability in Ireland is three years and in the case of minors, three years after the plaintiff's 18th birthday. The only legal grounds for extending the statute of limitations is that the plaintiff be of unsound mind. In the McColgan case, the plaintiff argued that she was unable to take action until her father was imprisoned. According to one author, the plaintiffs had great difficulty in finding doctors in the Republic of Ireland who were knowledgeable about the sequelae of child abuse and willing to testify in a civil liability suit against another doctor.[1] Sophie McColgan was awarded damages and the case was settled in 1998. There was no admission of liability by the health board or the general practitioner.

In 1998, the North Western Health Board (NWHB) established a group to review the board's involvement in the McColgan case. The report[m] found that the health board had taken a "non-legal interventionist approach towards child care" and that care options were insufficiently explored because of the emphasis on maintaining the family unit at the time. Overall, the review group found that the health board dealt with each sibling and event in isolation without reviewing the family as a whole. Information was never collated or shared and relationships between professionals were unstructured. As in the Kilkenny Incest Case, the abuse suffered by the McColgan children occurred during a time (1973–1993) when the Department of Health had issued guidelines on child abuse which were available to professionals.

Commission to Inquire into Child Abuse 1999–

In May 1999, the Government established a Commission to inquire into cases of child abuse which occurred in State institutions from the 1940s. It was known as the "Laffoy Commission" after Hon. Justice Mary Laffoy, the Commission chairperson. The Commission to Inquire into Child Abuse Act was enacted in April 2000.[n] The main aim of the Commission was to:

> . . . inquire into child abuse, to investigate child abuse in institutions in the State, to enable persons who have suffered such abuse to give evidence to committees of the Commission, to

---

[1] Sgroi, S.M. (1999). "The McColgan Case: Increasing Public Awareness of Professional Responsibility for Protecting Children from Physical and Sexual Abuse in the Republic of Ireland". *Journal of Child Sexual Abuse*, 8(1): 113–127.

[m] North Western Health Board (1998). *West of Ireland Farmer Case*. NWHB.

[n] Justice Laffoy resigned as Chairperson of the Commission in September 2003. The future of the Commission is uncertain.

provide for the preparation and publication of a report by the Commission containing the results of its investigation and any recommendations it considers appropriate for the prevention of child abuse, the protection of children from it and the actions to be taken to address any continuing effects of child abuse on those who have suffered it and to provide for related matters.

The functions of the Commission were:

- To listen to persons who have suffered abuse in childhood in institutions and give them an opportunity to recount abuse and make submissions to the Commission

- To conduct an inquiry into the abuse of children in institutions since 1940 or earlier and, where it is satisfied that abuse occurred, to find out why it occurred and who was responsible for it

- To report directly to the public on the results of the inquiry and to make recommendations, including recommendations on the steps which should be taken now to deal with the continuing effects of abuse and to protect children in institutions, as defined in the Act, from abuse now and in the future.

The Commission has two committees, the Confidential Committee and the Investigation Committee. The Confidential Committee provides a forum for those who have experienced institutional child abuse, who do not wish to become involved in an investigative procedures to report their experiences and have them noted as part of a public testimony to these events. The Investigation Committee facilitates persons who wish to recount their experiences and to have allegations of abuse investigated.

Interim Report 2001

In May 2001, the Commission published an interim report to inform the public of their work to date. The Commission decided not to publish any findings made during the course of the inquiry and intend to make public their findings only after the complete inquiry. According to the report, there were 524 requests to testify to the Confidential Committee and 714 for the Investigation Committee.

Issues of legal representation and compensation impeded the work of the Investigation Committee. It could not proceed without provision for legal representation for those who made allegations and for those against whom allegations were made. In February 2001, the Government made a public announcement that it had agreed a compensation scheme for the survivors of institutional abuse. At the time of writing, it was the view of at least some members of the Investigation Committee that the Government's decision had rendered redundant any recommendations they might have made on a compensation scheme. Furthermore, some persons, on the advice of their solicitors, withdrew their previous requests to testify, pending the establishment of a compensation scheme (Commission to Inquire into Child Abuse, 2001, p. 13). In May 2001, the Government informed the Commission that a scheme had been made available to cover legal expenses for the first phase of hearings of the Investigation Committee and that a further scheme would be made available for the second phase.

Since the Commission was established, there has been significant investment in the support services for those abused in institutional settings. A National Counselling Service for adults who experienced childhood sexual abuse was established in September 2000. This operates in each health board as a self-referral free service. Since its establishment, over 5,000 individuals have been referred for counselling[o] (a review of the experiences of 268 users of this service has recently been completed by this research group).[p] The Department of Health and Children also committed to providing funding for counselling for up to three years for those who were abused in institutional settings and now reside in the United Kingdom.

---

[o] Not all have been survivors of institutional abuse. The service now accepts referrals of all child abuse and neglect cases and approximately two-thirds of current clients have been abused in non-institutional settings.

[p] Leigh, C., Rundle, K., McGee, H.M. and Garavan, R. (2003) "SENCS: Survivors' Experiences of the National Counselling Service for Adults who Experienced Childhood Abuse". Dublin: National Counselling Service.

Second Interim Report, November 2001

Following the announcement of a closing date for the Commission, testifying requests to give evidence to both committees had increased from 1,238 to 3,149. In November 2001, 1,192 individuals had requested to give evidence to the Confidential Committee (with 254 hearings held) and 1,957 persons had requested to give evidence to the Investigation Committee (with two hearings completed). The Commission was due to publish its report before 23 May 2002 (two years after its establishment). However, because of the volume of requests to give evidence, the Commission sought and received an extension until May 2005. The Commission was under review by the government from December 2002 regarding the cost of the inquiry.

CRIMINAL LEGISLATION PERTAINING TO THE SEXUAL ABUSE OF CHILDREN AND RAPE

Offences Against the Person Act, 1861

Capital punishment was mandatory for rape, buggery and sexual intercourse with females below the age of consent in nineteenth-century Ireland. It was replaced with "transportation" (to a foreign location, e.g. Australia) in 1841. The 1861 Offences Against the Person Act created the sentence of life imprisonment for rape, which remains the maximum sentence today. Under the Offences Against the Person Act, the maximum sentence for indecent assault upon a female was two years but was ten years for indecent assault on a male (this was amended by the Criminal Law (Rape) Act 1981 and the Criminal Law (Rape) (Amendment) Act 1990).

Criminal Law Amendment Act, 1885

The growing problem of child prostitution resulted in the age of consent being increased from 13 to 16 years under the Criminal Law Amendment Act, 1885. Under the Act, a male charged with unlawful carnal knowledge of a girl aged between 13 and 16 had a defence if he had reason to believe that the girl was 16 years or over. Furthermore, the accused could not be convicted of an offence based on the uncorroborated evidence of a single witness. The sentence for rape was two years imprisonment. The Act also made homosexual acts in public or private an offence. Sections of the Act still enforced today relate to prostitution.

The Punishment of Incest Act, 1908

Incest was criminalised in Ireland for the first time by the Punishment of Incest Act 1908. It was an offence for a male person to have sexual intercourse with his mother, sister, daughter or granddaughter, regardless of consent. It was also an offence for a woman aged 17 years or older to knowingly permit her grandfather, father, brother or son to have sexual intercourse with her. Criminalising incest was intended to curb sexual relationships between family members in an attempt to avoid children being born with genetic defects. Consequently, "incest" did not include any sexual acts other than intercourse. Under the 1908 Act, the maximum sentence was seven years (and not less than three) for incest by a male with a female and seven years for incest by a female. Females under 17 years of age could not be charged with incest but there was no age limit for males.

The Carrigan Report, 1930–1933

In 1930, the Government established a committee to examine the Criminal Law Amendment Acts (1880–85). William Carrigan KC chaired the committee and its remit was to consider if new legislation was required to deal with juvenile prostitution. In particular, there was concern about the age of consent, which up to 1885 was 13, but which had been raised to 16 by the 1885 Criminal Law Amendment Act. The laws in relation to sexual offences were considered lenient compared to those of Northern Ireland and Great Britain.

In 1931, the Carrigan Committee reported that, according to the Garda Commissioner, there had been an increase in sexual crimes (in particular such crimes against children) in Ireland. The

Commissioner estimated that less than 15 per cent of cases were prosecuted because of the desire of parents to keep the abuse secret and their reluctance to have their child appear in court.[qr] In addition, some aspects of the law at that time made a prosecution unlikely. The evidence of children had to be corroborated and judges were required to warn the jury of the danger of convicting solely on the uncorroborated evidence of a child. The Garda Commissioner, in his memo to the committee, also criticised sentencing for sexual offences. He felt that sentences were too lenient and that legislation did not provide sufficient punishment to act as a deterrent. The Commissioner's remarks were not made public and the Carrigan Committee concluded that the law contributed to the frequency of assaults on children.

The Carrigan Committee made a number of recommendations, the most relevant of which are as follows:

- That the age of consent be raised from 16 to 18 years

- That grounds for acquittal based on "reasonable cause to believe" that the girl was above the age of consent be abolished

- That the time allowed for commencing a prosecution under the Criminal Law Act be extended (it was six months at the time of the Carrigan Report).

The Carrigan Report, known at the time as the *Report of the Committee on the Criminal Law Amendment Acts and Juvenile Prostitution*, was circulated to the government in 1931. The Department of Justice attached a cautionary memo to the report warning that the allegations made in the report were damaging to the standard of morality in the country. The Department also advised against publication of the report. In 1932, a general election was held and

---

[q] McAvoy, S.L. (1999). "The Regulation of Sexuality in the Irish Free State, 1929–1935", in Malcom, E. and Jones, G. (ed.) *Medicine, Disease and the State in Ireland, 1650–1940*. Cork: Cork University Press.

[r] Kennedy, F. (2000). "The Suppression of the Carrigan Report: A Historical Perspective on Child Abuse". *Studies*, 89 (356):354–363.

a new government led by Éamon de Velara was elected with a new Minister for Justice, Mr James Geoghegan. He was critical of the report and also felt that it should not be published. The Minister believed that raising the age of consent to 18 would increase the amount of crime and act as a mechanism whereby women could blackmail men. He was also reluctant to give any weight to the evidence of children, remarking that there "were grave doubts as to the value of children's evidence" and that a "child with a vivid imagination . . . will be quite unshaken by severe cross-examination". The government was dissolved in 1932 and a general election saw the appointment of a new Minister for Justice, Mr Patrick Rutledge, in 1933. A new committee of deputies chaired by former Minister, James Geoghegan, was established to deal with the Carrigan Report. This Committee opted for 17 as the age of consent rather than 18.

The Carrigan Committee sought to make the law more stringent to protect women and children. However, the Department of Justice saw their recommendations as being too harsh on men while overlooking the problem of the veracity of evidence given by women and children. Failure to publish the Carrigan Report meant that sexual abuse did not become an issue of public debate and the potential of the report to increase public awareness was never realised.[s] The existence of the Carrigan Report demonstrates that both the Gardaí and the Department of Justice were aware in 1933 that adults could sexually abuse children and "to say that in the 1960s and 1970s people in Ireland, particularly those who worked in the areas of child care, had no knowledge of child abuse suggests a level of ignorance clearly not shared by the authorities of either State or Church."[t]

---

[s] Kennedy, F. (2000). "The Suppression of the Carrigan Report: A Historical Perspective on Child Abuse". *Studies*, 89 (356):354–363.

[t] Raftery, M. and O'Sullivan, E. (1999). *Suffer the Little Children*. Dublin: New Island.

The Criminal Law Amendment Act, 1935

There was little change in the laws on sexual offences in the period between the foundation of the State in 1922 and 1981. However, one significant piece of legislation enacted during that period was the Criminal Law Amendment Act 1935. This followed the Carrigan Report and was partly in response to pressure from the National Council of Women in Ireland and the United Council of Christian Churches and Religious. Prior to the 1935 Act, sexual offences against children were governed by the 1885 Criminal Law Amendment Act. The 1935 Act set a maximum penal sanction for unlawful carnal knowledge of a girl under 15 years of life imprisonment and unlawful carnal knowledge of a girl under 17 years at five years' imprisonment for a first conviction and ten years' imprisonment for a second or subsequent conviction. Prior to the 1935 Act, the respective ages were 13 and 16 years. The girl was not subject to criminal liability, the male was always considered the instigator.[u]

Under the 1935 Act, 15 years was the age at which consent could not be given by either sex while 17 years was the age of consent. This was rather high by international standards.[v] A man proven to have had unlawful carnal knowledge of an under-age girl does not have any defence available to him. The original defence, under the Criminal Law Amendment Act 1885, that he believed the girl to be above the age of consent, was abolished by the 1935 Act. Once it was established that the accused had sexual intercourse with an under-age girl he was automatically guilty.[w]

---

[u] The Law Reform Commission (1990) recommended that this be retained as any attempt to make the female criminally liable might deter females from reporting the crime.

[v] The Law Reform Commission (1990) recommended keeping this age of consent adding that, where a girl was between the ages of 15 and 17, an offence would only be committed if the male were in a position of authority or at least five years older than the girl. Its view was that above a certain age, criminal law should not intrude on sexual relations between persons of the same age.

[w] The Law Reform Commission (1990) recommended that life imprisonment be applied only to cases where the child is under 13 years and that the maximum sentence be seven years' imprisonment for unlawful carnal knowledge of a girl

Time Limit for Prosecution

According to Section 2 of the Criminal Law Amendment Act 1935, unlawful and carnal knowledge of a girl under 17 years or attempting the same must be prosecuted within 12 months of the offence being committed. This was intended to avoid any malicious or vengeful attempts to falsely accuse a person. Charges such as rape and incest that are often used to prosecute perpetrators of child abuse, are not subject to any specified time limit.[x] Reforms that have taken place since the Criminal Law Amendment Act of 1935 reflect a more developed and aware society and have been informed by greater public exposure to the problem.

The Criminal Law (Rape) Act, 1981

Rape was first given statutory definition in Ireland under the Criminal Law (Rape) Act, 1981. However, the definition referred only to sexual intercourse with a woman and did not cover other acts such as forced fellatio or the forced insertion of objects into the vagina. Furthermore, sexual intercourse had to be "unlawful" which was taken to mean outside of marriage. This provided immunity for husbands. It was mostly a procedural act and provided for the anonymity of the complainant. It also restricted the questioning of the complainant about their previous sexual experiences with anyone other than the accused. The judge could, however, waive this restriction if he or she was satisfied that it would be unfair to the accused to refuse such evidence. The

---

between 13 and 17. The Commission also recommended that defence be available to those charged on the grounds of belief, at the time of the act, that the girl had attained the age of consent. It can be argued that the law as it stands, by not affording this defence, protects girls whose physical maturity has surpassed their emotional maturity and it discourages men from risking sexual relations with underage girls (Department of Justice, Equality and Law Reform, 1998). The Law Reform Commission also proposed that the girl's appearance be considered relevant to the case, although this proposal has been criticised on the grounds that it could result in the girl being exhibited as a piece of evidence.

[x] O'Malley, T. (1996). *Sexual Offences: Law, Policy and Punishment*. Dublin: Round Hall Sweet & Maxwell.

Criminal Law (Rape) (Amendment) Act also raised the maximum sentence for indecent assault on a female from five years to ten years. (The maximum sentence was five years under the Criminal Law Amendment Act, 1935.)

Criminal Law (Rape) (Amendment) Act, 1990

As soon as the 1981 Criminal Law (Rape) Act was passed, there was pressure to have it amended, particularly the issue of spousal immunity and the confinement of rape to vaginal intercourse. The issue was referred to the Law Reform Commission in 1987, which produced a consultation paper and report. The Government responded by producing a Bill in 1988 and eventually passed the Criminal Law (Rape) (Amendment) Act in 1990. The most significant aspect of the 1990 Act was "Rape under Section 4" which provided for penetrative acts other than penile-vaginal intercourse. There are now two forms of rape in Irish law:

- Common law rape — sexual intercourse between a man and a woman without the consent of the woman

- Rape under section 4 — bodily penetration other than penile penetration of the vagina.

Rape under Section 4 made penetration of the mouth or anus by penis or penetration of the vagina by any other object a felony with a maximum sentence of life imprisonment. However, penetration of the anus by an object is not included in the definition. It is proposed that sexual assault involving penetration of the anus by an object would be considered as aggravated sexual assault. Statutory rape and unlawful carnal knowledge of a female under 17 years of age are covered under the Criminal Law Amendment Act, 1935.

Prior to the 1990 Act, sexual intercourse had to be "unlawful" which was taken to mean outside of marriage. The 1990 Act abolished the law that a man could not be guilty of raping his wife. Also included in the 1990 Act was the provision that failure to offer resistance to the sexual act does not constitute consent.

Before the 1990 Act, there were separate offences of indecent assault upon a female and a male. These covered a wide variety of behaviours from unwanted touching to violent sexual attacks. The 1990 Act renamed "indecent assault" as "sexual assault" and introduced a new offence of "aggravated sexual assault" to cover more "vicious and degrading acts". The difference between sexual assault and aggravated sexual assault is one of degree. A sexual assault may become aggravated according to levels of violence or degradation. It is a gender-neutral offence that can be committed by or against persons of either sex. Aggravated sexual assault is a felony with a maximum sentence of life imprisonment whereas sexual assault carries a maximum sentence of five years' imprisonment. The clause that stated that a boy under 14 years of age was incapable of committing a sexual offence was also abolished by this Act.

The Criminal Evidence Act, 1992

Court Proceedings

Both reports from the Law Reform Commission (1990) and the Irish Council for Civil Liberties (1989) on child sexual abuse were critical of the hearing of children's evidence in criminal courts. The Criminal Evidence Act, 1992 was designed to make it easier for witnesses to give evidence in cases of physical and/or sexual abuse. Evidence by a witness under 17 years of age can be given by a live television link unless the court has good reason not to allow this. The television link could also be used for witnesses over the age of 17 with the permission of the court. A witness does not have to be the plaintiff to avail of the television link option. The Act also provides that any witness who gives evidence by television link may not have to identify the accused in court. The 1992 Act made a number of other changes, which were recommended by the Law Reform Commission in 1990. For example, judges, barristers and solicitors no longer wear wigs and gowns when young witnesses are giving evidence. In cross-examination, questions to child witnesses may be conveyed through an intermediary appointed by the court.

Status of Children's Evidence

The status of children's evidence was changed in the 1992 Act in accordance with some of the recommendations of the Law Reform Commission (1990). The video-recorded evidence of a person under 17 years of age is now deemed as admissible as if it were direct oral evidence given at the trial. Other recordings of statements given to Gardaí, made by persons alleged to have been physically or sexually abused under 14 years of age, are also now admissible. Under the Act, the court can now admit the evidence of children under 14, without an oath or affirmation, if they are considered capable of giving an intelligible account of events. The necessity to corroborate the un-sworn evidence of a child was abolished. Finally, the Act also allows evidence to be recorded by video outside of the courtroom, but only in certain circumstances.

The Criminal Justice Act, 1993

The 1993 Criminal Justice Act was one of the most important sentencing reforms in the history of the State. It was introduced as a direct result of two sexual assault cases in which the sentences were perceived to be lenient. The Act enabled the Court of Criminal Appeal to review lenient sentences. In the Kilkenny Incest Case, the defendant who pleaded guilty could have been charged with either rape or incest. The Punishment of Incest Act 1908 treated incest as a misdemeanour carrying a maximum sentence of seven years whereas rape, a felony, carries a maximum sentence of life imprisonment. The Director of Public Prosecutions charged the defendant with incest and the accused was given a four-year sentence. The sentence was widely criticised. Under the subsequently developed Criminal Justice Act (1993), the maximum sentence for incest was increased from seven years (Punishment of Incest Act, 1908) to 20 years.

Criminal Law (Sexual Offences) Act, 1993

The 1993 Criminal Law (Sexual Offences) Act decriminalised homosexual acts between consenting male adults.[y] The Act also abolished the common law offence of buggery between persons except with persons of either sex under 17 years of age or "mentally impaired" individuals. The penalty for buggery with a person over 15 but less than 17 years of age, was set at five years imprisonment for a first offence and ten years for any subsequent offence. The maximum penalty for buggery with a person less than 15 years of age is life imprisonment. The offence of gross indecency was replaced by an offence of "gross indecency with a male under 17 years of age". This carries with it a penalty of two years' imprisonment and consent does not provide a defence to a charge of buggery or gross indecency. Prior to the 1993 Act, the offences of buggery and gross indecency between male persons were covered in the Offences Against the Persons Act 1861 and the Criminal Law Amendment Act 1885.

The Criminal Law (Incest Proceedings) Act, 1995

The Criminal Justice Act of 1951 gives the courts discretionary power over publicity in any criminal proceedings "of an indecent or obscene nature". Up to 1995, some court proceedings were still governed by the Punishment of Incest Act of 1908. Section 5 of this Act stipulated that all court proceedings in an incest case must be held in private, i.e. admitting only immediate parties. The need for changes in the legislation became clear following two judgments by the Central Criminal Court in 1995, which ruled that it was

---

[y] Compared to other countries, Ireland was slow to decriminalise homosexual acts. In the United Kingdom, for example, homosexual acts were decriminalised in 1967. The Act followed a long campaign by Senator David Norris who, in 1977, issued a summons to the High Court seeking a declaration that sections of the Offences Against the Person Act of 1861 and the Criminal Law Amendment Act of 1885 were inconsistent with the Irish Constitution (O'Malley, 1996). The Law Reform Commission (1990) had also considered homosexual offences and the Criminal Law (Sexual Offences) Act 1993 implemented most of the Commission's recommendations.

prevented, under the Punishment of Incest Act of 1908, from disclosing information about cases. The Eastern Health Board had sought to establish whether an accused had been convicted of incest as it wished to apply for wardship to protect the children involved. As a result, the Criminal Law (Incest Proceedings) Act 1995 ensured that persons such as social workers and others with a genuine interest in child protection could have access to the information they required. The Act also provided for the verdict and the sentence to be announced in public. However, the name of a child defendant or witness in a sexual offence case is not usually published. It is not an offence to do so but this issue is addressed in the Children Bill of 1996, whereby the publication of reports or pictures of a child complainant or witness or information that could identify the child, is prohibited. The court does have the power to lift this prohibition but it must explain in open court why it sees fit to do so. The anonymity of those convicted of sexual offences is not legally protected.

The 1995 Act also increased the penalty for incest by a male with a female of 15 years of age or less from a maximum of 20 years' imprisonment (Criminal Justice Act, 1993) to life imprisonment. The maximum sentence for incest by a male with a female under 17 years of age was set at five years for first conviction and ten years for a subsequent conviction.[z]

Sexual Offences (Jurisdiction) Act, 1996

Sex Tourism

The Sexual Offences (Jurisdiction) Act 1996 was enacted in response to the increasing problem of sex tourism involving children. The Act had two main functions. First, it gave Irish courts jurisdiction in cases where Irish citizens, or persons who ordinarily reside in Ireland, are accused of engaging in sex with children

---

[z] An amendment was proposed with the 1995 Act to extend the offence of incest to include non-blood relationships such as a step or adoptive parent. However, it was concluded that this was unnecessary as unlawful carnal knowledge of a female and buggery with a male under 15 years of age already carried a maximum sentence of life imprisonment.

in foreign countries. The second function of the Act was to make it an offence to arrange transport for, or to transport, child sex tourists or to publish information on child sex tourism.

Criminal Justice (Miscellaneous Provision) Act, 1997

Search Warrants for Sexual Offences

The courts normally issue search warrants to enable Gardaí to search premises for items such as stolen goods, firearms and racist material. Up to 1997, there was no such statutory provision for issuing search warrants in relation to sexual and other serious offences. The Criminal Justice (Miscellaneous Provision) Act, 1997 made statutory provision for the search of any place or any person found at that place, where a District Court judge is satisfied that there may be evidence of a serious offence. Therefore, Gardaí can now search locations and seize evidence for cases of rape and other sexual offences, including offences against children.

Child Trafficking and Pornography Bill, 1997

The main features of the Child Trafficking and Pornography Bill (1997), as outlined by the Department of Justice, Equality and Law Reform (1998) are as follows:

- It will be an offence to knowingly produce, print or publish child pornography or to advertise it

- It will be an offence to knowingly import, export or distribute child pornography

- It will be an offence to knowingly possess child pornography for personal use

- It will be an offence to allow children to be used to produce such pornography.

The Bill will also make it an offence to traffic children in and out of Ireland for the purpose of sexual exploitation or to detain children for that reason. Maximum sentences of up to life imprisonment have been proposed.

Protection for Persons Reporting Child Abuse Act, 1998

The main provisions of this Act are:

- The provision of immunity from civil liability to any person who reports child abuse "reasonably and in good faith" to designated officers of health boards or any member of An Garda Síochána

- The provision of significant protections for employees who report child abuse

- These protections cover all employees and all forms of discrimination up to, and including, dismissal

- The creation of a new offence of false reporting of child abuse where a person makes a report of child abuse to the appropriate authorities knowing that statement to be false.

Sex Offenders Act, 2001

Under this Act, convicted sex offenders (convicted after June 2001) are obliged to notify the Gardaí of certain information. However, only those convicted of sex offences against persons under 17 years of age are subject to these requirements. Time periods for notification are:

- Five years for a non-custodial or suspended sentence

- Seven years for a custodial sentence under six months

- Ten years for custodial sentences from six months to two years

- Lifetime obligation for any custodial sentence over two years.

These time periods are halved where the person convicted is under 18 years of age. If a conviction is quashed by appeal the person is not subject to the requirements of notification. When a person is convicted, they must notify the Gardaí of their name and place of residence ten days before their release and once released they must notify the Gardaí if they are leaving the country for a continuous period of seven days or more and provide the address

at which they intend to stay. Failure to comply with these requirements is an offence and they may be subject to a prison sentence not exceeding 12 months or a fine of £1500 or both.

This Act also permits a member of the Garda Síochána (at or
above the rank of Chief Superintendent) to apply to the court for a
sex offender order. This order prevents the person from doing one
or more things specified in the order to protect the public from
death or serious personal injury whether psychological or physical. A sex offender order can be enforced for a period of five years
or longer as provided by the court. It is an offence (fine of £1500 or
prison sentence not exceeding 12 months or both) for a person
convicted of a sexual offence and subject to notification requirements to apply for work or enter into a contract of work that involves unsupervised access or contact with children or mentally
impaired persons. However, if the accused can prove that he or
she was unaware that the work involved contact with children
this can be used as defence. Once a sentence is determined for a
convicted sex offender, the court considers whether to impose
post-release supervision. The court may impose a sentence involving supervision once the offender is released from prison whereby
the person is under the supervision of a probation and welfare
officer. Additional provisions such as prohibitions from doing one
or more things the court considers necessary for the purpose of
protecting the public from serious harm and a condition of treatment or counselling may also be enforced. Non-compliance with
supervision orders is an offence (fine of £1500 or prison sentence
not exceeding 12 months or both).

The Sex Offenders Act 2001 also included amendments to the
Criminal Law (Rape) Act 1981 and the Criminal Law (Rape)
(Amendment) Act 1990. Under the Sex Offenders Act 2001, complainants in rape cases are entitled to have legal representation
and a person guilty of sexual assault is liable for a maximum
prison sentence of 14 years for the sexual assault of children and
ten years for any other case (this was five years under the Criminal Law (Rape) (Amendment) Act, 1990).

INDEX

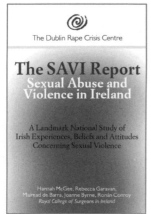